POWER, IDEOLOGY,
AND THE WAR ON DRUGS

PRAEGER SERIES IN CRIMINOLOGY AND CRIME CONTROL POLICY

Steven A. Egger, Series Editor

POWER, IDEOLOGY, AND THE WAR ON DRUGS

Nothing Succeeds Like Failure

Christina Jacqueline Johns

Praeger Series in Criminology and Crime Control Policy
Steven A. Egger, Series Editor

PRAEGER

New York
Westport, Connecticut
London

Library of Congress Cataloging-in-Publication Data

Johns, Christina Jacqueline.
    Power, ideology, and the war on drugs : nothing succeeds like
failure / Christina Jacqueline Johns.
        p.   cm. — (Praeger series in criminology and crime control
policy)
    Includes bibliographical references and index.
    ISBN 0–275–94167–1 (alk. paper)
    1. Narcotics, Control of—United States.   2. Narcotics, Control
of.   I. Title. II. Series.
    HV5825.J6   1992
    363.4'5'0973—dc20   91–35017

British Library Cataloguing in Publication Data is available.

Library of Congress Catalog Card Number: 91–35017
ISBN: 0–275–94167–1

First published in 1992

Praeger Publishers, One Madison Avenue, New York, NY 10010
An imprint of Greenwood Publishing Group, Inc.

Printed in the United States of America

∞™

The paper used in this book complies with the
Permanent Paper Standard issued by the National
Information Standards Organization (Z39.48–1984).

10 9 8 7 6 5 4 3 2

This book is dedicated to my parents, W. L. and Pat Johnson, who taught me to fight and loved me through forty years, and my dear sweet William, who died, as we all should, living a life he loved.

CONTENTS

SERIES FOREWORD

The Praeger Series in Criminology and Crime Control Policy is meant to provide a variety of perspectives and ideologies the regarding theory and policies of crime control. The intended audience is the academic community and governmental officials involved in developing and implementing crime control policy. Authors represented in this series will come from a variety of social science and behavioral disciplines. The series is open to all qualitative and quantitative methodologies and to contemporary and historical studies that address in some manner the focus of this series.

Power, Ideology, and the War on Drugs: Nothing Succeeds Like Failure by Christina Jacqueline Johns is the first monograph in this series. Johns presents a critical analysis of the federal government's crime control policy on dangerous and illegal drugs.

Wars on drugs have been waged in this country for quite some time. However, the problems of dangerous drug use had not been highlighted for the public nearly to the extent that it has been throughout the Reagan and Bush administrations. During this last decade the War on Drugs has indeed become a "war," with a national agenda and a political rhetoric encompassing politicians of both political parties in Washington, D.C., in large urban areas, and in small communities throughout the United States.

Johns focuses her discussion on the drug criminalization and enforcement policies of our federal government over the last decade, the seeming narrow-mindedness of continuing such a policy in light of evidence contrary to many assumptions, and (most important) the amount of social control such a policy invests in those in power. She convincingly argues throughout this work that the singular and seemingly overriding characteristic of the War on Drugs is that both the perception of success and the perception of failure can be used to justify the continuation of such a war. With success, governmental control mechanisms must be continued and enhanced to reach objectives. With failure, efforts require more resources and different levels of coordination to reach objectives. As the drug war continues unabated, it becomes increasingly evident that social control is indeed the real issue. As government at the federal, state, and local levels increases its repressive measures against drugs, societal members (particularly the middle and upper classes) seem more and more willing to accept these measures as necessary to combat the evils of dangerous drugs.

Politization of the drug problem through media campaigns results in a distorted image of the problem. Reported successes of law enforcement do not necessarily mean there has been a reduction in the use or availability of dangerous drugs on the street. Figures frequently cited as evidence of winning the drug war relate primarily to the middle class. There is an overemphasis on enforcement at the expense of treatment programs and education. Further, while education programs appear to be affecting only portions of middle-class youth, approximately 70 percent of the drug war effort continues to be allocated to enforcement strategies of interdiction and arrest of pushers in the streets.

As Johns aptly points out, crimes of the powerful are increasingly ignored while the War on Drugs expands. Money laundering, the savings and loan scandal, and corporate pollution receive only sporadic attention from government officials. Corruption of law enforcement officers, corrections officers, and others at all levels of government become almost commonplace as part of the drug war. Meanwhile, our prison population has increased by 45 percent since the early 1980s, and much of this increase can be attributed to increases in arrests for drug use.

Johns details our government's efforts to stop the flow of drugs into the United States, and she suggests that this effort has been as ineffective as the War on Drugs within our borders. Further, she identifies many of the drug war's social costs to Latin American countries, including human rights violations by military and police efforts funded by the United States, the corruption of local officials, secondary criminal activity, and the many health problems caused by the aerial spraying of toxic chemicals used in eradication efforts.

In Chapters 3 and 4 Johns focuses on her major theme of domestic social control. Four major arguments are presented as to why the U.S. government (the Reagan and Bush administrations) continue to pursue a policy of criminalization and enforcement: (1) to divert attention from the dangers of legal drugs, which are well integrated into our society and controlled by powerful interests; (2) to divert attention from fundamental social problems of our society, such as homelessness, the need for national health care, and the gross inequities among the population; (3) to legitimate our abandonment of the lower class and minorities by focusing the drug war on those segments of our society and making them appear as an enemy class; and (4) to legitimate a massive expansion of domestic state power and control.

In Chapters 5 and 6 Johns expands her discussion to our government's crime control policy on drugs in Latin America. She argues that the international War on Drugs is being pursued for two primary reasons. First, such a policy diverts attention away from structural inequalities and injustices in Latin America. Second, this policy allows our government to justify an ever-expanding control over and intervention into the governments of Latin America.

Johns concludes that the policy of criminalization and enforcement will continue, for the expansion of state power, both here and abroad, is clearly in the government's interest. Finally, the author warns proponents of drug legalization that their arguments must not be presented as a panacea to fundamental societal problems here and in the Third World, that their arguments must be expanded beyond their middle-class orientation, and that they must carefully consider the possibility of a greater erosion of civil and constitutional guarantees that could result from legalization.

In this work Dr. Johns offers a great deal of contemporary information, critical analysis, and argument for the reader to consider. *Power, Ideology, and the War on Drugs: Nothing Succeeds Like Failure* deserves careful reading and thoughtful consideration by criminologists and government policy makers alike.

Steven A. Egger

ACKNOWLEDGMENTS

I would like to thank:

—my close friend Carol Burgess whose love, laughter, and sense of humor have been a constant delight and support for me for over twenty years;

—my dear companions, Felipo, Goodman, and Fernando Rafael da Silva, who regarded it their duty to sit, sleep, and bathe on every draft page of this manuscript, and who spent innumerable nights with me in my study attacking my pens, playing tag over the computer keyboard, pushing my newspaper files on the floor, and generally making themselves useful;

—Gregg Barak, my friend and colleague, whose constant encouragement and feedback helped make the book possible;

—my students at Alabama State who have challenged me, amused me, and allowed me to hold a tiny part of their hearts;

—my friend Mary Boykin whose Monday visits were a welcome break and whose efforts helped give me the time to finish the book;

—Series editor Steven Egger, and Anne Kiefer and John Roberts at Praeger;

—and finally, all the men despite whom, not because of whom, this book was completed.

1

THE DOMESTIC COSTS OF THE WAR ON DRUGS

The use of any dangerous drug within society carries with it social costs. But it is evident that people in most societies have used and do use one form or another of dangerous drugs. The real question is not how to prevent drug use but how to minimize the social costs of dangerous drug use, legal and illegal. The Reagan and Bush administrations, however, have pursued a strategy that, far from minimizing the social costs of the use of certain dangerous drugs, has instead escalated those costs. By pursuing a strategy of criminalization on the one hand and eradication on the other (both of drugs and of the people associated with them), the Bush and Reagan administrations have guaranteed that society will pay a higher price for the use of certain dangerous drugs than would have been paid had a policy focused on decriminalization, treatment, and education been pursued.

And it is not as if the ineffectiveness and negative consequences of enforcement strategies to deal with "victimless"—or what are more accurately known as "complaintless"—crimes are unknown. In the 1920s, attempts to enforce the Eighteenth Amendment prohibiting the sale and use of alcohol not only failed to stop the sale and use of alcoholic beverages but brought about problems similar to those that characterize the present "War on Drugs" (see, for example, Woodiwiss, 1988).

One would think that if the government were sincerely concerned with reducing, if not stopping, the use of dangerous drugs, it would have learned from past mistakes and pursued a different strategy. The criminalization and enforcement strategies that characterized the prohibition era and now characterize the War on Drugs era have never been effective in stopping the manufacture, use, and trafficking of illegal substances. In addition, criminalization and enforcement strategies have brought about additional social costs (corruption, deflection of police resources, increased illegal profits, criminal justice system overloads, secondary crime, etc.). In this chapter the ineffectiveness of the criminalization-enforcement strategy will be examined along with the social costs brought about by that strategy.

THE INEFFECTIVENESS OF THE CRIMINALIZATION-ENFORCEMENT STRATEGY

A 1988 report by the American Bar Association noted:

Police, prosecutors and judges told the committee that they have been unsuccessful in making a significant impact on the importation, sale and use of illegal drugs, despite devoting much of their resources to the arrest, prosecution and trial of drug offenders. (1988:6, 44)

The authors of the report concluded that the drug problem was "severe, growing worse, and . . . law enforcement has been unable to control it."

City officials have also noted that the problems associated with criminalized drug use and drug trafficking are severe and growing worse. In a survey of elected officials conducted by the National League of Cities in January 1990, 58 percent of the chief officials of cities surveyed maintained that problems associated with drugs had grown worse during the previous year. An additional 31 percent reported that drug problems had remained the same (New York Times, 1/9/90b).

Almost every indicator points to the ineffectiveness of enforcement strategies to do more than temporarily decrease drug use and the problems associated with illegal drug use and trafficking. Temporary decreases, however, are widely hailed by the administration as evidence of the success of enforcement strategies.

Users

In May 1990, Senator Joseph Biden, chairman of the Senate Judiciary Committee, released a report that infuriated Drug Czar William Bennett and the administration by setting the figure for cocaine users in the United States at 2.2 million. The National Institute of Drug Abuse (NIDA) had been operating with a figure of only 862,000. Biden publicly stated that the new figures indicated that the administration's strategy for combatting drug abuse was faulty (New York Times, 5/15/90). Surveys in mid–1990 also showed that there were at least 8 million casual cocaine users in addition to the 2.2 million frequent or heavy users referred to by

Biden (Treaster, 7/1/90). The number of heroin addicts in 1989 was estimated to be half a million (Purvis, 12/11/89).

The High School Seniors Survey at the end of 1989 noted an increase in PCP use among high school seniors, and there has been an explosion of drug use in prisons (Malcolm, 12/30/89). The Atlanta-based Parents' Resource Institute for Drug Education (PRIDE), which conducts an annual survey of teenage drug use, released a report in September 1989 indicating that one in four teenagers smoked marijuana and six in ten drank beer. Figures for the teenage use of alcohol, tobacco, marijuana, and cocaine increased from figures in 1987–1988 (Earle and White, 9/27/89).

In early 1990, a report by the U.S. Conference of Mayors noted sharp increases in the abuse of drugs, including alcohol, among the homeless population (*New York Times*, 12/21/89). In 1989, almost one-third of the psychiatric patients in New York City hospitals were estimated to be using crack, and 60 percent were estimated to be drug abusers (Specter and Kurtz, 2/19–2/25/90). While drug use appeared to be declining among certain segments of the population, it was and continues to be increasing among minority populations (Hamm, 1988).

In September 1990, however, both Bush and Bennett were claiming that the enforcement tactics of the administration had been successful, that casual cocaine and other drug use was declining, and that hardcore addiction was declining (*Christian Science Monitor*, 9/7/90).

Prices

In July 1990, the press started to report that federal drug agents would tell Congress of increases in the price and decreases in the purity of cocaine. The Drug Enforcement Administration (DEA) released figures of an average increase in cocaine prices of 50 percent in five major cities. This increase in price represented a short-term reverse of an almost decade-old national trend toward greater availability, lower price, and higher purity of cocaine (Kelley, 7/17/90). The increases, however, were not consistent across the country and had been noted only for three to six months prior to the June press accounts (Treaster, 6/14/90).

The largest price jump reported was in Los Angeles, where the price of a kilo of cocaine was said to have increased 88 percent from $20,000 in December 1989 to $32,000 in mid–1990. The purity of cocaine was also said to have dropped from 87 percent per kilo in December 1989, to 74 percent per kilo, according to DEA analyses. Street dealers were said to be buying cocaine in ounces, rather than kilos because they could not afford the price (Kelley, 7/17/90).

Price increases from December 1989 to June 1990 reported in thousands for the five cities were as follows: Los Angeles, $20 to $32 per kilo;

Houston, $21 to $30; Chicago, $25 to $32; New York, $25 to $35; Miami, $22 to $23 (Kelley, 7/17/90). Others were reporting even higher prices. One researcher at the University of Illinois quoted a figure of $40,000 per kilo in Chicago (Treaster, 7/1/90). But these price increases may well have been merely a market adjustment. It is interesting to note that prices increased most in cities that had the lowest price before the increase, for example in Los Angeles. In Miami, the increase was negligible.

The reasons offered for the price increase noted by federal drug agents were (1) cocaine seizures in Colombia, Peru, and Bolivia that were decreasing supplies, (2) increased law enforcement in major U.S. cities, and (3) cocaine stockpiling and price gouging by dealers. Joseph Treaster, writing in the *New York Times* (7/1/90), noted that many researchers he interviewed at a NIDA conference in July 1990 felt that price increases were most likely due not to a decrease of supply, or disruption of the market due to interdiction, but to attempts of traffickers to drive up the price by holding back on the product. Bush and Bennett, however, used the price increases for cocaine as evidence of the success of the War on Drugs (*Christian Science Monitor*, 9/7/90).

Both the Reagan and Bush administrations have played a shell game with the figures about drugs, widely publicizing figures when they appeared to favor administration policies and conveniently ignoring them when they did not. In 1982, for example, Reagan's adviser on drug policy, Dr. Carlton Turner, argued that decreasing prices for cocaine, marijuana, and heroin did not indicate greater availability but less demand for the drugs (Freemantle, 1986:52). There have been other instances of manipulating the figures for drug use for political reasons. Edward Jay Epstein (1977), for example, has documented how the Nixon administration vastly exaggerated the heroin epidemic of the early 1970s in order to assist Nixon's reelection.

Drug Emergencies

The administration is also very selective in terms of quoting figures for "drug-related" deaths and emergencies. When the desire is to heighten public fear about drugs, figures indicating increasing deaths and hospital emergencies are publicized. When the goal is to convince the public that the War on Drugs is successful, other figures are used. There is no shortage of data to support either argument. For example, NIDA released a report indicating that between June 1988 and June 1989 cocaine emergencies increased greatly in most large U.S. cities. St. Louis had an increase of 153 percent, Atlanta 120 percent, and San Francisco 85 percent (Raber, 3/12/90). Eleven cities reported increases in heroin emergencies. San Francisco, for example, had an increase of 97 percent

(Meddis, 3/12/90). By July 1990, however, the Drug Abuse Warning Network (DAWN) was reporting a decline in cocaine-related emergencies nationwide. As usual, the figures were difficult to interpret. For example, in several large cities—Washington, Philadelphia, and Minneapolis—cocaine-attributed deaths rose while emergency room cocaine-related cases declined. The declines, however, were used as evidence of the success of the War on Drugs strategy. By September 1990, Bush and Bennett were claiming decreases in hospital-related emergencies due to drugs (*Christian Science Monitor*, 9/7/90). But Charles Rangel (N.Y.) remarked on the release of the study that the figures did not indicate success: "We have simply not succeeded in reducing hard-core addiction and drug abuse in our inner cities" (Treaster, 7/1/90).

Even if the reductions were real and proved to be more than temporary, what was ignored was that the problem was still severe. Philadelphia was a case in point. From a peak in mid–1989, cocaine-related emergency cases declined by 12 percent by the end of the year. The number of cases, however, was still several times greater than in the late 1970s and early 1980s. The coordinator for drug abuse programs in Philadelphia remarked: "You wouldn't know there was a decline by talking to the emergency room people. They're so overwhelmed they're at the point that they don't know where to turn." In addition, some decline in cocaine-related emergency cases in hospitals was the effect of street retail dealers choosing to dilute the product rather than raise prices (Treaster, 7/1/90).

Heroin emergency statistics present an equally mixed picture. In New York, heroin deaths declined 22 percent in 1989, while emergency-room episodes stayed virtually the same as in 1988. Nationally, heroin and morphine deaths fell 31 percent between 1988 and 1989, as the purity of the heroin on the street was rising. Purity levels for heroin of 3 to 5 percent were once common. The DEA has recently reported purity levels at 50 percent in two major East Coast cities and 35 to 40 percent in two other cities (Belsie, 8/1/90). Reports of health emergencies related to crack smoking, not mentioned by the administration, increased tenfold from 1985 to 1987 (*New York Times*, 5/28/89).

"Drug Babies"

Whatever the successes the administration was able to claim by selectively using emergency room figures for particular drugs, or temporary price increases, the statistics on drug-affected infants indicated not success, but failure. The number of babies born to drug-addicted mothers in New York City increased from less than a thousand in 1978 to 4,800 in 1989 (*New York Times*, 12/24/89). According to one survey in 1988, approximately 11 percent of U.S. infants tested positive for cocaine or alcohol. One New York City Health Department official estimated that births to drug-abusing mothers had increased in New York City by about 3,000 percent over the past decade (Dorris, 6/25/90). In one study in Rhode Island, 7.5 percent of 465 women whose urine was tested had used cocaine, marijuana, speed, or opiates two days before giving birth (Byrd, 4/13/90).

Crime

Both Republican administrations have also played a shell game with crime statistics, at times making it sound as if almost all the increases in crime were drug-related. But the entire issue of drug-related crime is problematic. There is little agreement about what drug-related crime is. The exact relationship between drugs and crime is not specified in major national data bases, and as the moral panic about drugs being engendered by the administration has increased, the willingness to cite drugs as the cause of all forms of crime has increased.

The conventional conception of drug-related crime is crime engaged in due to the influence of drug ingestion. A more useful breakdown of the ways in which drugs and crime can be related, however, has been formulated by Paul Goldstein et al. (1989), who have posited that drugs and crime can be related in three different ways: psychopharmacologically, economic compulsively, and systemically. These models are described as follows:

The *psychopharmacological* model suggests that some persons, as a result of ingesting specific substances, may become excitable and/or irrational, and may act out in a violent fashion. Psychopharmacological violence may also result from the irritability associated with withdrawal syndromes from addictive substances. Psychopharmacological violence may involve substance use by either victims or perpetrators of violent events. In this regard, substance use may contribute to a person behaving violently, or it may alter a person's behavior in such a manner as to bring about that person's violent victimization. Finally, some persons may ingest substances purposively in order to reduce nervousness or boost courage and thereby facilitate the commission of previously intended violent crime.

The *economic compulsive* model suggests that some persons feel compelled to engage in economic crimes in order to finance costly drug use. Sometimes these economic crimes are inherently violent, as in the case of robbery, and sometimes the violence results from an unintended or extraneous factor in the social context in which the economic crime is perpetrated. Such factors include the perpetrator's nervousness, the victim's reaction, the presence or absence of weapons carried by either victim or perpetrator, the intercession of bystanders, and so on.

The *systemic* model refers to the normally aggressive patterns of interaction within the systems of drug use and distribution. Most systemic violence is posited to arise from the exigencies of working or doing business in a black market. Examples of systemic violence include territorial disputes between rival dealers, assaults and homicides committed within particular drug dealing operations in order to enforce normative codes, robberies of drug dealers, elimination of informers, punishment for selling adulterated or bogus drugs, assaults to collect drug related debts. Systemic violence may also occur between users, as in cases of disputes over drugs or drug paraphernalia. (Goldstein et al., 1989:3)

In terms of these models, crime engaged in due to economic compulsive or systemic factors can be said to be attributable to the illegality of drugs, not to drugs themselves. A great deal of what is popularly considered drug-related crime, therefore, is in actuality Drug War–related crime.

For example, drug-related bombings were said to have almost doubled between 1988 and 1989. In 1989, there were sixty-four drug-related bombings. There were thirty-three in 1988. But the spokesman for the Treasury Department's Bureau of Alcohol, Tobacco, and Firearms (which issued a report in mid–1990) noted that most of these bombings were related to turf battles or disagreements between different factions of traffickers. "I don't think," the spokesman said, "there's any question but the street level of activity in narcotics is becoming increasingly violent" (*Montgomery Advertiser*, 6/22/90). In March 1990, a DEA office in Florida was gutted by a large firebomb (*Montgomery Advertiser*, 3/18/90). This was certainly due not to drug-crazed addicts but to hard-nosed drug traffickers competing in an illegal market.

Between 1988 and 1989, Federal Bureau of Investigation (FBI) estimates were that the national homicide rate increased 5 percent. In 1987 there was a killing every twenty-six minutes; by the end of 1988, that figure was a killing every twenty-five minutes. Much of the increase in homicide rates was said to be drug-related. Many experts, however, argued that the increases were due to turf wars among drug dealers, the increased availability of lethal weapons, greater social acceptance of violence, and demographic changes. Some criminologists, for example Jim Fyfe at American University, argued that the violence could be directly attributed to turf wars, especially for sales of crack (Malcolm, 12/31/89).

Homicide rates continued to rise in the first half of 1990. More than a dozen major cities reported 10 to 50 percent increases in homicide rates over rates for the first six months of 1989. Nationwide, FBI statistics indicated a 5 percent increase in violent crime in 1989 and a 4 percent increase in homicides. The increase was even greater in cities with populations over one million (6 percent to 7 percent). Many experts attributed this rise to an increase in drug disputes and deadlier weapons on the streets (Hinds, 7/18/90).

The increases in and of themselves are a significant indicator that enforcement tactics are not having the impact claimed for them. For example, the murder rate in cities like New York and Boston continued to rise even though officials were reporting a decline in cocaine use (Treaster, 7/1/90).

The murder toll in the United States may break a record of a decade in 1990. The Senate Judiciary Committee placed the blame on rising stockpiles of assault weapons and shrinking supplies of cocaine, not drug-crazed addicts. If the trend continues, the committee predicted that 23,220 people could be murdered in 1990. Senator Joseph R. Biden said it could turn out to be "the bloodiest year in American history." The United States is already the most murderous industrialized nation in the world. The dwindling supply of cocaine in some major cities has caused increasingly violent turf wars, and there is a growing arsenal of assault weapons in the hands of drug dealers (Robinson, 9/1/90).

In claiming success in their War on Drugs in September 1990, Bush and Bennett failed to note this rising murder rate, a fact pointed out by Biden, who maintained that the rate might be up 2,000 from the figures for 1989 (*Christian Science Monitor*, 9/7/90).

WHY ENFORCEMENT FAILS

It should come as no surprise that enforcement strategies have been ineffective in stopping the use and trafficking of drugs. Human beings have historically been adept at securing the goods and services they desired despite government prohibitions, and business entrepreneurs (legal and illegal) have always invested considerable time and effort circumventing any restrictions of the law that inhibit their activities. In the drug business, stepped-up law enforcement efforts in one neighborhood or region frequently result only in a move of the activity to another locale. Several highly publicized police sweeps in neighborhoods of Washington, D.C., for example, had the result of temporarily moving drug activity to other neighborhoods. The selling of drugs resumed as soon as the television cameras left and the police presence decreased.

Similarly, arrests, prosecutions, and the incarceration of dealers, far from eliminating the problem of drug trafficking, only result in others moving in to take their place. As one ex-dealer noted to a *New York Times* reporter, "The police can arrest me. But as soon as they take me away there are two or three people who come in and take my place. There's too much money involved for it to be any other way" (Marriott, 6/1/89). In fact, arrests of drug dealers often serve only to destabilize the market, and consequently they increase the violence of turf battles between new dealers competing over territories. In New York City, for example, the FBI, the DEA, the U.S. Attorney's Office, and the City Police Department coordinated efforts in Operation Horse Collar, which was widely acclaimed for its elimination of the turf battles between government agencies. Between 1986 and 1989, Operation Horse Collar is said to have resulted in the conviction of 150 drug dealers. However, federal and local authorities admitted that drug sales, especially of cocaine, did not even decrease in the areas where these drug dealers had operated (Holmes, 1/21/90). This operation may have decreased turf battles among government agencies, but it fostered them on the street.

A professor of sociology at UCLA wrote the following in the *Washington Post*:

Prosecutorial shocks given to the higher levels of drug markets commonly produce chaotic violence at lower levels. Drug arrests and seizures break established deals and leave unpaid debts, raise a host of suspicions about treachery and create a series of interconnected scrambles to supply suddenly unmet user demands and to fill suddenly vacant distribution positions. Such ripple effects are a leading explanation for the dramatic fluctuations in drug-related violence across American cities in recent years. (Katz, 6/5–/11/89)

In addition, the fact that police action may decrease blatant sales of drugs on the street frequently means only a change in operating procedure. For example, a 1989 federal report on New York City's illegal drug industry noted that the city police had reduced some of the more blatant street traffic but that dealers had merely moved to fortified apartments or abandoned buildings, where they were even more difficult to root out (Marriott, 6/1/89).

In addition, stepped-up enforcement tends to distort the drug market. Stepped-up enforcement targeting marijuana, for example, drove up prices to such an extent that crack cocaine became a cheaper alternative (Passell, 9/5/89). In some areas of New York City in mid–1989, crack prices had decreased from $5 a vial to $3, and in addition, tokes were being sold for pocket change (Marriott, 6/1/89).

Harvard economist Mark Kleiman, in his book *Marijuana: Costs of Abuse, Costs of Control*, has argued that efforts to interdict marijuana coming over the border succeed only in stimulating the domestic market and encouraging the development of more potent strains of marijuana. Kleiman also argues that the assumption that every ton of marijuana confiscated is one less ton consumed is a fantasy (Passell, 9/5/89).

According to government estimates, domestic production of marijuana rose 10 percent from 1982 to 1986, during the Reagan administration's stepped-up border interdiction. It is now estimated that one-quarter of the marijuana sold in the United States is home-grown (Passell, 9/5/89). In one state, Alabama, the marijuana *destroyed* in 1989 by state officials was worth more than any other legal cash crop grown in the state (Harper, 2/18/90).

Stiffer border controls also have the effect of increasing the risks to importers and therefore driving the more poorly capitalized importers out of business, which further centralizes the control of the market. The risks to larger importers are offset by the rise in prices. For those remaining in the trade, the profits are higher than ever (Passell, 9/5/89).

Among economists there is little disagreement that interdiction efforts have a perverse effect on the drug market (Passell, 9/5/89). As UCLA sociologist Jack Katz has noted, "Recent studies indicate that increases in enforcement pressures do not even seem to raise the street price of drugs. They are most likely to increase and concentrate the wealth of the surviving drug dealers" (Katz, 6/5–/11/89).

Stepped-up enforcement also frequently leads to substitution. In July 1990, for example, participants in a conference held by NIDA were maintaining decreases in cocaine use and no evidence of substitution. By August 1990, however, after more than a decade of decline, heroin use in some cities was on the rise. Federal drug authorities were saying in August 1990 that heroin was then more abundant and cheaper and was sold in purer forms. In addition, according to DEA estimates, between 1985 and 1989 the world production of opium more than doubled (Belsie, 8/1/90).

If an increase in cocaine prices simply results in what the DEA has referred to as an "explosion" of heroin production, we will have gained little. Heroin has become a routine alternative to cocaine. And as the purity of heroin increases, so does the possibility of smoking it rather than injecting it, thereby decreasing the aversion to needles and AIDS.

The crackdown on imported drugs has also raised fears that new synthetic substitutes, which are more dangerous, will take their place. The High School Seniors Survey at the end of 1989 noted an increase in the use of phencyclidine (PCP). Even though the process of manufacturing the drug is dangerous because of its explosive potential, it is very easy to make and is highly profitable. The explosive potential (drug officials maintain that five gallons of liquid PCP can explode with the force of a stick of dynamite) means that the risks of manufacturing the drug also affect third parties (Lait, 4/17/88).

THE ILLUSORY BENNETT-BUSH VICTORY

Despite these facts, William Bennett began declaring a victory in the War on Drugs after only a year in office. One of the real beauties of the War on Drugs is that failure and progress can be claimed as an excuse to continue and expand the war. Evidence of expanding drug abuse can be used to frighten the public into allowing even greater efforts and expenditures in the drug war. Evidence of limited successes can be used to support the notion that progress is being made, victory is in sight, if only the fight is continued. For example, just before the drug summit in Colombia, Bennett maintained that the war was "clearly winnable" and that there were "clear signs" of the beginning of a victory. "The Scourge," he said "[was] beginning to pass" (Berke, 2/3/90). As Richard Berke (2/18/90) noted in the *New York Times*, Bush spoke so much of "success" and "headway" and "cooperation" before he left for Colombia that it was unclear why he even needed to go.

But when Bennett was appointed "Drug Czar," his initial targets for drug use reduction fell well into line with trends that had been apparent before he took office. Mark Hamm (1988) argued that an examination of official statistics indicates that drug use rates were decreasing as the nation began its drug war. Hamm cited data from NIDA and the Gallup polls that indicated a decline in drug use in the mid–1980s.

In addition, most of the widely touted reduction in drug use, even by official estimates, has come from middle-class and not lower-class users. For example, Bennett used as evidence for an administration victory before the Colombia summit the continuing decline in middle-class drug use (*Washington Post*, 1/28/90). Middle-class users, however, have not been and are not likely to be targets of police enforcement tactics and new harsher penalties. If a reduction has occurred within the middle class, it is likely to be an effect of education and not increased enforcement tactics.

The supposed reduction in middle-class drug usage is always measured by survey responses. The fact that the administration, through a media campaign, can alter the number of people who approve of drug taking or who are willing to admit using drugs demonstrates very little except the power of the media on the one hand and the increasing fear of surveillance and thus the admission of drug use on the other. Survey responses only show a decline in the number of those admitting drug use, not necessarily a decline in actual usage.

Government surveys, for example, indicated a decline in drug use among high school seniors in 1989. But one out of every two seniors indicated that they had tried an illicit drug. And as the survey's authors noted, the figures did not include students who had dropped out of high school, who are commonly thought to be more involved in illicit drug use. In some major metropolitan areas, this dropout rate is estimated to be as high as 50 percent (*Criminal Justice Newsletter*, 3/15/89). The dropout rate for teenagers overall is 27 percent (Isikoff, 2/19–/25/90). But even considering the figures for those still in school, the evidence is that the War on Drugs is not having a significant impact on the availability of drugs. For example, 85 percent of high school seniors surveyed said marijuana would be easy to get; 55 percent said cocaine would be easy to obtain (*Criminal Justice Newsletter*, 3/15/89).

The government-sponsored survey of high school seniors at the end of 1989 was much touted by Bush and Bennett. But aside from the other inadequacies of the survey, reported PCP usage increased, as did the reported use of heroin. The percentage of students reporting use of crack remained the same. Democratic Representative Charles Rangel noted quite rightly that the study was of "extremely limited value" (Isikoff, 2/19–/25/90).

Even though Bush and Bennett declared victory shortly before the drug summit in Colombia in February 1990, by April, administration officials were scrambling to explain a report that indicated that Bennett's "test case" in the District of Columbia had been a failure. Federal officials (including Bennett) blamed D.C. city officials for the fact that drugs were still cheap and plentiful in the District of Columbia and that "drug-related killings" had not decreased after a year of federal intervention (Shenon, 4/5/90). In a news conference after the release of the report, Bennett maintained that "the length of a baseball season may be enough to establish a winner of the World Series. It's not enough to win the war on drugs in this city or any other city." Bennett argued that despite the figures from the District of Columbia, there had been "successes" such as raids on 209 suspected crack houses (Berke, 10/20/89).

Bennett's report noted some other "successes" in the District of Columbia, such as the creation of a special DEA team that had made scores of arrests and seized millions of dollars of drug assets (Shenon, 4/5/90). It is difficult, however, to see how this can be considered a success unless the intent of this "test case" was to expand the DEA and enrich its coffers. Jack Blum, former special counsel on narcotics to the Senate Foreign Relations Committee, called the administration's figures "macho numbers" (Berke, 2/18/90).

And the battle of the macho numbers goes on and on and on. After Biden released the new figures for cocaine addicts that so infuriated Bennett, the response of the administration was to release figures a week later showing that cocaine-related hospital emergencies had declined 20 percent in the fourth quarter of 1990. Bennett proclaimed a "leveling-off of addiction" and a "peaking of the addiction problem" (*New York Times*, 5/15/90). Secretary of Health and Human Services Lewis Sullivan, whose agency released the figures, defensively stated that they were not "smoke-and-mirror projections" or "hunches." But even though the 8,627 cocaine emergencies in the fourth quarter of 1989 was lower than the 1988 peak of 11,094, it was triple the figure for cocaine emergencies in the fourth quarter of 1985 (Kelley, 5/15/90). In addition, no one in the administration pointed out the possible effects of harsher penalties on cocaine use and, therefore, a doctor's or a patient's reluctance to report it. Nor was it even considered that the quality of the cocaine on the street is directly related to cocaine emergencies.

Bennett's deputy chief of staff maintained that the data on cocaine emergencies indicated that drug abuse was no longer "spiraling out of control" and (with the elegance that has characterized official statements in the Reagan and Bush administrations) that "bodies [were] not piling up as a result of cocaine or any other drug." He added, however, that this did not mean any reduction in proposed spending on the drug war (*Montgomery Advertiser*, 5/24/90).

In a press conference in September 1990, Bennett and Bush released a new white paper on drugs, and Bush claimed "progress" in the War on Drugs. However, Representative John Conyers, Jr., (D-Mich.) stated that the administration "cannot deny that we are losing the drug war in our inner cities." Conyers pointed out that measures directed at the "educated middle class appear to be having a dramatic effect." Conyers continued: "Treatment programs have room for clients who can afford to pay. However, the chronically addicted cannot pay when they are poor and unemployed, as is often the case." Representative Charles B. Rangel, chairman of the House Select Committee on Narcotics Abuse and Control, agreed, arguing that the statistics used by the administration primarily applied to the middle class (Skorneck, 9/6/90).

In a survey of almost 400,000 junior high and high school students conducted by the Parents' Resource Institute for Drug Education, and released in September 1989, it was reported that the percentage of students reporting use had dropped but that those using cocaine were getting higher. Even though the number of students who reported using cocaine decreased, the percentage reporting "very high" or "bombed/stoned" from cocaine increased (Skorneck, 9/27/89).

Even while announcing "progress," Bush admitted that there was "still too much violence, too much destruction, too many innocent victims." "Drugs" he said, were "still an international menace" (Skorneck, 9/6/90).

Therefore, failure and success in the drug war called for the administration doing more of the same. But more of the same (i.e., a continuation of criminalization, stepped-up law enforcement tactics, and harsher penalties) has not only been ineffective at decreasing drug use and trafficking, it has brought about additional social costs as well.

SOCIAL COSTS OF THE WAR ON DRUGS

Enforcement Costs

The costs of the enforcement and interdiction strategy are staggering if one considers their failure to adequately address the root causes of the problem of drug trafficking and abuse, and the other purposes to which all this money could be put. The Reagan administration conducted an eight-year, multi-billion dollar war against drugs. In one year, 1988, the federal government spent an estimated $3 billion to fight the War on Drugs. The Bush administration asked Congress for $150 million in anti-drug grants to state and local agencies alone. Lawmakers sought $275 million for fiscal year 1990. Under the initial Bush proposals, the DEA would receive even more money ($551 million) than it received under the Reagan administration ($546 million). The real costs of the War on Drugs are difficult to assess since many appropriations are hidden within other budgets. Under the Bush proposals for 1990, for example, an additional $68 million was to go to the DEA through a separate appropriation (*Criminal Justice Newsletter*, 3/1/89).

The costs of the War on Drugs are also reflected in increased personnel. The Bush proposal for 1991 included the addition of some 6,000 federal agents, prosecutors, and support staff, including an additional 700 U.S. attorneys and 75 new federal judges. The official figure for the drug war for fiscal year 1990 was $9.5 billion (Corn, 5/14/90). The federal budget for drug programs has quadrupled in five years. And the Pentagon budget for drug interdiction has doubled over the last year (Shenon, 4/22/90). In 1989, there was an estimated $986 million being spent on anti-marijuana enforcement alone (Wenner, 6/22/90).

Much of the money to fight the domestic drug war is expected to come from increasing the demands on the states. For example, it is expected that the states will spend from $5 to $10 billion on new prison construction to meet the goals of Bush's national drug strategy. Bush has in addition called for drug testing at almost every phase of the criminal justice process. This would add to the costs of the states, which are already strapped for money (Weinraub, 9/8/89).

Other funds are coming from cutbacks in social programs. In late 1989, for example, Bush proposed shifting $50 million from public housing subsidies to the drug program. He also proposed abolishing the Economic Development Fund and thereby releasing an additional $194 million (Herman, 11/89). In an especially self-defeating move, the administration also proposed shifting some $40 million from juvenile justice programs (Silk, 9/8/89). As Carl Rowan has written, Bush's War on Drugs is being "waged with money that the Congress is supposed to shave off the very programs that offer millions of Americans the slim hope that stands between them and submission to the drug peddlers" (Rowan, 9/8/89).

These expenditures come amid cries that the money being spent for the War on Drugs is not enough (see, for example, Morgenthau, 9/27/89). The Democrats, who have ceased to be an effective party of opposition, could react to Bush's proposals only by complaining that more money should be spent (Silk, 9/8/89).

The largest share of the 1988 appropriation for the drug war, $962.2 million, was allocated to interdiction. The concentration on enforcement in the expenditure of funds can be clearly seen by comparing the percentage of money devoted to treatment, education, and prevention in 1970 (55.9 percent) with the percentage of money devoted to treatment, education, and prevention in 1987 (23.7 percent) (Drug Policy Foundation, 1989). Even amid Reagan administration rhetoric about drug prevention education, the budget of the Department of Education for programs to combat drug abuse was reduced to $2.9 million in 1985 from $14 million in 1981 (MacDonald, 1988:10). These reductions were supported by Bennett (Berke, 2/3/90).

The Bush administration's plan for 1991 called for $617 million to be spent on drug education and treatment programs through the Department of Education. Even though this represented an increase in funding from $562 million in 1990, Senator Biden pointed out that with that level of funding only around 40 percent of grade school children would have access to drug treatment funds on a regular basis (Berke, 2/3/90).

The Bush administration proposed that for fiscal year 1991 the basic split of funds—70 percent for enforcement and 30 percent for treatment—be maintained (Berke, 1/25/90). Bush proposed to funnel roughly $40 million into five areas called "high intensity" drug abuse zones in 1990, to be spent exclusively for law enforcement (Johnson, 12/13/89). Bennett reaffirmed the administration's lack of faith in education as a means of doing anything about drugs in his testimony before the Senate Judiciary Committee in February 1990. When Bennett was secretary of education under Reagan, he even sought a cut in drug education funds (Berke, 2/3/90). But even former members of the DEA have argued that more funds are needed for treatment. Robert Stutman, who resigned in 1990 as the chief of the DEA's New York City office, supported increased funding for treatment even if it meant taking money away from law enforcement. "The drug war," he stated, "will be won or lost based on our education and treatment programs and not on how many people we arrest" (Meddis, 3/12/90). Bush's proposals for fiscal year 1991, however, included only $102 million for community treatment programs and $150 million for a public housing program (Rosenthal, 1/24/90). Only 14 percent was earmarked for treatment. In 1990, the Bureau of Justice Assistance (BJA) money for drug treatment in jails was slashed (Corn, 5/14/90).

Again, the Democrats, showing a complete lack of vision, could only respond to Bush's budget proposals to fight the War on Drugs by recommending the expenditure of $14.5 billion, instead of the $10.6 billion recommended by Bush (*Washington Post*, 1/28/90).

The experience of New York City in terms of enforcement-related expenditures to combat drug use is instructive. In fiscal year 1988, New York City spent $500 million on drug-related enforcement, more than twice the money spent in 1986. According to New York State statistics, however, the figure of 182,000 estimated regular cocaine abusers in 1986 grew to an estimated 600,000 in 1988 (Berke, 4/7/89). And there is evidence that the populace at large does not agree with the emphasis on law enforcement to deal with the drug problem. In a Media General-Associated Press poll conducted in late 1989, for example, 60 percent of respondents said that treating drug users would accomplish more than punishing them (Langer, 10/2/89).

As S. H. Kadish noted some time ago, "It seems fair to say that in few areas of the criminal law have we paid so much for so little" (1971:63).

Deflection of Police Resources

The time, resources, and energy devoted to policing complaintless crimes, like drug use and trafficking, also deflects police time and resources away from other more serious crimes, crimes that are associated with just as much violence and that are arguably more destructive to the social fabric—white collar crimes, corporate crimes, environmental crimes, and political crimes (Reiman, 1984; Hills, 1987).

The House Subcommittee on Oversight and Investigation estimated that in 1976 unnecessary surgery cost the nation $3.5 billion and led to 12,000 deaths. The director of public health in California has argued that medical quackery kills more people than all crimes of violence taken together (Eitzen and Timmer, 1985:190, 195). In early 1990, a major study of medical malpractice revealed that 7,000 people died in New York State hospitals in 1984 due to negligent care. Sidney Wolfe, director of the Health Research Group, a Washington-based consumer advocacy organization, commented that the New York State study of medical malpractice suggested that approximately 89,890 people die each year because of medical malpractice inside hospitals nationwide (Winslow, 3/1/90). But a police force consumed with fighting the War on Drugs has no time for these types of crimes.

In fact, the crimes of the powerful are increasingly being ignored, especially if they primarily affect marginalized segments of the population. In the New York State study, for example, it was estimated that 70 percent of in-hospital injuries that occurred in the emergency room were the result of negligence, and that the rates of negligent injury were higher in hospitals with a high proportion of minority patients than in those treating primarily white patients. The economic losses suffered by injured patients measured in lost wages and fringe benefits, uninsured medical costs, and household production was estimated to be $894 million in 1989 dollars (Winslow, 3/1/90).

However, due to shifts in resources to fight the War on Drugs, Bush's budget proposals for 1990 would mean that the FBI (which has traditionally been at least partly involved in investigations of crimes of the powerful) would experience a 4 percent manpower cutback in 1990, while the DEA would gain 380 new agent positions, a 12 percent increase (Barrett, 1/30/90).

During the Reagan administration, oversight of crimes of the powerful decreased drastically. For example, regulation of financial institutions eased rather than tightened. Money laundering and savings and loan fraud flourished while the Reagan administration fought the War on Drugs and implemented a hiring freeze that limited the number of bank examiners and Internal Revenue Service agents (Morley, 10/2/89). In 1979, after exposés in *Parade* magazine and on *60 Minutes*, an interagency task force (Operation Greenback) was launched in an effort to curb drug banking. Within a year of George Bush's appointment to lead the nation's anti-drug strategy, however, Operation Greenback had been downgraded to a unit within the office of the U.S. Attorney in Miami. Charles Blau, Chief Prosecutor in Operation Greenback, said that Bush "wasn't really too interested in financial prosecution" (Morley, 10/2/89). In April 1990, the House Government Operations commerce subcommittee accused the Bush administration of failing to match rhetoric with manpower over the S&L crisis. Using information from an FBI study, the subcommittee noted that the agency lacked sufficient agents to investigate the S&L fraud (Barrett and Brannigan, 4/3/90).

The shift of concentration to drug cases has also led to a de-emphasizing of the crimes of the powerful in the courts. Increases in federal drug cases have meant that civil cases in the federal courts are increasingly delayed. One example of the seriousness of this delay in processing civil cases is *Florida v. Great Lakes Chemical Corporation*. In this case, Great Lakes Chemical Corporation is charged with exposing residents in Florida to a cancer-causing chemical (Wermiel, 2/6/90). But with current priorities being what they are, the prosecution of a corporation exposing countless citizens to cancer-causing chemicals for profit can be delayed while individual drug consumers or dealers are prosecuted.

Enforcement Primarily Affects Street Criminals

The enforcement tactics that are the primary focus of the War on Drugs primarily affect lower-class individuals, even within the drug-using and drug-trafficking community. Middle- and upper-class dealers and users are seldom targeted. Police officials use the same "difficulty of enforcement" argument to explain this disparity as they use to explain the lack of enforcement of laws against white collar crime. The police maintain that the drug use and trafficking of the middle and upper classes is more difficult to detect because it does not commonly take place in the street (Jordan, 2/26/88).

But the disproportionate impact on the lower class of enforcement tactics cannot always be explained away as due to difficulty of enforcement. In New York City, for example, enforcement tactics with regard to crack have purposefully been focused on street dealers rather than big-time suppliers (Kifner, 9/8/89).

The President's Commission on Law Enforcement and the Administration of Justice noted as long ago as 1967 that "the application of these laws [against complaintless crimes] often tends to discriminate against the poor and subcultural groups in the population." The report concluded that because of this differential enforcement, "poverty itself becomes a crime" (1967:103–4).

Profit Margin and Organized Crime

The criminalization of any drug increases the profit margin associated with its production and distribution. *High Times* magazine has estimated that due to interdiction efforts, the wholesale price and therefore the profit margin of the sale of medium-grade marijuana rose from $90 to $175 per pound in 1968–1970 to $1,100 to $1,400 in early 1990. In the 1989 trial of Guillermo Tabraue, a Bay of Pigs veteran, federal prosecutors maintained that the single drug syndicate operated by Tabraue and his son earned $75 million between 1976 and 1987. Tabraue also increased his profits by taking $1,400 a month from the Central Intelligence Agency (CIA) to provide information about drug trafficking among Bay of Pigs veterans (Corn and Morley, 4/17/89a). Thomas Mickens, described as being part of the middle management of drug traffickers around Kennedy Airport, was sentenced in 1990 to thirty years in prison. In four years of drug trafficking, Mickens was estimated to be worth $3.5 million in assets (Holmes, 1/24/90).

The huge profits to be made from criminalized drugs virtually guarantee organized crime involvement. The profits gleaned during the prohibition era virtually established organized crime in the United States. Paul Eddy, Hugo Sabogal, and Sara Walden (1988:43) have argued that the U.S. Mafia was the first to recognize the enormous potential of the cocaine market and the role that smugglers in Medellín could play as suppliers. Criminalization, therefore, has helped to create new organized crime groups. In fact, organized crime is often dependent on new criminalizations for its profits.

Investment in the Legal Economy

The profits from illegal drug transactions are reinvested not only in other illegal activities but in legal business activities as well. For example, Max Mermelstein, a former drug dealer in Miami turned FBI informant, related stories of delivering cash to legitimate banks in duffel bags (Engelberg, 3/6/89). In April 1989, the Justice Department filed a civil suit seeking to seize $433.5 million in laundered drug money that moved through the accounts of nine U.S. banks and foreign banks with U.S. branches (Wines, 4/3/89). Some of this money was invested in U.S. real estate (Wines, 3/30/89).

Bank regulators have also noted unusually large numbers of cash sales of real estate, automobiles, and boats in Dade County, Florida, thought to be financed with drug money. It is estimated that as much as 2 to 10 percent of Dade County's legal business boom has been driven by drug profits. Local prosecutors note that this large increase in cash transactions has had the effect of increasing property taxes and inflating the price of real estate (Labaton, 12/6/89). One economist, Charles Kimball, has argued that Florida's economy is dependent on drug money and that if the flow of money was cut off, there would be a real estate recession in Florida (Freemantle, 1986:45).

As Robert B. Reich, a political economist at the John F. Kennedy School of Government at Harvard University, pointed out to a *New York Times* reporter, "narcotics is one of America's major industries right up there with consumer electronics, automobiles, and steelmaking" (Labaton, 12/6/89).

Corruption

The clandestine nature of drug investigations and the enormous profits associated with illegal drugs inevitably lead to police corruption. Questionable, if not illegal, practices are characteristic of investigations of complaintless crimes. The use of low visibility tactics such as decoys, informants, bugging devices, wiretapping, and no-knock raids is commonplace in drug investigations, and it increases opportunities for corruption. The President's Commission on Law Enforcement and the Administration of Justice noted over twenty years ago the negative consequences of such tactics of enforcement:

The practical costs of this departure from principle are significant. One of its consequences is to communicate to the people who tend to be the object of these laws the idea that law enforcement is not a regularized, authoritative procedure, but largely a matter of arbitrary behavior by the authorities. (1967:103–4)

Police. The examples of law enforcement involvement in drugs are legion; they involve every level of police from local police to federal agents. In 1986, for example, thirteen officers from New York's Seventy-Seventh Precinct in the Bedford-Stuyvesant section of Brooklyn were charged with selling cocaine and accepting bribes (Marriott, 6/1/89).

In 1987, the U.S. Attorney's Office began investigating charges that

Washington, D.C., police officers had routinely lied under oath to obtain search warrants of homes in vice cases. Investigators were told that in some cases the informants whose testimony was cited did not exist. In other cases the informants were real, but the alleged drug transactions never happened. In response to this investigation, U.S. Attorney Joseph E. di Genova was forced to drop 300 to 400 drug cases (Walsh and Lewis, 6/27/87).

The Miami police force was plagued by drug-related corruption scandals in the 1980s. In 1984 and 1985, fifteen Miami police officers were charged with robbing drug dealers (*New York Times*, 1/25/90). In October 1986, seven Miami police officers were charged with reselling drugs stolen from users and dealers. The officers were said by prosecutors to have made at least $700,000 each from the sales. The officers were accused of being part of a drug-theft ring responsible for the sale of over $15 million of cocaine. The ring is also said to have been responsible for four deaths, including setting up the death of one of the drug dealers (*Washington Post*, 10/24/86).

In July 1987, a federal grand jury indicted twelve former Miami policemen on racketeering, drug, and civil rights charges. Six other former Miami police officers were also indicted in the case involving the deaths of several drug-smuggling suspects. The officers were charged with conspiracy; racketeering; possession and sale of cocaine, marijuana, and Quaaludes; tax evasion; and civil rights violations (*Washington Post*, 7/15/87).

The acquittal of a police officer in the beating death of a black businessman helped touch off riots in Miami in 1980. The riots left eighteen people dead and resulted in $80 million in property damage. In April 1989, this same police officer was arrested on drug charges along with a federal drug agent. The two men had offered to provide protection for a man working with an undercover sting operation who said he wanted to smuggle large quantities of cocaine into the United States from the Bahamas. For this protection, the two demanded a fee of $300,000 (*Anchorage Daily News*, 4/11/89b).

In January 1990, three Miami police officers were charged with plotting the theft of 110 pounds of cocaine, a ton of marijuana, and more than $1 million in cash from drug dealers. The prosecution argued that these three, along with several businessmen, a former sheriff's deputy, and a former Nevada narcotics officer, had been involved in shakedowns of drug dealers from 1981 to 1987. The officers were additionally alleged to have arranged for the transfer of "honest" police officers out of their area to facilitate the robberies they were conducting. Thirty-nine separate acts of theft were listed in the indictment, one of which involved $415,000 in cash from a home in 1982. In a separate case, a Florida grand jury indicted another Miami patrolman for conspiracy and intent to distribute cocaine (*New York Times*, 1/25/90).

The New York Police Department has considered the problem of police involvement in illegal drug trafficking so serious that it has found it necessary to establish a special undercover squad to try to control drug-related criminal activity among police officers. The initiation of the special squad was in response to findings in 1986 that officers had been systematically robbing drug dealers of cash, narcotics, and guns (Pitt, 9/30/88).

Police officers in most major metropolitan police departments have been involved in drug corruption—in Miami (*New York Times*, 1/25/90); in Houston (Belkin, 12/10/89); and in Detroit, to name a few. In December 1989, a federal grand jury in Detroit began investigating what had happened to over $1 million from a secret account administered by the Detroit Police Department established to pay for undercover operations, including drug buys (Schmidt, 12/14/89). There have also been numerous incidents of law enforcement personnel convicted on drug charges in smaller cities—for example, in Selma, Alabama (*Montgomery Advertiser*, 12/29/89). In May 1990, a federal grand jury in Montgomery, Alabama, indicted an investigative technician with the Department of Public Safety for alerting the operators of an illegal drug laboratory of an impending raid (Ingram, 5/23/90).

In early 1990, a police officer in Montgomery, Alabama, Brad Sims, was convicted on charges that he sold crack cocaine to a police informant. Sims's defense attorney argued at his trial that Sims had been set up by other officers because he knew of their involvement in protecting drug dealers. Sims was convicted. In February 1989, however, four policemen were forced to resign from the Montgomery, Alabama, Narcotics and Intelligence Bureau after they failed to turn in money seized in a drug raid set up to test their honesty (McCartney and Gerome, 2/15/90). Sims (who is black) was denied a new trial even though three of the four officers (who are white) were involved in the search of his home that turned up $360 in marked money that was the basis of his conviction (Foss, 2/20/90).

In August 1990, four county sheriffs in eastern Kentucky were arrested for taking more than $85,000 in bribes during a one-year period from traffickers transporting cocaine through their jurisdictions. The sheriffs and two other officers were charged with conspiracy, drug distribution, and protecting others transporting drugs (*New York Times*, 8/17/90).

A federal inquiry into drug use and distribution in Dauphin County, Pennsylvania, resulted in the resignations of two former deputy state attorneys general after they pleaded guilty to cocaine possession. Also indicted on cocaine-related charges was a top aide to Attorney General

Thornburgh when he was governor of Pennsylvania (*New York Times*, 8/19/90).

The record at the federal level is no less disturbing. In 1988, three former DEA agents were charged with laundering more than $608,000 accumulated apparently while they were dealing in drugs. The narcotics trafficking and money laundering by the three men went on during and after their employment with the DEA (*New York Times*, 11/25/88). In December 1989, there were press reports of declining morale in the DEA due to pending trials of seven veteran DEA agents in four cases in Los Angeles, Miami, and Washington. The agents were accused of being deeply involved in illicit drug trafficking while they were employed to fight it. Agents in the Los Angeles case were charged with taking drugs from traffickers and stash houses and then travelling around the world arranging drug deals and hiding the proceeds (Berke, 12/17/89). In early August 1990, the Philippine military filed murder charges against three DEA agents and thirteen Filipino policemen for the killing of three soldiers during a seizure of narcotics (*USA Today*, 8/2/90).

In 1988, four coastguardsmen were convicted of drug trafficking and passing confidential information to drug smugglers. In May 1990, indictments were pending against ten more coastguardsmen (*USA Today*, 5/23/90b). Consistently denying the extent of corruption, officials persisted in presenting these cases as exceptions. Admiral Paul A. Yost, Jr., Commandant of the Coast Guard, commenting on the 1990 indictments, remarked to reporters: "We have a few bad apples" (Shenon, 5/23/90).

In August 1990, a fifteen-year veteran of the Internal Revenue Service was charged with passing on key information about an investigation into a drug-smuggling ring to one of the participants in the ring, and helping the members of the drug ring launder some of the illegal drug profits (*Atlanta Journal Constitution*, 8/11/90).

Prisons. Correctional personnel have also been repeatedly linked to drug transactions. There are reportedly more drugs in prisons than ever before. In late 1989, prison personnel in Michigan were charged with accepting bribes to arrange for some inmates to transfer from one institution to another to facilitate the operation of prison drug rings. In Illinois over the three-year period 1987–1989, a total of sixty-six employees of the Department of Corrections were arrested on drug and other illegal contraband charges. In Chicago in the spring of 1989, three deputies were charged in federal indictments along with nineteen others with running a drug ring to supply inmates in the county jail. Two prison guards in Connecticut were arrested for drug smuggling in 1989. A federal-state task force in Michigan began investigating reports in 1989 that state corrections officials had allowed visitors to smuggle illicit drugs into the prisons and had protected inmates from searches in return for payments of up to $1,000 a week by dealers (Malcolm, 12/30/89).

In June 1990, seven guards in a D.C. prison were charged with distributing marijuana, crack, or powdered cocaine to inmates. According to federal prosecutors, guards were recruiting inmates to make drug sales and arrange payments outside the prison (*Montgomery Advertiser*, 6/24/90).

As former U.S. Supreme Court Justice Earl Warren noted a decade ago, "the narcotics traffic of today . . . could never be as pervasive and open as it is unless there was connivance between authorities and criminals" (quoted in Eitzen and Timmer, 1985:233).

Others. The corruption is not only confined to law enforcement or correctional personnel; it permeates the society as well. Lawyers, merchants, and real estate agents frequently connive to hide the origins of drug money invested in legitimate business. Even mid-management drug dealers, who do not have access to offshore corporations or Swiss bank accounts, have no difficulty finding an array of legitimate businesses to launder their money (Holmes, 1/24/90). In South Florida, hearings to inform a defendant that his or her lawyer may have a conflict of interest in negotiating with the prosecutor on the defendant's behalf because he or she has been indicted on drug charges have become so frequent that they have their own name: "Orta hearings" are named after Michael Orta, a convicted Miami lawyer (Lewis, 2/9/90).

When arrests were made in early 1990 of those involved in what the *Wall Street Journal* referred to as "the nation's most efficient money laundering operation," it was discovered that dozens of "legitimate" businesses were involved, including the New York branch of the Chicago-based Continental Bank Corporation (Fialka, 3/1/90). Small inner-city businesses through which immigrants send money to relatives are also used to launder drug money. The illegal transmitting business takes a customer's money and deposits it in a legitimate bank, sometimes under the name of a fictitious corporation. From the bank, the funds are electronically transferred to another bank, leaving no trace of the real depositor. The Bush administration, however, did not even mention illegal money transmitters in the anti-drug strategy (Labaton, 9/25/89). Nor did Bennett comment on the morality of the $8 billion in currency surpluses in Miami and Los Angeles reported by the Federal Reserve Bank in Washington in the spring of 1989 (Morley, 10/2/89).

Middle-class involvement in the drug economy receives little attention. Notables who have been convicted in money-laundering deals include former Representative Robert Hanrahan (R-Ill.), right-wing Republican Pat Swindall, and a leading fund-raiser for Jerry Brown's 1980 presidential race, Richard Silberman (Morley, 10/2/89).

There are certain other segments of society that are using the facilities created by drug traffickers even though they are not directly involved in drugs. In a Senate subcommittee on narcotics report issued in early 1990, there was strong evidence that much of the money stolen from savings and loan institutions had been laundered by U.S. and foreign banks (Barrett, 2/9/90). But the involvement of all levels of society in sharing the proceeds of the drug trade is largely ignored.

Secondary Crime

The criminalization of drugs creates a whole host of secondary criminal activity. For example, criminalization creates an environment in which users often have to resort to illegal means to get money to buy drugs at costs inflated by criminalization. In addition to this is the violence that is associated with managing any illegal activity and disciplining an illegal work force. The FBI has estimated that the homicide rate in 1989 increased 5 percent over that of 1988. The rise in homicide is attributed by many to drugs, but the common wisdom is that drug use is *causing* higher crime and higher homicide rates (Malcolm, 12/31/89). There is ample evidence, however, that most of what is considered to be drug-related crime is not drug-related in the sense that drug use caused the crime; rather, it appears that these are crimes committed by drug sellers in turf battles caused by criminalization.

There is also some indication that law enforcement exacerbates the problems of violence related to drugs. In a 1987 federal grand jury probe of police officers in the District of Columbia, sources reported that the police connivance with certain drug dealers by arresting their rivals sparked violent battles between competing groups. Authorities were told that officers gave protection against arrest and advance notice of drug raids to some drug dealers. In addition, allegations were being investigated that officers diverted police funds intended to be used to pay informants and make undercover drug purchases to their own use. This investigation came at the end of an undercover FBI investigation into allegations that some of the officers were personally profiting from their work in drug enforcement (Anderson and Lewis, 10/16/87).

Disrespect for the Law

Since full enforcement of laws against illegal drugs is virtually impossible, discriminatory enforcement common, and police tactics questionable (if not illegal), criminalization promotes even more disrespect for the law and the legal system than already exists. The President's Commission on Law Enforcement and Administration of Justice has noted the following:

It is costly for society when the law arouses the feelings associated with these laws in the ghetto—a sense of persecution and helplessness before official power and hostility to police and other authority that may tend to generate the very conditions of criminality society is seeking to extirpate. (1967, 103–4)

An administration that presents itself as concerned with preserving respect for "law and order" must surely take note of a Bronx jury's decision to acquit Larry Davis on charges that Davis tried to kill nine police officers. Contrary to what the police maintained, the jury believed the defendant's arguments that he had fired in self-defense. The police officers, Davis's lawyer maintained, came to kill Davis to silence him because of his knowledge of corruption and drug dealing in the local police precincts (Blair, 11/21/88). The jury forewoman stated after the trial: "[The police] wanted him dead so he couldn't squeal on them." The 1990 acquittal of Mayor Marion Barry of Washington, D.C., on all but one count also demonstrates the growing disenchantment of the public with government tactics in the War on Drugs.

As Justice Brandeis wrote when dissenting in *Olmstead v. United States*, 277 U.S. 438, 48 S. Ct. 564, 72 L. Ed 944 (1928):

Our Government is the potent, the omnipresent teacher. For good or for ill, it teaches the whole people by its example. . . . If the Government becomes a law-breaker, it breeds contempt for law; it invites every man to become a law unto himself; it invites anarchy.

Some sixty years later, Justice William Brennan, Jr., dissenting in *United States v. Verdugo-Urquidez*, echoed Brandeis: "If we seek respect for law and order, we must observe these principles ourselves. Lawlessness breeds lawlessness" (Greenhouse, 3/1/90).

Labeling

By criminalizing the use of certain drugs, the society labels as criminals a group of people who would not for any other reason be so labelled. In 1985, for example, 45 percent of the total arrests for drug law violations were for the possession of marijuana (*Sourcebook of Criminal Justice Statistics 1986*, 1987:325). In 1988, 391,600 people were arrested for marijuana offenses (Wenner, 6/22/90). More recently, the deputy chief of New York's Tactical Narcotics Team admitted that the vast majority of arrests in New York had been of small-scale dealers and users (Marriott, 2/20/89). Small-time dealers and users then become criminals and face discrimination in employment and housing that helps ensure that continued drug involvement will be an attractive, if not the only, alternative.

The criminal label remains with the convicted person forever, no matter what his or her behavior. Longitudinal research on heroin users in London, however, has indicated the futility of labeling users as criminals early on in their lives, since drug use tends to decline on its own with increasing age (see Hamm, 1988).

Health Problems

Another cost of criminalization is that it makes dealing with the health problems associated with drug use much more difficult. Many of the deaths due to overdose can be attributed to a lack of control over dosages and qualities of drugs circulating in the market. In addition, users are reluctant to seek medical care if they are afraid of being reported as addicts. In New York City, for example, doctors recently discovered a potentially fatal condition called crack lung that could be properly treated only if the patient's drug use was known. But with increasingly harsh enforcement, patients are even more reluctant than in the past to reveal this information.

The problem of needle sharing and AIDS is another example of a health problem that potentially threatens the entire population but cannot be dealt with effectively because of criminalization. In the United States, drug users and their partners are the fastest-growing segment of AIDS victims, and intravenous drug users are considered to be the primary link between AIDS and the heterosexual population. The National Academy of Sciences has recommended that needle exchange programs be allowed to help curb the AIDS problem. The 1988 Anti-Drug Abuse Act, however, prohibited the use of most federal treatment funds for any program providing clean needles to drug users, or even bleach to clean needles (Drug Policy Foundation, 1989). In New York City, 60 percent of the estimated 200,000 intravenous drug users are believed to carry the AIDS virus. Even so, the sale and possession of hypodermic needles in New York has been illegal. Mayor Koch advocated prosecution of those who distributed free needles (Raspberry, 1/11/88).

Shortly after he became mayor of New York City, David Dinkins halted a study that was being conducted there about the effectiveness of a free needle program (the first in the nation). The program, which initially was to include four centers, was scaled back after considerable community pressure to one center near City Hall. The program therefore drew only around 300 participants. Dinkins, long a critic of the program, called it a "surrender" to drug abuse. Bennett phoned his congratulations after Dinkins cancelled the program. Even though the program did not run long enough or have enough participants to be a reliable test, roughly 50 percent of the participants went on to enroll in drug treatment programs (Purdum, 2/18/90).

As serious as the AIDS problem is, the War on Drugs ideology effectively prevents adequate responses. Needle exchange programs are suspended and even methadone is considered suspect. Intravenous drug users account for around one-third of AIDS-infected cases. It is estimated that drug users receiving methadone are about half as likely to get the AIDS virus as those not on methadone. But a report released in March 1990 by the General Accounting Office noted that most of the methadone programs it investigated were dispensing doses of methadone inadequate to effectively keep users off heroin. The doses being administered were kept at moderate levels due to fears that larger doses would lead to methadone's diversion into the illegal market, and fears of methadone's addictive qualities. Some argued that methadone was merely replacing one addiction with another (Hilts, 9/19/90). Again, though, the fear is of addiction itself. The fact that addiction to a less harmful substance is preferable is not considered.

An additional problem caused by the refusal of the society to legalize and adequately control drug use is the selling of tainted blood plasma to commercial collection centers. In one study conducted by the Johns Hopkins School of Hygiene, researchers found that 23 percent of the almost 3,000 intravenous drug users they surveyed in the Baltimore area in 1988 and 1989 reported having sold blood plasma or donated blood after they began injecting themselves with drugs. Of those surveyed, 24 percent were infected with the AIDS virus (*New York Times*, 4/25/90).

The illegality of drugs also prompts measures to smuggle drugs into the country, which can endanger the lives of those not directly involved. In July 1990, for example, a young man drank a cocaine-laced soft drink imported from Colombia that contained 1,000 times the lethal dose of cocaine, and he went into a coma. It was estimated that there were possibly 8,000 other bottles of potentially contaminated soft drink unaccounted for (*Montgomery Advertiser*, 8/15/90).

Criminalization also denies health benefits from drugs such as marijuana. At the end of 1989, the DEA rejected the recommendation of its own chief administrative judge to reclassify marijuana as a Schedule II drug, which would have made marijuana available on a prescription basis. The judge, Francis L. Young, called marijuana "one of the safest therapeutically active substances known to man." Marijuana has been used to treat patients with cancer for nausea and to suppress muscle spasms in patients with multiple sclerosis. Young argued: "It would be unreasonable, arbitrary and capricious for DEA to continue to stand between those sufferers and the benefits of this substance in light of the evidence in this record" (*New York Times*, 12/31/89b).

The DEA administrator, Frank Lawn, explained DEA's refusal to accept the recommendation by saying that Young had "failed to act as an impartial judge in this matter" (*New York Times*, 12/31/89b). Legalization of drugs would allow a control over the price of drugs, thereby allowing price to guide users toward safer drugs. Britain, for example, at one time manipulated the price of ale so that it became a cheaper alternative to gin. However, enforcement tactics against marijuana made crack cocaine a more dangerous drug than marijuana, the cheaper alternative. In one study of the health effects of crack on teenagers, it was reported that one out of ten frequent crack users had brain seizures that could result in serious illness or death (Elias, 5/3/90). The cost of caring for one infant born to a mother taking crack is estimated to be $648,000 for only eight months (Foster, 6/13/90).

It is estimated that each year 375,000 children are born having been exposed to cocaine and other drugs. It is argued that many of these children exhibit tremors, hyperactivity, listlessness, and an inability to organize their thinking (Henry, 9/2/90). Regardless of highly publicized administration lamentations about drug babies, the administration opposed legislation introduced in Congress by Senator Daniel Patrick Moynihan (D-N.Y.) in December 1989 to extend Medicaid financing to cover drug abuse treatment for pregnant women who were addicted to crack or cocaine (Johnson, 12/13/89).

Criminal Justice System Overcrowding

The War on Drugs has resulted in an overburdening of an already strained criminal justice system. In a report issued by Chief Justice William H. Rehnquist in January 1990, it was noted that in the federal district courts there had been a threefold increase in drug cases since 1980 (Greenhouse, 1/1/90). The figures for state courts reflect a similar trend. The increase in drug cases measured as a percentage of all felony cases between 1985 and 1987 was 175 percent in Boston; 114 percent in Jersey City, New Jersey; 109 percent in the Bronx, New York; 95 percent in Oakland; 74 percent in Miami. The increase has been more rapid since 1987, according to the National Center for State Courts. In DeKalb County, Georgia, drug indictments rose 235 percent between January 1988 and April 1989. In January 1988, drug cases made up 13 percent of the total indictments. In April 1989, that figure was 37 percent. In Bibb County, Georgia, the increase was 300 percent (Whitt, 9/5/89).

Edward R. Becker, a federal appeals court judge in Philadelphia, remarked on the increased number of drug cases filed in federal courts: "We're becoming drug courts." The percentage of drug-related cases on the federal docket has increased from 17 percent in 1985 to 26 percent in 1989. This increase has produced unprecedented delays in the processing of federal cases, especially for civil litigants, some of whom are seeking resolution to civil rights actions and personal injury disputes (Labaton, 12/29/89). One of the cases on hold in Florida, for example, is a job discrimination lawsuit affecting many people (Wermiel, 2/6/90). The harsher sentences mandated by new federal sentencing guidelines have also meant that fewer defendants plea bargain and therefore more go to trial (Labaton, 12/29/89). This has affected federal courts in Arizona, Arkansas, Tennessee, West Virginia, New Jersey, New Mexico, North Dakota, and other states (Wermiel, 2/6/90).

Officials in state courts as well report a shift in resources from civil to criminal (Labaton, 12/29/89). In January 1990, for example, Vermont suspended civil jury trials until July. Delaying civil trials means that plaintiffs often settle for less, for example, from insurance companies in personal injury disputes. Insurance companies, knowing of the delays, offer lower settlements in anticipation that plaintiffs will settle rather than wait for their cases to go to court (Pereira and Hagedorn, 1/29/90).

The number of drug filings in federal courts rose 229 percent in the 1980s, largely due to federal funding patterns (Beale, 2/8/90). In 1988, drug cases represented 44 percent of criminal trials in federal courts. Soon, over half the criminal cases will be drug cases (Wermiel, 2/6/90). The administration and Congress are directing a large share of federal anti-drug funding to federal prosecution, while these funds could be redirected to the state level. The federal courts, with just six hundred trial judges, are ill equipped to handle the influx of cases. And it is argued that drug cases consume more resources than non-drug cases (Beale, 2/8/90). They frequently involve at least two defendants and last at least six weeks (Wermiel, 2/6/90). In one trial of twenty defendants in a narcotics case in Reno, Nevada, in 1989, the case lasted over a year and had more than a hundred witnesses. Many of these cases could be prosecuted just as successfully at the state level (Beale, 2/8/90).

Jails and Prisons. Never before in the history of the country have so many people been in prisons. There are currently almost one million people locked up in either prisons or jails. Court orders mandating measures to control overcrowding are in effect in over three dozen states. At the end of June 1989, state and federal prisons housed 673,565 inmates. This figure represented an increase of 7.3 percent since January 1989—an increase larger in six months than prisons have experienced in the past in one year (Malcolm, 12/30/89). A large percentage of these inmates have been convicted of drug offenses, and it is estimated that 60 percent to 80 percent of those in correctional facilities are in need of some kind of drug treatment (Corn, 5/14/90). In Georgia, half of those in prison or on probation report having a cocaine problem. Correctional officials estimate the real figure to be 70 percent in the prisons. In Georgia, prison admissions for drug offenses have more than doubled in five years after six years of relative stability (Whitt, 9/5/89).

In 1988, the cost to the taxpayer for state and federal prisons alone was over $16 billion. For the whole enterprise—courts, corrections, jails, and police—the cost was $25 billion. This is ten times the expenditure ten years ago, and an estimated two-thirds of those released from prison return within three years (Crittendon, 12/29/89). Because of system overcrowding, it is estimated that in some sections of New York City arrested dealers are back on the street within seventy-two hours (Kifner, 9/8/89).

Even amid this prison crisis, states are expected to absorb even greater populations brought in by increased drug enforcement. State prisons hold roughly 85 percent of drug convicts, and the problem is expected to worsen. The commissioner of corrections in Pennsylvania, for example, estimated that the Pennsylvania system was operating at 48 percent over capacity, and he expected the inmate population to double in nine years (McWilliams, 1989). In Georgia, the legislature funded the construction of more prison beds in the past seven years than were built in the past century (Whitt, 9/5/89).

Even with the evident failure of the prison system to perform a deterrent or rehabilitative function (it is, for example, estimated that 70 percent of drug abusers return to jail within one year of release; see Whitt, 9/5/89), Bush's anti-drug program proposed an 85 percent increase in federal funds for prison construction (Malcolm, 12/30/89). Of the $9.5 billion anti-drug budget, $1.5 billion was allotted to prisons (Wenner, 6/22/90).

The executive director of the Metropolitan Atlanta Council on Alcohol and Drugs has recommended that the state "tear down prisons instead of build them." A corrections spokesman for the Georgia Department of Corrections commented, "We're never going to build our way out of this problem" (*New York Times*, 5/28/89). However, build we have done and are going to do. For example, from 1983 to 1989, California built 21,000 new prison beds (and it has plans to build 16,000 more). The cost was $3.2 billion. Between 1983 and 1989, New York spent roughly $900 million to build 17,780 cells (*New York Times*, 5/28/89). There is indication, however, that the public does not agree with the notion that building more prisons is the way to solve the drug problem. For example, a Media General-Associated Press poll conducted in late 1989 revealed that 57 percent of the respondents felt that building more prison cells (as the administration was proposing) would fail to reduce drug abuse (Langer, 10/2/89).

Parole and Probation. The situation of parole and probation is no brighter. In Georgia, for example, the number of drug offenders on parole increased from 886 in 1984 to 3,129 in 1989. It is estimated that drug offenders represent 20.5 percent of the parolee population (Whitt, 9/5/89). The probation system is similarly overcrowded, with probation officers in some states carrying a case load as high as 1,000. While President Bush's drug control strategy made provisions for prisons and prosecutors and judges, there was no mention of probation. Rand Corporation studies have indicated that in the past ten years, the prison population has increased by 45 percent. The number of offenders on probation has increased by 75 percent. It is estimated that as many as 70 to 75 percent of probationers are addicted to drugs, including alcohol, but only a small number are receiving any treatment (Labaton, 6/19/90).

Expansion of the Availability of Guns

The War on Drugs has led to an increasing escalation in firepower on the street. Due to the expansion in the availability of guns driven by the War on Drugs, police departments have also stepped up their firepower. In September 1990, for example, it was reported that many police departments, without much public debate, were replacing their standard .38-caliber revolver with a high-capacity 9-millimeter semiautomatic weapon. Some arms makers are estimating that the change will be complete in four to five years. Darrel Stephens, executive director of the Police Executive Research Forum, argued that "we've got a full-blown arms race going on in the streets" (Malcolm, 9/4/90). Even though many officers support the change, others argue that the increased firepower means that more innocent people will be shot. This change comes at a time when fatal shootings of police officers have actually declined. In 1989, more police officers were killed in accidents (seventy-seven) than were killed by suspected criminals (sixty-seven) (Malcolm, 9/4/90).

SUMMARY

The criminalization and enforcement tactics of the War on Drugs have been ineffective in accomplishing the stated goals of the drug war and have brought about additional social costs that we as a society are expected to bear. It is easy to see the failures and the costs on the domestic level. The War on Drugs has been similarly ineffective and has brought about additional social costs on the international level as well.

2

THE INTERNATIONAL COSTS
OF THE WAR ON DRUGS

The War on Drugs has been just as ineffective in stopping the flow of drugs into the country as it has been in stopping drug trafficking and drug use within the country. The interdiction-eradication strategy pursued by two Republican administrations has been so ineffective, in fact, that in 1989 there was a cocaine glut (Lernoux, 2/13/89). Cocaine production in Colombia alone is estimated to be 6,000 metric tons per year, and it is estimated that some 265,000 pounds of cocaine are smuggled into the United States annually from South America (Treaster, 6/14/90). Drug seizures are insignificant in relation to the traffic, and the street price of drugs declined rather than increased during a decade of "war." In 1983 a "street" gram of 35 percent pure cocaine cost $110. In 1986 a 50 percent pure street gram cost $100 (*Sourcebook of Criminal Justice Statistics, 1986*, 1987). According to the Drug Policy Foundation (1989), by 1989 the price of cocaine had dropped to one-third of its 1981 rate.

As was noted in Chapter 1, in the fall of 1990 administration officials and the DEA were widely publicizing what was reported to be a reversal in the trend of decreasing prices, citing increases in the prices that DEA undercover officers were being asked to pay for large buys. But city police and federal agents noted that prices for individual customers on the street had not changed. There were reported to be indications that dealers were diluting cocaine rather than raising their prices. But dilution would merely ensure that users would buy more cocaine to reach familiar highs.

Some in the DEA argued as well that there was really no problem with supply on the streets. The only problem they noted was whether the individual dealer had the money to pay for it (Treaster, 6/14/90). The comments of the DEA agents supported the arguments of many at a NIDA conference in July 1990, which were reported by Joseph Treaster (7/1/90) and mentioned in Chapter 1. Many of the researchers at the conference argued that price increases were not due to interdiction-eradication efforts but to producers using the current political situation as an excuse for driving up prices.

In the war of macho statistics, however, the price increases for cocaine being publicized by the administration in the fall of 1990 were used to argue that "progress" was being made in the War on Drugs. The rise in price for a particular drug, cocaine (which might well prove temporary), was used as evidence that the interdiction-eradication strategy had been a success.

But success has been claimed many times before. Ronald Reagan, for example, claimed a breakthrough in the War on Drugs in 1982, citing an increase of drug arrests and seizures. By early 1983, however, the General Accounting Office (GAO) had issued a report revealing that the figures used by Reagan were the result of double counting, that is, that the DEA and Customs, for example, were claiming some of the same seizures (Freemantle, 1986:52). There was no breakthrough in 1982, and temporary price increases for cocaine in certain parts of the country (even if they are real) do not constitute a breakthrough in 1990.

Tina Rosenberg, a writer based in Chile, has written about the effect of nearly a decade of war in the Andean countries:

From 1980 to 1988, Washington spent more than $10 billion on law enforcement to make cocaine unavailable or prohibitively expensive in the United States. Over the same period the supply of cocaine in the United States multiplied by 10 and coca fields in the Andes increased 250 percent.

The Andean countries can now produce seven times more coca than U.S. drug buyers can absorb. In 1980, a kilogram (2.2 pounds) of cocaine cost $60,000 wholesale in Miami. In 1988, it cost $10,000. And the cocaine was stronger and more plentiful.

Measured by seizures in Colombia, 1989 was an excellent year for the war on drugs. More cocaine was seized by last August than in all of 1988, and seizures of processing chemicals soared.

Yet measured by the price and the probable quantity of drugs available in the United States, it was as if none of this ever happened. In August 1989, coke cost $11,000 a kilo in Miami, close to the all-time low. The seizures seemed to have almost no effect on the cost or supply of drugs in the United States. (Rosenberg, 1/30/90)

Even after the much-touted enforcement efforts in Colombia in 1990, U.S. officials in Colombia noted that there might be some curtailing of processing but that new refineries were opening up in Peru, Bolivia,

Brazil, Ecuador, and Venezuela (Treaster, 6/14/90). A report released by the Colombian government in July 1990 echoed the comments of U.S. officials. It was noted that the crackdown, while perhaps forcing traffickers to move their laboratories to neighboring countries, had not reduced drug trafficking (*Christian Science Monitor*, 7/24/90). The estimate was that government pressure had decreased the output of cocaine-refining laboratories in Colombia by 15 to 20 percent, but that even after this, more than 700 tons of refined cocaine were leaving Colombia annually.

The peace plan initiated by Colombia's president César Gaviria Trujillo in September 1990, in which cartel leaders were allowed to plead guilty to one crime and in exchange were guaranteed not to face extradition or the seizure of their property, led to a decrease in the violence associated with the War on Drugs. But there was no indication that the plan had had any effect on the cocaine business itself. The surrender of important figures like Jorge Luis Ochoa (said to rank second in the Medellín cartel) did not ensure that the business would not go on as usual run by subordinates. In addition, Gaviria's peace plan was focused on the members of the Medellín cartel. The most likely result of the plan is that the power of the more efficient and less violent Cali cartel would increase (Treaster, 1/21/91). In fact, the elimination of important cartel leaders often only creates a power vacuum, which increases the violence surrounding drug trafficking. This happened after the killing of Rodríguez Gacha in December 1989 (Moody, 7/23/90).

Bush officials were predictably hostile to the peace plan initiated by Gaviria. Some even characterized it as a kind of capitulation, but officials were reluctant to alienate Gaviria and were preoccupied by the war in the Gulf when the plan was initiated (Treaster, 1/21/91).

Jack Weatherford, a professor of anthropology at Macalester College who researched coca cultivation in Bolivia, was in Bolivia during the government's Operation Blast Furnace, which was designed to eliminate the coca crop in the Bolivian jungles. Weatherford has written the following:

Despite the government's efforts to portray the operation as a success, I saw the true results in the coca-producing Chapare [region].

The program actually helped to increase production by clearing exhausted coca bushes from old fields and by carting away the unproductive boys who had been crippled by months of stomping coca leaves in vats of toxic chemicals. The program even improved roads in an effort to develop alternative agriculture and give the authorities better access to remote areas, but those roads now serve as landing strips for airplanes hauling chemicals in and cocaine out of the jungle.

With such help from our government, it is small wonder that coca production in Bolivia has increased dramatically in the eight years that the United States has been trying to eradicate it. (Weatherford, 9/27/89)

Similarly, Brian Freemantle (1986:150) has noted that the eradication campaign targeting opium production in three of Mexico's northwestern states—Sinaloa, Durango, and Chihuahua—in the early 1980s merely resulted in the expansion of production into surrounding states. In addition, farmers developed methods of scoring mature plants to collect the opium gum before the plants died and hosing the plants down to diminish the effect of the herbicide. Aerial spraying of coca plants in San José del Guaviara in Colombia in 1984 and 1985 resulted in strengthening rather than eliminating the plants (*U.S. News and World Report*, 3/25/85, cited in del Olmo, 1987).

Increased interdiction to prevent drugs entering the country has been similarly ineffective. Increased interdiction has frequently resulted only in the shifting of the locus of activity. Increased interdiction in the Caribbean and along the Florida coast, for example, resulted in an increase in drug trafficking through Mexico (Rohter, 4/16/89a; Applebome, 4/17/89). It is estimated that 70 percent of the cocaine entering the country now comes through Mexico. The figure was 30 percent only a few years ago (Weiner, 2/9/90). Mexico in fact has proved to be such a convenient route for the Medellín cartel that the cartel reportedly considered dispensing with Mexican middlemen and running the entire distribution network themselves. This is said to have generated some of the increase of violence that has occurred along the U.S.-Mexican border (Rohter, 4/16/89a).

Because of the shift of smuggling activity in response to interdiction efforts, the General Accounting Office (GAO), the investigative arm of Congress, has argued the futility of putting more money into surveillance technology on the border. A GAO report in 1989, for example, noted that as the administration's efforts to block airborne drug smuggling intensified, smugglers merely switched airports or found other ways of getting drugs into the country (Berke, 6/9/89).

Nevertheless, the administration has continued to pour more and more money into sophisticated interdiction efforts. The 1989 GAO report noted that

federal spending on radar suspended from balloons, tracking aircraft and other measures to detect air-borne smugglers has increased dramatically, to nearly $205 million in the 1989 fiscal year from about $18 million in the 1982 fiscal year. (Weiner, 2/9/90)

It is estimated that in 1990 the administration will spend over $2 billion in an effort to seal off the border to drug smuggling (Treaster, 4/29/90). In response to these high-tech interdiction methods, however, smugglers have merely resorted to low-tech means. Tramp steamers out of Haiti, tomato trucks out of Mexico, and large cargo containers have replaced planes and large ships as the preferred form of transport (Magnuson, 1/22/90). For example, in 1990 the U.S. Customs Service noted an increase in the use of containers to smuggle drugs and estimated that one-third to one-half of the cocaine entering the country was smuggled in containers through commercial ports. One senior DEA official interviewed by the *New York Times* was quoted as saying, "Everybody's concerned about small planes and fast boats coming in with 500 or 1,000 kilos.... It's cargo containers coming in with thousands of pounds. You're talking bulk. You're talking containers, containers, containers" (Treaster, 4/29/90).

This DEA official noted as well that most of the discoveries of drugs in containers were the result of informant tips, not high-tech surveillance. "Unless you have an informant providing definitive information that a shipment has cocaine in it," he stated, "it usually goes right through." When Customs tried targeting containers from "producing" countries, traffickers merely set up shell companies and shipped drugs in containers originating in other countries (Treaster, 4/29/90).

In the eighteen-month study of surveillance technology on the border, the GAO found that the latest drug detection technology often did not even work (Berke, 6/9/89). It was estimated that the radar balloons were down for maintenance as much as 50 percent of the time. Each radar balloon with support computer equipment costs $18 million and $700 per hour to operate, but the balloons had to be pulled down in bad weather, required a great deal of maintenance, and could be easily seen by pilots. In December 1989, one of the balloons broke free, had to be electronically deflated, and plummeted to the ground, destroying the expensive radar equipment inside. Shortly afterward, Customs grounded two other balloons (Weiner, 2/9/90).

Even when the balloons were flying they did not, according to the GAO study, have much of an impact on the quantity of illegal narcotics entering the country from Latin America and the Caribbean (Berke, 6/9/89). Nor did these radar balloons stop other means of getting drugs into the country. In May 1990, for example, law enforcement officials found a 300-foot tunnel in Arizona, which they estimated had been used to smuggle cocaine into a warehouse four blocks from the U.S. Customs border checkpoint for at least six months (Squitieri, 5/21/90). It was estimated that this one tunnel was used to smuggle at least a ton of cocaine into the country (Rotstein, 5/19/90).

Shifting tactics to foil increased surveillance is characteristic not only of smuggling drugs into the country but of smuggling money out as well. When restrictions on banks became more stringent, for example, money launderers merely shifted to non-bank financial institutions (currency exchanges, check-cashing operations) or enterprises that regularly deal in large amounts of cash (race tracks, restaurants, liquor stores). In addition, it is possible for traffickers to ship money out of the United States via the same channels they use to ship the drugs into the United States—airplanes and cargo containers (Barrett, 12/14/89). It is suspected that the tunnel discovered in Arizona in 1990 was used not only to smuggle drugs into the country but also to smuggle cash and guns out (Squitieri, 5/21/90).

The U.S. border is simply too large and too porous to be adequately sealed. Florida, for example, has a coastline of 395 miles and 6,000 miles of inland waterways (Freemantle, 1986:47).

In addition, if interdiction efforts along the border were significantly stepped up, there would be a massive disruption in the flow of trade. For example, it is estimated that 8 million large cargo containers passed through U.S. borders in 1989. Roughly 3 percent of them were checked. If this percentage was increased substantially, the delays would cause havoc and provoke an outcry due to the interference with trade (Magnuson, 1/22/90). Customs officials estimate that even if they had the personnel, they could never search more than 10 percent of incoming containers without causing extensive disruption of trade through U.S. ports (Treaster, 4/29/90).

In 1969, the Nixon administration tried just such a blockade on the U.S.-Mexican border. Two thousand customs and patrol agents were stationed along the 1,700-mile border with Mexico. The operation caused traffic delays of up to half a day, and 5.5 million travelers were searched, without one dramatic seizure of drugs. The response of the Mexican government was so strongly negative that the State Department finally had to warn the White House that its Operation Intercept was threatening relations with Latin America. The blockade was lifted and the name of the operation was promptly changed to Operation Cooperation (Freemantle, 1986:148). The seizures had little effect. Even after these and other interdiction efforts, witnesses in the trial of some of those accused of being involved with the murder of DEA agent Enrique Camarena testified about vast plantations of marijuana in Mexico, some of which employed as many as nine thousand workers and had hundred-yard-long sheds for curing marijuana plants (*New York Times*, 7/17/90).

Other measures that are proposed to stem the flow of drugs, chemicals, and money are similarly unworkable because they interfere with business interests. In late 1989, the Treasury Department made proposals to require banks to maintain detailed records of any customer transferring money abroad. But one bank alone, Citibank, makes forty thousand wire transfers every day, and it is argued that the complexity of keeping such detailed records would be prohibitive. In addition, the proposals of the Treasury Department would not have covered foreign banks that use U.S. facilities. Senator John Kerry called this a "gaping loophole"

(Isikoff, 11/6-/12/89). Reluctance to interfere with business, therefore, makes many interdiction efforts and regulatory measures unworkable.

For example, a treaty signed in 1988 by eighty nations, which was designed to decrease drug trafficking in part by decreasing the chemicals used in processing drugs, has yet to be ratified by most of the nations whose representatives signed it. It is acknowledged that some nations, especially those with large chemical industries (such as Switzerland), may resist attempts that interfere with international trade (Browne, 10/24/89).

Efforts to place restrictions on the chemicals used to process drugs are doomed to fail also because of the almost endless alternatives. Just as the flow of drugs changes direction in response to more stringent border interdiction, countries importing large quantities of precursor chemicals change. For example, when Colombia and some other Latin American countries imposed strict regulations on ether and acetone shipments in 1982, Mexico's imports of precursor chemicals increased 1,160 percent between 1983 and 1986 (Rohter, 5/13/90). Brazil and Ecuador are also becoming increasingly important sources for chemicals needed to refine cocaine (Moody, 7/23/90).

Even the drugs themselves can be synthesized, including drugs usually derived from plants. If coca leaves, for example, should ever be in short supply, cocaine could be made synthetically. And, as chemists note, the new synthetic drugs that require no natural base are more dangerous than either cocaine or heroin. Government policies may only drive producers to switch to these more dangerous synthetic drugs (Browne, 10/24/89).

New regulations imposed by the Anti–Drug Abuse Act of 1988, requiring that transactions of chemicals used in the processing or making of drugs be recorded by sellers and be made open to government inspection, are said by the government to be intended to hamper the processing or manufacturing of drugs especially in warehouses, private homes, vans, and other temporary locations. But the raw materials and processes that can be used for making drugs are practically limitless. When one illicit process is disrupted, others spring up to replace it. One chemist, who asked not to be named in an interview with the *New York Times*, remarked:

You might decide to curb the sale of corn, which can be fermented to make moonshine. But the bootlegger would merely switch to barley or prunes or any of the thousands of natural substances containing carbohydrates. Curbing the precursors of many drugs involves similar problems. (Browne, 10/24/89)

Another chemist, Dr. Gary L. Henderson, has argued that anti-drug enforcement may well drive illicit producers to switch to exceptionally dangerous substances. Henderson, an associate professor of pharmacology at the University of California at Davis, has noted: "Dangers increase drastically whenever people start concentrating drugs or consuming them in new ways" (Browne, 10/24/89).

The drug 3-methylfentanyl, a depressant that is roughly 1,000 times more potent than heroin, is one of these dangerous new synthetic drugs. In fact, 3-methylfentanyl was mistaken for heroin when the first overdose cases showed up in hospital emergency rooms. One industrial chemist made enough fentanyl in a single, relatively simple laboratory synthesis for up to 10 million doses. This synthesis required only a few pounds of starting materials, the most essential of which was purchased in a retail store (Browne, 10/24/89).

Fentanyl is only one of the new synthetic drugs that will be difficult, if not impossible, to control. Others are Ketamine, a legal anesthetic that has effects similar to those of heroin and is reportedly more easily acquired than heroin in some areas of the country; Eu4ria, an amphetamine-like stimulant made from materials found in some legal pharmaceuticals, most notably diet pills; "ice," a form of methamphetamine that produces symptoms described as often indistinguishable from those of acute paranoid schizophrenia; and other methamphetamine drugs that can be produced from ingredients found in many over-the-counter cold remedies (Browne, 10/24/89).

At the moment, cocaine and heroin are still cheap and plentiful enough to make bothering with synthetic processes only marginally profitable. This may change, however. The economics are determining. If it is possible to become rich from one simple laboratory operation, dealers will always be able to hire the professional expertise. Therefore, the price increases for cocaine being reported in cities such as New York and Los Angeles of as much as 40 percent (Treaster, 6/14/90) are not the success the administration is claiming. These price increases may well spur the advent of other more dangerous chemically synthetic drugs.

The chemicals needed to manufacture drugs synthetically are commonly available, so much so that controlling them poses almost insurmountable difficulties. Cocaine typifies the problem. Besides coca leaves, the producer needs only a small variety of cheap chemicals to make pure cocaine. All are used in large amounts for legitimate purposes. As Malcolm Browne has noted,

the required chemicals are kerosene; ammonia, commonly used to make cleansing agents, fertilizers and synthetic fibers; lime, used to make bricks and mortar; sodium carbonate, used in glass, soap and cleansers; sulfuric acid, used in automobile batteries; potassium permanganate, used in tanning leather, and purifying water, ethyl ether, a common solvent, and hydrochloric acid, used for cleaning metal and preparing food products. . . . The law now regulates transactions involving several common solvents used for making cocaine, heroin and dozens of other street drugs. The new regulations apply to ethyl ether; acetone, the chemical in nailpolish remover; methyl ethyl ketone, found in rubber cement, and toluene, used in paint thinners. (Browne, 10/24/89)

In addition, the law regulating the sale of chemicals does not apply to the sale of less than fifty gallons a month domestically and foreign sales of less than five hundred gallons, unless the sales are deemed to be suspicious by dealers. But these solvents are manufactured and sold in such immense quantities that it would be virtually impossible to detect all small transactions (Browne, 10/24/89).

R. Garrity Baker, director of international affairs for the Chemical Manufacturers Association in Washington, D.C., has commented:

In this country alone, 6 billion pounds of toluene and 2 billion pounds of acetone are sold each year. Our 170 members, which produce more than 90 percent of the basic chemicals made in the United States, will keep the sales and distribution records required under the new law. But it will be up to the D.E.A. to make use of those records in tracking down illicit drugs, and it will be no easy task. (Browne, 10/24/89)

Browne (10/24/89) has noted that most chemists are reluctant to make public statements critical of the new regulations. "Not to go along with the patriotic anti-drug bandwagon can place a chemist under suspicion of being soft on drug dealers," one chemist said. "The truth is, nearly all of us are against drugs, but a lot of us feel the current regulatory efforts are as self-defeating as Prohibition was in the 20s."

After the expenditure of vast amounts of public monies on enforcement, we see that more drugs rather than less are being produced and are entering the country, and new synthetic drugs are being developed. In March 1989, the State Department released a report detailing increases in arrests, seizures, and eradicated acreage, and the successful extradition of a small number of drug traffickers. However, the report also acknowledged global increases in production and demand. In the report it was estimated that from 1987 to 1988, coca production increased 7.2 percent among Bolivia, Colombia, Peru, and Ecuador. Global marijuana crop increases were estimated to be 22 percent, opium crop increases 15 percent, and hashish crop increases 11 percent (Sciolino, 3/2/89). Drug production had increased not only in Latin America: In Asia's Golden Triangle, which produces roughly 80 percent of the world's opium, production is expected to be over 2,500 tons in 1990—a near doubling of production (Gemini News Service, 1990).

At the end of a *New York Times* article about the State Department report, Elaine Sciolino (3/2/89) noted: "The report was printed in a small quantity and will not be available to the public." While this report was not available to the public, disinformation about drug seizures has been widely available to the public. In November 1988, the Justice Department agreed to review a DEA practice of allowing local police forces to make well-publicized seizures of drugs brought into the United States in federal undercover operations (*New York Times*, 11/30/88).

The pattern of failure of the international War on Drugs, then, mirrors the domestic failure of the War on Drugs. And like the domestic War on Drugs, it has also brought about additional social costs.

SOCIAL COSTS OF THE WAR ON DRUGS

Enforcement and Interdiction Costs

The costs of international enforcement are high. The federal government spent $900 million on interdiction in 1986 (Data Clearinghouse for Drugs and Crime, 1989). The DEA planned to spend $50 million between 1988 and 1991 in Bolivia alone in eradication programs (Kerr, 4/17/88). Mexico receives $14.5 million a year for drug eradication (Rohter, 3/1/89). Colombia was expected to receive $89 million in assistance to fight drug trafficking in 1990 (Brooke, 12/18/90). The Bush administration asked for $2 billion in funding for the Andean nations and to send U.S. advisors to Bolivia and Peru to teach them how to control drug production (Weatherford, 9/27/89). This is so even after a GAO report issued in June 1989 suggested that the government spend more on treatment, prevention, research, and education rather than on increased enforcement measures (Berke, 6/9/89).

In fiscal year 1988, efforts to stop the flow of drugs into the United States accounted for $1 billion of the $3.8 billion in anti-drug money spent by the government. A GAO report maintained that the 55,346 pounds of cocaine seized from private aircraft in 1987 represented more than one-third of all seizures from smuggling but only a small fraction of the volume of illegal drugs thought to have entered the country (Berke, 6/9/89).

"If we measure the success of the current Federal drug abuse control strategy by looking at the number of drug users and amounts of drugs entering the country," the report said, "we must conclude that our present strategy, which emphasizes supply reduction, is not very effective" (Berke, 6/9/89). The government cannot even prevent the domestic cultivation of drugs like marijuana. Department of Agriculture and DEA statistics indicate that one of the largest sources of domestic marijuana is illegally cultivated fields on government-owned land such as national forests and parks (Weatherford, 9/27/89).

The Deflection of Police Resources

Massive U.S. aid to the military and police in Latin American countries has been unsuccessful in decreasing, much less stopping the production and distribution of drugs. In addition, while the United States funds the police and the military in Latin America to fight the drug war, gross violations of human rights are commonplace in many Latin American countries, and many of these violations are committed by the military and police. The Colombian general staff, for example, has been accused of covering up human rights abuses by the military. An international human rights panel headed by Nobel Peace Prize laureate Adolfo Perez Esquivel concluded that some Colombian military officers were involved in death squad activity (Collett, 4/11/88). But the preferred strategy of the administration is to pour money into the Colombian military and other military organizations in Latin America. Most of the $89 million appropriation from the United States to fight drug trafficking in Colombia in 1990 would go to the police and military (Brooke, 12/18/90).

While money pours into the military in Latin America with the excuse that the United States is fighting drugs or "narco-terrorism," the military in many of these countries continues abuses. At times, these abuses are perceived as particularly outrageous when they are committed against U.S. citizens or people in sympathetic categories such as nuns or priests. The November 1989 slaying of six Jesuit priests, their housekeeper, and her daughter roused public attention to the human rights abuses of the Salvadoran military. Months later, however, a congressional report disclosed in September 1990 that top Salvadoran military officers were continuing to block the investigation into the deaths. Congressional investigators alleged that military officers ordered the slaying and that some of the evidence in the case, specifically an army duty logbook, was suspected of having been forged (Krauss, 9/25/90). Despite this, funding for the Salvadoran military, which had been temporarily decreased by Congress, was restored by Bush in late 1990.

The U.S. administration is not fighting a "War against Human Rights Abuses." In fact, the War on Drugs is funding those abuses.

Enforcement Primarily Affects Lower Rungs of Trade

Even though there have been some notable successes in the prosecution of big-time drug traffickers, for the most part they remain outside the criminal justice net. As Senator Kerry's congressional report documented in 1989, the more powerful drug kingpins are often ignored for political reasons. The prosecution of Carlos Lehder was presented by the U.S. media as having been a major law enforcement coup. Many have argued, however, that Lehder was caught and prosecuted only because the drug lords themselves wanted Lehder out of the way. Lehder's overtly aggressive political statements attracted attention and interfered with business. Eduardo Martinez Romero, the reputed money launderer, extradited to the United States in September 1989, corroborated this story. He reported to DEA agents that Lehder offended powerful Mafia bosses by shooting to death a bodyguard of Pablo Escobar Gaviria in a conflict over the bodyguard's wife. Martinez said that Escobar "gave" Lehder to the DEA (Epstein, 9/8/89).

After the arrest in 1989 of Miguel Angel Félix Gallardo, one of Mexico's most important drug traffickers, even law enforcement officials were referring to "the hydra-head phenomenon." In other words, they were warning that the arrest of an important drug trafficker does little to slow the drug trade. At best, such arrests temporarily disrupt trafficking patterns; at worst, they open up the field for new aspiring drug kingpins and therefore spark increased violence as the aspirants compete to establish their hegemony (Rohter, 4/16/89a).

In addition, enforcement tactics do not apply as harshly on the upper- and middle-class complicity in the drug trade. Banks, for example, are largely considered to be unwitting accomplices to drug money laundering. Attorney General Thornburgh, for example, has stated that most banks are unaware of money laundering (Wines, 4/3/89). It should be noted that this presumption of innocence extended to banks holding large amounts of laundered money does not extend to individuals who, for example, live in public housing projects and do not know that their houses or cars are being used for drug selling.

In April 1990, the House of Representatives voted to set up a process that would allow, but not insure, the closing of banks and savings and loans institutions convicted of laundering drug money. The closing of the financial institution would depend on the extent to which it had cooperated with the investigation and whether it agreed to adopt measures to prevent money laundering in the future. Under intense pressure from the Bush administration and the banking industry, the House voted down a measure that would have required the Treasury Department to undertake a project that would test the advisability of requiring banks to keep records of international wire transfers, the most widely used method of money laundering. Representative Charles E. Schumer (D-Brooklyn) remarked, "We're telling the drug lords to transfer this way because if you do it by wire, you won't be affected." Opponents of the measure argued that it would add a $350 million annual paperwork burden, and described the bill as "well meaning" but "overkill" (*New York Times*, 4/26/90).

Profit Margin and Organized Crime

International efforts to fight the War on Drugs have also ensured that the profit margin on drugs is high. The profits are so large that the

Colombian Mafia at one point reputedly offered to pay off the Colombian $10 billion external debt (U.S Senate, 1989). The Kerry Commission Report estimated that the Colombian drug cartels earn $8 billion annually (U.S. Senate, 1989:29), and *Forbes* magazine listed Colombian cartel leaders Ochoa and Escobar as among the richest men in the world (7/25/88:64; cited in U.S. Senate, 1989). The personal fortune of the Honduran drug trafficker Juan Ramon Matta has been estimated at $1 billion (Rohter, 4/16/88).

One Mexican drug trafficker, Félix Gallardo, is believed to have smuggled two tons of cocaine into the United States every month (Rohter, 4/16/89) and to have been paying off the police officials arrested along with him in monthly bribes of five figures. Gallardo is thought to have made hundreds of millions of dollars in his fifteen-year career (Rohter, 4/16/89a).

The economies of a number of the more important drug-producing and drug-trafficking countries depend on drug profits. Freemantle (1986:211), for example, maintains that nearly 36 percent of Colombia's gross national product comes from drug profits and that drugs are Colombia's largest source of foreign income.

Eddy et al. (1988:48) detail the steps in the processing and distributing of cocaine and the profits at each step based on a DEA report from as long ago as 1979. The basic ingredients needed to produce a kilo of cocaine cost $625. Once the coca leaves had been turned into paste, then base, and finally one kilo of cocaine hydrochloride, the value in Colombia was $9,550. By the time this kilo reached the United States, the value was $37,000. The distribution process increases the amount of the product. First, the wholesaler cuts the cocaine to 50 percent purity and sells two kilos for $37,000 each. The distributor cuts it and sells four kilos, and the street dealer (after cutting) sells eight kilos at $70 or more a gram. Thus, $625 worth of coca leaves becomes $560,000 on the street. As Eddy et al. (1988:49) note, cocaine is "the most valuable commodity on earth."

A report by a Senate subcommittee on narcotics in early 1990 estimated that some $300 billion in worldwide drug money is disguised through laundering every year (Barrett, 2/9/90). The assistant treasury secretary for enforcement, Salvatore R. Martoche, has estimated that 80 percent of this is pure profit (Isikoff, 11/6–/12/89). The profits from drug trafficking are said to be worth as much as oil to the world banking system.

Investment in the Legal Economy

Internationally, the illegal profits do not remain outside the legitimate market. It is estimated that the value of the Latin American drug trade is between $80 and $150 billion. Most of this money remains in the United States or is deposited in Swiss bank accounts (MacDonald,

1988:5). The banking industry is heavily implicated in money laundering. Robert Stankey, a former Treasury Department analyst who started compiling currency surplus figures in 1979, estimated that much of the $6.4 billion cash surplus of southern Florida banks in 1988 (compared to $3.3 billion in 1978) came from drug payments (Corn and Morley, 4/17/89b). Federal officials consider bank surpluses to be a strong indication of drug activity. The Federal Reserve branches with the largest cash reserves in the first six months of 1989 (compared with the first six months of 1988) were in Miami; Los Angeles; Jacksonville, Florida; San Antonio; and El Paso. Increases in cash reserves in these areas correspond to large drug seizures in these cities (Labaton, 12/6/89).[1]

In February 1989, thirty-three people were charged in Los Angeles with laundering more than $500 million in Colombian cocaine profits, which were destined for legal reinvestment. It was estimated that this operation alone had hidden the source of $1 billion in drug money over the past two years and that it involved bank accounts in New York, Panama, and Uruguay (*New York Times*, 2/23/89).

Juan Ramon Matta invested heavily in legitimate businesses in Honduras including hotels, cattle ranches, factories, a tobacco plantation, and a processing plant that employed several hundred people (Rohter, 4/16/88). Penny Lernoux (2/13/89) estimated that $600 million of the $3 billion earned in Bolivia annually through drug trafficking was reinvested in the economy. The areas of investment included the agriculture and construction sectors. Cartels in Colombia invest heavily in real estate both in Colombia and the United States, and they own newspapers and broadcasting companies. The Kerry Commission Report (U.S. Senate, 1989:29) estimated that one-third of the drug income in Colombia was invested in industry, real estate, and agriculture. The Herrera family of Mexico, whose profits come largely from heroin, are said to control banks, hotels, and cattle ranches (Freemantle, 1986:152).

An indication of the extent of economic power that can be wielded by the drug trade is illustrated by events that took place following the Lara assassination in Colombia in 1984. Just after the assassination, several important drug traffickers were forced to move from Colombia to Panama as a result of government pressure. They took with them a sizeable amount of capital. As a consequence, the value of the dollar on the black market rose (the black-market value of the dollar was 140 pesos; the official rate was 100 pesos). In an attempt to negotiate their return to Colombia, the traffickers later released some of their funds back into the Colombian economy. The dollar value on the black market subsequently fell in relation to the peso (by the end of June the dollar was worth 115 pesos) (*Latin American Regional Report Andean*, 1984:4, cited in MacDonald, 1988:36).

Corruption

The War on Drugs has also had negative effects on police institutions in Latin America by promoting even more questionable police tactics and even more widespread corruption than existed before the U.S.-initiated War on Drugs. DEA agents are reportedly as afraid of the police they work with in Latin America as of the drug traffickers they are supposed to arrest. In 1987, a State Department report criticized "endemic" corruption extending into the highest levels of the Mexican government. The report characterized this corruption as the "single most important factor undermining meaningful narcotics cooperation" (Sciolino, 3/1/89). During the presidency of Jose Lopez Portilla, Mexico City's police chief, Arturo Durazo Moreno, was one of Mexico's biggest traffickers and protectors of traffickers (Freemantle, 1986:149). In large drug busts in Mexico in 1987 and 1988, a number of those arrested were members of the Mexican Federal Judicial Police, the state police, and Customs personnel (Branigin, 2/26/88).

The complicity of the Mexican police in the death of Enrique Camarena has been detailed in Elaine Shannon's book about drug cartels, *Desperados*. Notwithstanding these events, Mexican president Carlos Salinas de Gortari appointed as his attorney general the governor of the state of Jalisco, who U.S. officials had complained dragged his feet on the Camarena investigation (Rohter, 12/12/88). U.S. sources have maintained that others implicated in the Camarena murder are the ex-head of the federal security directorate (José Antonio Zorrilla Peréz), the former chief of the federal police (Manuel Ibarra Herrera), and the former leader of Mexico's anti-drug program (Miguel Albana Ibarra) (*Time*, 1/22/90). The assistant U.S. attorney for the Central District of California, Manuel Medano, who prosecuted some of those involved in the Camarena case, argued that members of the Guadalajara narcotics ring responsible for Camarena's death thought that they operated above the law, since there was complicity from almost all of the law enforcement agencies working in the city (*New York Times*, 7/17/90).

When the Mexican authorities arrested Miguel Angel Félix Gallardo in 1989, a reputed drug lord called by the attorney general of Mexico "the No.1 drug trafficker in Mexico," they also arrested the top federal anti-drug official of the state of Sinaloa, six police officials, and every policeman on the force of Félix Gallardo's home town of Culiacan (*Anchorage Daily News*, 4/11/89a). A spokesman for the State Judicial Police noted that when a new state administration took power in 1987, they found "the police body to be completely infiltrated by narcos" (Rohter, 4/16/88).

The head of intelligence for the Mexico City police resigned in 1989 after he was indicted in the United States on charges of operating a car theft and smuggling ring. His name has also surfaced in testimony given to U.S. grand juries considering drug trafficking across the Mexican border (Rohter, 3/1/89).

A former chairman of the Joint Chiefs of Staff noted to the *Washington Post* (Collett, 4/11/88) that drug traffickers had "thoroughly penetrated" the National Police force in Colombia. Joaquin Matallana, the former head of Colombia's state security agency, noted in 1988 that official corruption extended into the 1,800-member anti-narcotics unit partially funded by the United States (Collette, 4/11/88). U.S. officials commenting after the killing of drug trafficker Rodríguez Gacha in December 1989 said that part of the difficulty of capturing Gacha had been due to the presence of paid informants in the police and the military who had tipped off Gacha and Escobar about operations. A U.S. official was quoted in the *New York Times* as saying: "All levels of the military and the police are riddled with informants. . . . The vast majority, if not all, aircraft control towers in the country have informants in them" (Treaster, 12/16/89).

A State Department report issued in 1989 noted that the corruption of the criminal justice system in Colombia was so complete that it was "virtually impossible" to arrest and convict drug dealers or to do serious damage to their organizations (Sciolino, 3/2/89).

In 1989, Colombia's president at the time, Virgilio Barco, conducted a widespread purge of police officials thought to be involved with the drug cartels. Even after this, the security problem was considered so serious even by the Colombian government that anti-drug helicopter units were given precise information on location only after they were airborne (Brooke, 12/24/90). In 1989, an army lieutenant, Javier Wanumen, was arrested on charges of maintaining an espionage network that kept the Medellín cartel informed of private discussions in the Justice Ministry, the Attorney General's Office, and the Supreme Court.

The State Department issued a report in 1988 noting "drug-related corruption" in the Bahamas. A 1989 report noted that drug-related corruption in the Bahamas continued to be a problem (Sciolino, 3/2/89). Evidence of official connivance in trafficking has been noted as well in Bolivia (Lernoux, 2/13/89), Haiti (Sciolino, 3/1/89), and Paraguay (Riding, 2/27/89), among other countries.

The corrosive effect has been not only on police institutions but on leading government and military officials as well. For example, U.S. authorities indicted Colonel Jean-Claude Paul of Haiti in March 1988 on narcotics counts (Collett, 4/11/88). A close associate of Prime Minister Lynden Pindling of the Bahamas was indicted in March 1989 on charges of taking part in smuggling more than $1 billion worth of cocaine into the United States. Another Pindling associate was indicted in Florida for receiving bribes in exchange for allowing the Bahamas to be used for drug trafficking (Efron, 2/1/89). Witnesses at the trial of Carlos Lehder Rivas testified that Prime Minister Pindling himself was involved. Even Reagan administration officials admitted that Honduran military officers were involved in drug trafficking (Collett, 4/11/88).

Secondary Crime

The enforcement tactics against illegal trafficking in drugs create a whole host of secondary criminal activity, from murder to arms trafficking to document forging.

Violence. Groups that organize to provide illegal substances use violence to intimidate enforcement officials and competitors and to discipline an illegal work force. The toll this violence has taken is especially great in countries like Colombia. The Medellín drug cartel has been accused of killing thousands of Colombians in 1989 and 1990 in gunfights, assassinations, and bombings (*New York Times*, 1/16/91). In December 1989, a school bus filled with a ton of dynamite was blown up outside the headquarters of the Security Department in Bogotá, killing sixty-seven people and wounding seven hundred others (Brooke, 12/24/90). The cartels have, in addition, kidnapped and killed relatives of those involved with the government. In 1990, reported kidnappings nationwide rose to 1,274 from 789 in 1989 (not all of them cartel-related) (Brooke, 1/9/91). In 1991, for example, the kidnapped sister (Marina Montoya) of a former presidential aide who helped plan a large-scale anti-drug crackdown was found dead on a Bogotá street (*Montgomery Advertiser*, 2/1/91). The woman was one of nine people who had been taken hostage in August and September 1990 in an effort to force the government to meet drug traffickers' demands for pardons, leniency, and freedom from extradition to the United States. A day after the discovery of the body of Ms. Montoya, the body of another hostage, Diana Turbay, was discovered. Ms. Turbay, a magazine editor, was the daughter of former president Julio César Turbay Ayala. Four of the nine hostages were released (*New York Times*, 2/1/91). Between August 1990 and the end of January 1991, nine journalists (including Ms. Turbay) were kidnapped in an effort to end hostile press coverage (four were released). The publisher of *El Espectador*, a Bogotá newspaper, Guillermo Cano, was killed in 1987, and since then there have been bombings of the newspaper's printing plant and news offices. Three circulation managers were killed in Medellín (Brooke, 1/28/91). There were an estimated seven news employees slain in 1990 and nineteen in 1989. Many journalists have gone into exile.

The stepped-up campaign against drug traffickers, which was pressed by the United States and which began in August 1989 after the assassination of presidential candidate Luis Carlos Galán, has had the effect of increasing the number of kidnappings and the level of violence in general. James Brooke (1/9/91) maintained in the *New York Times* that the disruption within the Medellín cartel caused by the stepped-up campaign put many assassins and hired killers out of work. These young men, who are used to what one university sociologist in Medellín called "a life style of easy money, of high consumption," resort to kidnapping to gain money. One German television journalist who was kidnapped for several months said that one of his captors claimed to have participated in the kidnappings to earn money to buy his mother a washing machine.

After the Colombian government offered a reward of $400,000 for the capture of Pablo Escobar, Escobar responded by offering $500 to $2,000 a head for each policeman killed in Medellín. By July 1990, 140 lawmen in the city had died (Moody, 7/23/90).

In Colombia the violence associated with illegal drug business was considered so serious that after initially implementing a crackdown supported and pressed for by the United States, the government finally initiated a peace plan that had widespread support among the population. A university student interviewed by the *New York Times* stated: "It's time to stop pursuing a war that only interests the United States" (Brooke, 12/18/90).

The government came to realize that the criminalization itself was creating much of the violence. It was estimated that 550 people had been killed in drug war–related violence between mid-1989 and the end of 1990. The violence subsided after the beginning of talks for a peace plan (*New York Times*, 1/25/91b).

Arms. U.S. Army General Paul Gorman, former commander of the U.S. Southern Command, testified before a Senate subcommittee: "If you want to move arms and munitions in Latin America, the established networks are owned by the Cartel." Gun running and drug distribution go hand in hand. In February 1988, Mexican Police authorities in a series of raids captured over 360 AK-47 assault rifles and over 145,000 rounds of ammunition. According to Mexican and U.S. officials, the weapons had been smuggled into Mexico from the United States and were destined for Colombia. In another series of raids in Durango, Mexico, the capture of three suspected drug dealers led to the seizure of 180 AK-47s. The raid came after federal indictments in San Diego of twelve Mexicans—eight of whom were members of the Federal Judicial Police, three of whom were state policemen, and one of whom was a Mexican customs official—for the smuggling of semiautomatic assault rifles from California (Branigin, 2/26/88).

It is estimated that 29,000 domestically manufactured semiautomatic weapons are smuggled across the border to Mexico every year. One Mexican newspaper, which conducted an investigation of gun smuggling, estimated that 60,000 firearms enter Mexico illegally each year (Squitieri, 5/15/90).

In early 1990, the Colombian government disclosed that Israel had sold a large consignment of automatic weapons to Antigua that wound up in the hands of Rodríguez Gacha (Moody, 7/23/90).

Official Secondary Crime. The criminalization of drugs and the subsequent War on Drugs has created a situation in which the military and the paramilitary can conveniently blame their own violence on the cartels. And the cartels can attempt to claim themselves defenders of human rights. In February 1991, for example, the death of the sister of a former presidential aide who had helped plan a large-scale anti-drug crackdown was said by the Medellín cartel to be in retaliation for human rights abuses by the police (*New York Times*, 2/1/91).

Disrespect for the Law

The U.S. administration has shown clearly its disdain for international law in the War on Drugs (and in other areas), and this disdain has led to the perception in Latin America of the United States as an outlaw nation. As Thomas Bodenheimer and Robert Gould (1989:223) note in their book *Rollback!*, it is difficult for the American people to understand the depth of the resentment people in other countries feel for the United States.

Rosa del Olmo, a professor at the Universidad Central de Venezuela in Caracas, terms the war on drugs "a type of crime committed on the pretext of preventing another crime," even though it has not been successful in doing so. She also notes that "the sole preoccupation is to . . . protect North American youth, regardless of the consequences for Third World youth" (del Olmo, 1987).

The Supreme Court decision in *United States v. Verdugo-Urquidez*, 110 S. Ct. 1056 (1991), which declares warrantless searches outside the country to be constitutional, is an excellent example of the double standard of U.S. law. The Justice Department argued that "the right against unreasonable searches and seizures does not extend to all persons throughout the world" (Greenhouse, 4/18/89). In his dissenting opinion, Justice Brennan wrote: "By respecting the rights of foreign nationals we encourage other nations to respect the rights of our citizens" (Greenhouse, 3/1/90).

Health Problems

In the Chapare region of Bolivia it is estimated that 42,000 farming families depend on coca production for their livelihood. However, the State Department has taken the position that the area should be sprayed with chemicals to destroy the coca fields, a measure the Bolivians oppose (Kerr, 4/17/88). A State Department report issued in 1988 maintained that aerial spraying was the only way to curb cocaine production (Sciolino, 3/2/89), but even other government agencies (such as the GAO) have noted that eradication programs are largely ineffective (Lernoux, 2/13/89). In fact, rather than decreasing production, eradication programs most commonly have the effect of expanding drug production into other areas and increasing domestic production, as was the case with programs to eradicate marijuana in Latin America (Perkins and Gilbert, 1986, cited in del Olmo, 1987).

The earliest attempts in Latin America to use aerobiology to destroy drug-producing plants were carried out in Mexico in the 1970s. In 1975, paraquat was used massively in Mexico, especially in the Sierra Madre, to eradicate marijuana. As del Olmo (1987) has noted, from 1975 to 1978 the United States spent approximately $30 million a year for a program to eradicate marijuana with paraquat and opium-producing poppy fields with 2-4 dichlorophenoxyacetate (2-4-D), which causes birth defects. The subsequent panic over the use of paraquat was so great that Congress made it illegal, through the Percy Amendment, to support fumigation programs in other countries. As del Olmo (1987) has pointed out, however, the primary concern was the amount of paraquat being ingested by smokers of marijuana in the United States, not the environmental and health risks to those living in the producing regions in Mexico. By 1981, Congress had annulled the Percy Amendment and, for fiscal year 1982–1983, appropriated $37.7 million to begin using herbicides again to eradicate crops not only in Mexico but in other countries as well.

In 1977, the U.S. government claimed to have destroyed 33,000 acres in Mexico as a result of spraying paraquat. In 1978, an additional 8,200 acres were destroyed and in 1979, over 3,700 acres (Freemantle, 1986:149). In 1984, the Colombian government conducted serial pesticide spraying of marijuana (MacDonald, 1988:36). In 1985, marijuana and poppy fields were sprayed in a joint U.S.-Mexican operation (del Olmo, 1987). More recently, however, some Andean countries have resisted administration pressure to agree to aerial spraying of coca and have pointed out that this sort of spraying was not being conducted in the United States. Bolivia, for example, has rejected the use of chemicals to destroy coca plants for environmental reasons (Skorneck, 2/21/90).

In response to the objections of Andean countries and criticism of the House Select Committee on Narcotics Abuse and Control over DEA use of paraquat, the DEA spent $1.5 million on environmental impact statements in an attempt to justify eradication with paraquat. The DEA also began using another toxic chemical, gliphosphate. In order to get around some of the objections over the use of paraquat in Latin America while it was not used in the United States, the DEA also started sprayings in the United States. But it was promptly prevented from doing so by the courts (del Olmo, 1987).

Eradication programs have created health problems by destroying not only coca but other crops, and by their use of toxic chemicals. Paraquat, which has been used to destroy marijuana in Mexico and Colombia, is associated with especially disturbing health problems. As del Olmo (1987) notes, the pesticides cause "food contamination, and unnecessary poisoning of Third World people who are the main victims of those pesticides for lack of adequate medical care, chronic malnutrition, and other health problems." A report by the Centers for Disease Control and the National Institute for Environmental Health Sciences noted the severe consequences of paraquat exposure, including pulmonary fibrosis, irritative dermatitis, damage to the nails, optical injury, and severe epistaxis (del Olmo, 1987).[2]

Nevertheless, the U.S. government has continued to apply pressure especially on the government of Colombia to permit aerial spraying. In the mid–1980s the Colombian government permitted the aerial spraying of gliphosphate despite the peasants' protests (del Olmo, 1987). Effects on wheat crops, animals, and human health were subsequently reported in the region that was sprayed (Santós Calderon, 1986, cited in del Olmo, 1987). In 1985, the Environmental Protection Agency (EPA) noted that even though gliphosphate did not attack the lungs directly, like paraquat, it created liver damage (del Olmo, 1987). The director of the U.S. Customs Service, William Von Raab, argued when he was in Colombia that aerial spraying of gliphosphate in the United States was not profitable because the marijuana fields were too small (*El Impulso*, 8/5/86 cited in del Olmo, 1987).

In 1988, Eli Lilly disrupted the Reagan administration's plans to implement coca eradication programs that would have affected thousands of acres in South America. After reaching a tentative agreement with Peruvian officials to begin trial spraying in the Huallaga Valley, Eli Lilly and Company announced that it would refuse to sell tebuthurion (more popularly known as "spike") to the government for eradication (Gladwell, 6/1/88).

There had been a great deal of pressure from environmental groups against the use of spike. These groups especially stressed its environmental effects on the fragile tropical ecosystem in Peru. Lilly's response was in part due to this pressure. Environmentalists argued that among the effects were the destruction of endangered plant species, the leaching of chemicals into the Amazon, and risks to the health of farmers. The EPA shared some of these concerns (Gladwell, 6/1/88).

The long-term environmental effects of current chemical spraying in Latin America are especially serious because it is a region where the poorest segment of the population is totally dependent on the land. The intensive use of pesticides on cotton fields in the 1960s and 1970s in Central America was reported to have caused high levels of pesticide poisoning. Toxins such as DDT accumulated in humans, livestock, and the entire food chain (Fagan, 1987:49). Rosa del Olmo (1987) quotes a Colombian journalist who conducted a detailed study of the effects of aerial spraying programs: "According to evidence gathered from growers in the region, the spraying is being done indiscriminately, not only against marijuana, but also against every type of food crop of the peasants, and their farms are being destroyed by the helicopters."

In 1986 the Colombian newspaper *El Tiempo* noted that farmers in affected regions were protesting that aerial spraying was threatening an economic collapse in the region. An Indian leader was quoted in the newspaper as saying:

My brothers are dying there and what the doctors are doing, the medicines they leave, is not sufficient because this is an unknown and deadly epidemic. We believe that it is a poisoning produced by spraying with gliphosphate because the symptoms are vomiting of blood, intense headaches, and shivering all over the body until death. (del Olmo, 1987)

The War on Drugs, which is conducted like a real war, has serious environmental and health implications in Latin America. There is a U.N. convention prohibiting the use of agents that modify the environment for military purposes (del Olmo, 1987). It would seem that the environmental effects of other wars in the region would provide a clear lesson. For example, after ten years of civil war (largely funded by the U.S. administration), El Salvador is suffering ecological disaster. In May 1989, the Environmental Project on Central America released a report entitled "El Salvador: Ecology of Conflict." The authors of the report noted that 95 percent of the country's deciduous trees were gone, that 50 percent of the land had been turned over as pasture for cattle exports, and that "the average Salvadoran eats less meat than the average North American house cat" (Cockburn, 6/26/89).

Alexander Cockburn noted in *The Nation* magazine:

Only one in ten Salvadorans has access to safe drinking water. The coffee processing plants that have swollen the bank accounts of Christiani . . . spew boron, chloride, and arsenic contaminated wastewater into rivers and streams. To boost crop yields the cotton magnates drench the Pacific coastal plains in poison, which leaches into the Pacific Mangroves, killing them off and with them the shrimp and fish that were among El Salvador's most important export earners. (6/26/89)

But the use of environmentally unsafe agents to fight the drug war continues. Scientists are working to develop plant viruses to attack coca plants that would be spread through aerial spraying. Although it is maintained that these viruses would attack only coca plants and would pose no danger to the local ecology or to humans (Bishop, 12/28/89), as the *Washington Post National Weekly Edition* (2/26–3/4/90) noted in an editorial, biologists have many stories of pest-control strategies gone wrong.

In February 1990, the Bush administration was reported to be pushing for the development of research into a caterpillar (the malumbia) that would defoliate coca plants. The *Washington Post National Weekly Edition* (2/26–3/4/90) characterized the plan as "dangerous, arrogant and foolish." However, the Bush administration increased the drug budget proposal for the Agricultural Research Service by $5 million for fiscal 1991. Marlin Fitzwater maintained that the administration was "not undertaking any biological war" in developing research into what was described by one official of the Agricultural Research Service as "quite a voracious caterpillar." Fitzwater also maintained that "neither troops nor caterpillars will go in [to Latin America] without prior request or consultation" (Skorneck, 2/21/90).

The reports of the research were greeted with some concern, however, by officials from Latin American embassies who asked not to be identified in several news reports. The ambassador of Peru was said to have met with administration officials after the research was reported by the *Washington Post*, and he received assurances that the administration would not proceed to introduce the caterpillars without approval (Skorneck, 2/21/90).

The introduction of a pest that could defoliate coca and other crops has horrifying implications for peasants in countries like Peru and Bolivia. The head of the Confederation of Bolivian Peasants labor organization remarked that the plan indicated the lack of U.S. "political will to solve the social and economic problems in Bolivia, Peru and Colombia" (Skorneck, 2/21/90).

Even considering the serious environmental implications of eradication programs and their effect on human health, a report issued by the State Department in early 1989 suggested that the United States should explore ways of using the Third World debt in order to force countries to cooperate on drug control (Sciolino, 3/2/89). Use of an economic stranglehold to force compliance with administration objectives is nothing new. In July 1986, aid was suspended to Bolivia and U.S. troops were sent to "assist" anti-narcotics forces after Bolivia objected to chemical spraying (del Olmo, 1987).

The use of dangerous chemicals to destroy drug cultivation in Latin America can be conducted because of the lack of administration concern for the health of people in Latin America and because of the lack of adequate environmental laws in Latin America to prevent such use (del

Olmo, 1987). Rosa del Olmo (1987) notes that because the chemicals are considered to be subjects of national security, it is often difficult to discover exactly what is being sprayed and where. Added to this is the lack of U.S. law preventing companies from exporting chemicals to the Third World that are prohibited from use in this country. The president of the U.S. National Agricultural Chemical Association has said: "It is not the affair of the United States to draw up the laws of the world. We do not have to impose on those countries the standard we have imposed on ourselves" (del Olmo, 1987).

NOTES

1. The Federal Reserve reports that cash surpluses in branches in the first six months of 1989 were as follows: $2.8 billion in Miami, $2.7 billion in Los Angeles, $1.5 billion in Jacksonville, $1.2 billion in San Antonio. Surpluses in Miami and Los Angeles are reported to be growing at 10 percent per year (Labaton, 12/6/89).

2. Farm workers in Malaysia who worked with paraquat organized a campaign to ban the use of this and other dangerous agricultural chemicals because of the health implications including blindness, paralysis, and death (*Workers World*, 1/1/87).

3

WHY THE ADMINISTRATION CONTINUES TO PURSUE A POLICY OF CRIMINALIZATION AND ENFORCEMENT

It is evident from the preceding two chapters that the War on Drugs has been ineffective, both domestically and internationally, in stopping the use, manufacture, or trafficking of drugs. The War on Drugs has also created a host of subsidiary problems. Given the failure of the War on Drugs to accomplish its stated goals and the negative consequences of the criminalization-enforcement strategy, why has the administration chosen to pursue this course? The answer is this: While the War on Drugs has been ineffective and destructive in some ways, it has been highly effective and highly successful in other, more important ways.

First, the focus on the dangers of illegal drugs diverts attention away from the dangers of legal drugs, which are well integrated into the culture and the economy and are represented by powerful interests. The serious consequences of the legal drugs (like tobacco, alcohol, and the more dangerous prescription drugs) in terms of public health, violent behavior, spiritual deterioration, family disruption, death, and disease are downplayed in the quest for a so-called drug-free culture. The drug-free culture is in fact one in which citizens are free to consume their own culturally and economically integrated drugs and the drugs of other cultures are excluded. The population is encouraged to absorb the social costs of the use of legal dangerous drugs but not the social costs of the use of illegal drugs whose profits are not under control.

Second, the War on Drugs has been highly successful in diverting public attention away from fundamental social problems that plague the society. The Reagan and Bush administrations have managed to convince a substantial proportion of the American people that the dangers emanating from the use of cocaine, marijuana, crack, and heroin are among the greatest dangers threatening not only the health of the population but the very fabric of their existence as a society. Drug abuse is portrayed as a cause rather than a symptom of severe social problems, which are the predictable outgrowth of a social order that has failed, even with all its wealth, to provide a satisfying, enriching quality of life for its citizens.

Third, by primarily focusing on drug use and trafficking by members of the lower class and minority groups, the War on Drugs has aided in legitimating the virtual abandonment of minority and marginalized segments of the population and has assisted in making them appear as an enemy class deserving of marginality and impoverishment. Fourth, the War on Drugs has been used to legitimate a massive expansion of domestic state power and control. In this chapter, the first three successes of the War on Drugs will be explored. In Chapter 4, the domestic expansion of state power will be discussed.

THE LEGAL DRUGS

It is evident that the ideological work of the state has been successful in shaping the extent and focus of public concern about particular drugs and the intensity of concern about these drugs at particular times.[1] Immediately after the Bush administration blitz surrounding the release of William Bennett's first drug plan in September 1989, for example, public concern about drugs increased phenomenally. In a *Wall Street Journal/NBC News* poll at the height of the media blitz, drugs were named as the most important issue facing the society by 43 percent of those polled. By mid-January 1990, however, the intensity of concern had declined. By January, only 20 percent of those polled named drugs as the top issue of concern (*Wall Street Journal*, 1/19/90).

Similarly, the public perception about the dangers of certain drugs has been manipulated. The dangers of illegal drugs are perceived to be much more serious than the dangers of legal drugs, partly because they are constantly discussed and presented in graphic (if overblown) form. The use of marijuana, cocaine, heroin, and crack, therefore, has come to be perceived as "real" drug use. Evidence of this can be seen in references to "drug and alcohol abuse"; the phrase implies that alcohol is not a drug. While the dangers of legal drugs (like alcohol and tobacco) are not ignored completely, they are hardly presented in the panic terms of the targeted drugs in the drug war. The public is not subjected to extensive media campaigns dramatizing the dangers of over-the-counter or prescription drugs. Nor are the destructive effects of alcohol and tobacco presented as eroding the very fabric and internal security of the nation.[2]

But the negative health effects of these drugs and their pervasive use and misuse are well known. According to the U.S. surgeon general, for example, 5 million of today's children will die in their later years of smoking-related illnesses if the current rate of tobacco usage continues. Even though 3,000 teenagers start smoking every day, cigarette companies are allowed to spend an estimated $3.3 billion every year to advertise cigarettes. An estimated 1 billion packs of cigarettes are sold to minors every year, but according to the Centers for Disease Control (CDC), despite these violations only three states reported citations against thirty-two vendors in 1989 for sales to minors. Researchers at the CDC found only minimal enforcement of laws restricting sales of cigarettes to children in other states (Duston, 6/1/90).

Alcoholic beverage companies are allowed to spend hundreds of millions of dollars each year on advertising that encourages alcohol use. When former surgeon general C. Everett Koop was still in office, he called for a ban on alcohol advertising. William Bennett, however, has refused to add alcohol to his mandate as Drug Czar, and predictably enough, advertising trade groups have opposed attempts in Congress to introduce any restrictions on alcohol advertising. These trade groups have even gone to the extent of denying a connection between advertising and consumption. Dan Jaffe, executive vice president of the Association for National Advertisers, was quoted in the *Wall Street Journal* as saying: "Research has yet to document a strong relationship between alcohol advertising and alcohol consumption. Let's not go off down a blind alley" (Lipman, 2/23/90). That they are going off down a blind alley should be news to the companies who spend so much money advertising alcohol.

The Partnership for a Drug Free America, a coalition of advertisers, ad agencies, and media groups that produces some of the most gruesome of the anti-illegal drug advertising,[3] produces no alcohol abuse advertising and reportedly has no plans to do so. This is not surprising, since the coalition's major corporate sponsors include the Miller Beer parent company, Philip Morris (Lipman, 2/23/90).

Because of the powerful interests behind legal drug production, the negative health effects of legal drugs are not portrayed in graphic form, nor is their addictive quality stressed. The panic over the addictiveness of illegal drugs completely ignores the fact that tobacco is probably the most addictive drug of all the drugs, legal and illegal, that are now available. According to NIDA's chief clinical pharmacologist, 90 percent of casual cigarette smokers escalate to the point of addiction. In addition, there are an estimated 106 million users of alcohol in the country, and one of every eight is considered a "problem" drinker.

Similarly, the population is not bombarded with public service ads portraying the dangers of prescription drugs, even though the dangers are considerable. The dangers not only include side effects; drug companies are putting unsafe drugs on the market as well. Cases in which drug companies distort or withhold information from the Food and Drug Administration (FDA) in order to secure approval for their drugs are commonplace (see, for example, Leary, 1/24/90).[4]

It is estimated that controlled legal substances are responsible for one-third of all drug overdoses that turn up in hospital emergency rooms—a total of 80,000 a year. This figure is three times the rate of heroin overdoses. Even so, there is a lack of simple oversight on almost 200 types of controlled substances like Valium and Xanax as well as dangerous sedatives and amphetamines. Nationally, there are 1.5 billion prescriptions issued each year for dangerous drugs, and it is estimated that something like 2 million senior citizens are needlessly addicted to tranquilizers. Lower-class drug traffickers are not responsible for the distribution of these drugs. In New Mexico, in 1989 one doctor alone was responsible for 28 percent of all Valium prescriptions to Medicaid recipients in the state.

Simple programs such as those that require doctors prescribing dangerous drugs to use multiple-copy prescription forms are in place in only nine states. Programs in which one copy of the prescription is kept by the doctor, one copy is given to the patient to take to the pharmacy, and the remaining copy goes to the state health agency have resulted in a 35 to 50 percent decrease in prescriptions written for dangerous drugs in states where they have been implemented.

Even though the dangers of prescription drugs are evident and simple oversight programs combined with education could reduce their use, it is difficult to implement programs to further control the use of dangerous prescription drugs. The prescription drug industry composes a powerful lobby within the country. Pete Stark (D-Cal.), chairman of a House subcommittee on health, has noted that the reason that other states do not implement oversight programs is opposition from the drug manufacturers, who fear losing up to 50 percent of their sales of sedatives, tranquilizers, and amphetamines. Stark asks: "How can the U.S. drug companies reasonably defend a system that invites fraud and forgery? How can the pharmaceutical lobby advocate the needless addiction of millions of senior citizens to powerful psychoactive drugs?" The answer: profits. Stark himself continues: "Instead of defending their profits, drug companies and organized medicine should join with consumer, elderly and law enforcement groups to support multiple-copy prescription plans" (Stark, 8/12/90). The questions is: Why should they? The state offers no incentives for drug companies to protect the health of citizens. In a free market economy, drug companies are in business to make money, not to protect health.

While the dangers of legal drugs are understated, the dangers of illegal drugs are blown out of all proportion. For example, what Larry Martz calls in *Newsweek* the "dirty little secret" about crack is that it is possible to smoke it without becoming addicted. It is estimated that at least 2.4 million Americans have tried crack, but that less than half a million use it once a month or more. An op-ed piece in the *New York Times* denounced "Bennett's Sham Epidemic," accusing him of manipulating figures to create a false sense of emergency over drugs such as crack (Martz, 2/19/90).

The Marion Barry case illustrates well the panic over crack and the distortions of its effects. The U.S. government spent over $3 million to entrap Barry, who was accused of crack use. But the question that was never asked in the media even after Barry's arrest and indictment was how he could have run the capital of the country for years while smoking a drug that (according to the administration and the media) turns people into violent, out-of-control zombies.

The real concern of the administration is not the negative health effects, misuse, or addictive qualities of drugs in the society. If that concern was real, the dangers of legal drugs would receive just as much attention as those of illegal drugs, and stronger measures would be taken to control or stamp out the use of dangerous legal drugs.

SOCIAL PROBLEMS

The moralistic rhetoric about drugs and drug traffickers that is a fundamental part of the War on Drugs has overwhelmed the reality of the situation and has complicated any attempt to find realistic solutions to what is referred to as the drug "problem." The war against illegal drug taking and drug trafficking has been converted into a holy war, an almost religious crusade. In the ensuing fervor, the real factors that underlie the problem of drug trafficking and abuse are obscured. They are obscured for a very good reason: They are factors that the more powerful segments of the society do not want to confront; if they were confronted, something might have to be done about them.

The two main factors that underlie the problem of drug trafficking and drug abuse and that the moralistic rhetoric has been so successful in masking are (1) the effects of economic exploitation and inequality, and (2) the reality of social life that has been constructed in advanced capitalist countries, a reality so unbearable and so stressful that most people (even the well-off) spend a great deal of their time trying to escape from it in one way or another.

Social and Economic Inequality

The ideology of the War on Drugs has functioned to mask the society's failure to establish fundamental economic and social justice domestically.

The problems generated by that social and economic inequality have been redefined, transformed in the popular consciousness as being at least partly, if not primarily, caused by drug use and drug trafficking. Almost every social problem (especially crime) is portrayed as and perceived of as a drug problem. Almost every homicide, every assault, and every robbery is now presented in the media as drug-related. Newspaper stories contain estimates by various government officials of the amount of crime that is drug-related. Almost never, however, is the concept of drug-related crime defined. There is no uniform definition of drug-related crime among criminal justice agencies or researchers, much less among those in the media. Its increasing application is a reflection of the moral panic that has been manufactured over illegal drugs and the desire to write off profound social problems as problems of drug use and trafficking. In one study, for example, researchers seeking to probe the lack of definitional clarity noted that a crime might be considered drug related if arresting officers *suspected* the perpetrator or victim of being involved with drugs (Ryan et al., 1989). Through the label of drug-related crime, the survival strategies of the marginalized and their violence, desperation, and alienation have been redefined into a contemporary version of "reefer madness."

It should come as a surprise to no one that urban inner-city ghettos are filled with drug dealers. It is predictable that the segment of the population facing the most obstacles to attaining the rewards of the social system would opt for a fast and easy route to the affluence that all are taught to expect. The question for them becomes, Why be poor forever?

The virtual abandonment, economically and socially, of already marginalized segments of the population has ensured that drug trafficking will be an attractive economic alternative, and that drug taking will provide one of the few cheap sources of recreation and escape from lack of opportunity, discrimination, and poverty.

Decline in the Standard of Living

After decades of struggle to secure even minimum access to equal opportunity, marginalized segments of the population have seen those victories stripped away in the past decade. The standard of living of the poorest segments of the population in this country has decreased substantially during the past ten years. In the late 1970s, an estimated 25.5 million U.S. citizens lived below the official poverty level. In 1988, that figure was almost 32 million. This means that the percentage of the population living in poverty (as officially defined) rose from 11.5 percent to over 13 percent. This figure includes almost one-fifth of all children, one-forth of Hispanics, and one-third of blacks (Prowse, 1990).

According to a report by the House Ways and Means Committee, average family income (adjusted for family size, government benefits, taxes, and inflation) declined from 1979 to 1987 by 9.2 percent. For families with children, the decline was an even greater 13.8 percent. For families with a head of household under age thirty-five, the decline was 23.3 percent (Passell, 3/4/90).

The gap between rich and poor families is now larger than any in the last forty years. According to the Center on Budget and Policy Priorities, in 1987 the poorest fifth of U.S. families received only 4.6 percent of the national family income. The richest fifth received 43.7 percent. The top 10 percent of the population may hold nearly 65 percent of the wealth (Prowse, 1990). The number of citizens who were without adequate housing, were poorly educated, and were without health care is also the largest reported in forty years (Bell, 1/14/90). Inequality of wages for the same type of work is even increasing.[5]

As Henry Aaron, senior fellow at the Brookings Institution in Washington, D.C., has noted, in the past decade "we went backward on poverty and homelessness, and the distribution of income became dramatically less equal" (Prowse, 1990). This kind of economic decline and the growing disparity between rich and poor is itself criminogenic. That the groups most affected by these declines would opt to become involved in the most profitable enterprise available to them, drug trafficking, is predictable.

It is interesting to note that the conservative approach to explaining the causes of criminal behavior has always been based on a rationalistic model. According to the conservative model, in deciding whether or not to commit illegal acts, individuals rationally weigh the benefits of crime and the potential costs (arrest, imprisonment, etc.). If the benefits of the crime outweigh the costs, the individual will most likely choose to commit the crime. The conservative response, however, has always been to increase the costs of the crime (e.g., administer harsher penalties), never to decrease the benefits (e.g., provide meaningful employment, job training and retraining, or an adequate social service net). In fact, government economic policy has done just the opposite. It has increased the relative benefits of crime—first, by having no employment policy, thereby ensuring that some segments of the population are condemned to lives of drudgery; and second, by criminalizing drugs and therefore driving up the profits to be gained by selling them.

The administration and right-wing media pundits like to talk about the number of jobs that have been created during the two recent Republican administrations. Many of these jobs, however, are poorly paid and lack any possibility for advancement; or they are jobs that have been created in sectors of the economy in which lower-class individuals cannot compete because they do not have the proper training. For example, it is estimated that thousands of Americans have simply stopped looking for work because they have given up. These people are part of a "hidden unemployment" problem that some analysts say boosts the real jobless rate to around 8 percent. It is estimated that there were about 827,000 discouraged workers in the final quarter of 1989. Added to this is the percentage of "under-employed" workers, or those who hold part-time jobs but who need full-time employment. These people should be included in the unemployment statistics to give a more accurate picture of the nation's jobless problem (Ball, 2/4/90).[6]

As Elliott Currie (1985:103–141) has noted in a discussion of research on the relationship between unemployment and street crime, the real impact on street crime comes not from merely providing jobs but from providing jobs that furnish an adequate quality of life for employees. The benefit side of the cost-benefit equation of selling drugs will continue to be high in competition with badly paid, insecure, benefitless drudgery.

Even given the obvious connection between a lack of jobs and opportunity and the attractiveness of drug trafficking, the Bush administration decided against proposing any new strategies to deal with poverty in the United States. Bush's 1991 budget, for example, cut discretionary programs for low-income families to half of what they were ten years ago, adjusting for inflation (*New York Times*, 3/18/90). After an interagency group meeting at the White House in July 1990, the president's Domestic Policy Council concluded that new strategies were "too expensive or would stir up too much political controversy." One White House official was quoted as saying that the group had decided to "keep playing with the same toys. But . . . paint them a little shinier" (Pear, 7/6/90).

The administration uses the excuse that because of the budget deficit, the society can no longer afford social programs. As Daniel Patrick Moynihan (D-N.Y.) has pointed out, the Reagan-created budget deficits are "doing their intended work," that is, "providing an automatic obstacle to any new program" (Moynihan, 7/16/90). But as the *New York Times* (3/18/90) editorialized, "Americans may not *want* to help the poor. . . . But they can surely afford to." Choices about where to cut to reduce the budget deficit and how much to decrease it are just that, choices. The determination to make the poorest segments of the population pay for a budget deficit caused largely by the Reagan military buildup and massive giveaways to the rich reflects the increasingly crude and blatant abandonment of the lower class in the society. The War on Drugs has helped to create a political environment in which this abandonment can proceed not only without real opposition, but without need of even apologizing for it.

Encouraged by the Republican administrations and their rhetoric blaming the marginalized for their own plight, large segments of the population have increasingly adopted a callous attitude toward the least privileged in the society. The general attitude is reflected by the question, Why help a bunch of pushers and drug addicts? Problems of the ghetto are presented as drug-related and therefore come to be seen as problems that are created by the people themselves. Poverty, death, disease, and crime are perceived of as drug problems. But in Harlem, to take but one example, the death rate for black men over age sixty-five is three times that for whites, and the leading causes are not drugs or even homicides, but cancer, heart disease, and cirrhosis of the liver (Terry, 5/6/90). However, there is little administration rhetoric about lack of health care, AIDS education, and jobs for the people of central Harlem. The poverty, the illness, and the despair of people merely struggling to survive is not an administration priority. It is not a priority in and of itself and it is not even a priority when these conditions lead to both drug trafficking and drug use.

The War on Drugs has functioned to harden attitudes toward the disadvantaged by creating the impression that if people would just stop trafficking in and taking drugs, everything would be fine. But the policies of two Republican administrations have ensured that more people rather than less will be attracted to drug trafficking and use, and the posture of the administration that it is concerned with the socially destructive effects of drug use and trafficking is simply a lie. This is easy to see if one looks at some of the administration policies that have directly contributed to drug trafficking and abuse and that have led to far more devastating social damage than the use and trafficking of illegal drugs.

Housing

Part of the abandonment of the poor in U.S. society is the refusal to provide adequate, affordable, low-income housing. During the Reagan administration, for example, the appropriations for low-income subsidized housing were cut by 82 percent (Nader and Green, 4/2/90). Consequently, the poor or near-poor who rent housing now spend roughly 70 percent of their incomes on rent and utilities (Prowse, 1990). At the end of 1989, the Conference of Mayors released a survey of officials in twenty-seven U.S. cities. According to the survey, requests for emergency shelter had increased 25 percent between 1988 and 1989 alone. Requests for food increased 19 percent. Authors of the report identified decreases in affordable housing as the primary cause of growing homelessness and hunger (*New York Times*, 12/21/89).

The decline in the availability of affordable housing and the quality of life has affected not only the poor in urban areas but those in rural areas as well. A report issued in 1989 by two nonprofit research organizations noted that poor people living in rural areas were even more likely to live in substandard housing than poor people in urban areas. The authors of the report noted that in 1970 there had been a surplus of low-rent housing. In 1970 there were 500,000 more low-rent housing units available than low-income families to rent them. By 1985, however, there were 500,000 fewer low-rent units than low-income families. The authors noted that the causes of the crisis in rural housing were fewer rental housing units, a large increase in the number of poor people, and reductions in federal housing programs (*New York Times*, 12/18/89).

The refusal to provide adequate low-income housing is a form of state violence and the toll is great. In the past year in New York City alone, seventy-nine homeless people died while seeking shelter in the subway, fifteen were crushed by trains, and nine were electrocuted (Kiley, 2/17/90). In March 1990, Mitch Snyder and other advocates for the homeless began a fast to protest cutbacks of $19 million for shelters and other services for the homeless. This cut represented a reduction in the budget for homeless people by almost one-third, and almost one-half in the fiscal year beginning October 1990. "We've got to use ourselves as lightning rods," said Snyder, who had often argued that the homeless had nothing to fight with but their bodies (Sanchez, 3/11/90). By the middle of 1990, Snyder had used his own body to call attention to the plight of the homeless: He hung himself, evidently in despair over the refusal of those in power to provide even the most basic of human needs, shelter.

Health

The administration claims that the War on Drugs is necessary in large part because of the disastrously negative health effects of illegal drug consumption. But the administration has shown itself to be unconcerned with health in other arenas. There are, for example, only two other industrialized countries in the world besides the United States that have no national system of health insurance for the entire population (Lewis, 2/20/90). One American out of six has no health insurance at all, and an equal ratio have inadequate insurance (Cohn, 8/13–/19/90). This situation is likely to grow worse as medical costs rise and companies cut benefits and ask employees to help pay for more of their expenses (Lawlor, 7/25/90).

Even amid this obscenity, there is talk of further "rationing" of health care. In 1984, Richard Lamm, the Democratic governor of Colorado, stated: "We've got a duty to die and get out of the way." But the "we" in question is obviously the poor, since the rich can afford private medical care (Cohn, 8/13–/19/90).

Hospitals in major cities across the country are experiencing debilitating overcrowding due to federal cutbacks, drugs and AIDS cases, and the effects of increasing poverty (see, for example, King, 2/19/90, for a discussion of Chicago's health care system). Forty-one states have reported severe overcrowding in emergency rooms, and conditions have become so serious in some areas that health care workers themselves have felt impelled to take action. In February 1990, for example, physicians in a Bedford-Stuyvesant emergency room briefly threatened to resign over conditions they considered "brutal" and "inhumane."

Because of a refusal to provide adequate treatment facilities, many drug cases end up in these overcrowded and inadequately funded hospitals. The inadequacies of the health care system, especially in urban areas, combined with poverty ensures that the poor receive no medical assistance until there is an emergency and more serious illness is inevitable. The director of medical affairs for the New York Health Department blamed the dismal state of health care on five years of a federal policy that essentially said, "If you are poor, it's your problem" (Specter and Kurtz, 2/11/90).

The administration is certainly not concerned with the general health of the country's low-income groups. Nor is it really concerned with the health effects of the drugs it so widely decries. One doctor at the Congressional Office of Technology Assessment noted that only 10 to 20 percent of intravenous drug users receive treatment, and even those receive inadequate AIDS testing and counseling (Holts, 9/19/90). In Dade County, Florida, to give but one example, there are 173 beds for substance abusers. Every one of these beds is filled and there is a waiting list of over a thousand names (Reveron, 2/18/90).

In addition, while repeatedly pointing out the costs of taking care of illegal drug users and "crack babies," the administration ignores other health costs such as the estimated $40 billion in health care and related costs brought about by industrial pollution (*The Nation*, 7/3/89).

Children

There is a great deal of talk about concern for children in the rhetoric of the Drug Warriors. But no matter how politically appealing posing in hospitals holding crack babies is for politicians in terms of photo opportunities or sound bites, there is little evidence of real concern on the part of those in power for the health of children. During the Reagan administration, drastic cuts in social services affected the quality of life for many children, especially those from the lower socioeconomic sectors who are most likely to have their lives destroyed by either drug abuse or the criminalization strategy of the War on Drugs.

Columbia University's National Center for Children in Poverty released a report in April 1990 in which it was noted that the group of people most affected by poverty in this country are children. Approximately 5 million children live in families that are below the poverty line.

These children, the report noted, are more likely to be exposed to drugs, abuse, and neglect.

Between 1981 and 1990 (during two Republican administrations), the percentage of children living in poverty increased to almost 20 percent. This is the highest figure in the industrialized West (Nader and Green, 4/2/90). Children in this country are more likely to live in poverty than children in eleven other industrialized countries, and they are more likely to die before their first birthday than children in any of these countries except the Soviet Union. In 1986, 10 American children per 1,000 births died before their first birthday; in Japan the figure was 5 per 1,000 (*New York Times*, 3/19/90). These children living in poverty are more vulnerable to disease, more likely to do badly in school, more likely to become involved with the criminal justice system, and more likely to earn less and wind up on public assistance. But, as Michael Prowse, a writer for the *Financial Times* of London, has pointed out, "Bush's strategy is to sound extremely concerned but do very little" (about the dismal social problems facing marginalized populations) (Prowse, 1990).

Administration policy has also negatively affected foster care, where many of the children it so loudly claims to be concered about end up. In California alone, over 60 percent of drug-exposed babies have been placed in foster care. Nationwide, many drug exposed babies abandoned in hospitals by parents too sick to care for them are destined for foster care, as are the children of families that cannot find adequate housing. Families with children are one of the fastest growing groups among the homeless. But the Reagan administration opposed funding for services that might have prevented much of the need for foster care, left state foster care plans unreviewed, and conducted few audits despite growing evidence of fiscal mismanagement and soaring costs in the foster care system (Downey and Miller, 7/10/90).

If those in power were seriously concerned with children, infant mortality rates would be decreasing, not increasing. Only Greece and Portugal have higher infant mortality rates than that of the United States (Prowse, 1990). More than six out of ten black infants are born to unmarried mothers, and the infant mortality rates for these infants is higher than for infants born into two-parent families. These black women with children are the most severely affected by cutbacks in government programs. According to the Census Bureau, 36 percent of black families with a child under age eighteen are classified as living in poverty. This compares to 12 percent of white families (Byrd, 8/3/90). In addition to increases in infant mortality, the rate of low birth weight babies rose in 1989, especially among African Americans (Nader and Green, 4/2/90).

In 1990, a White House group considered a major new initiative on children but rejected it because it would not provide immediate results

(Moynihan, 7/16/90). Recommendations for expanding family planning services by establishing clinics in schools were rejected by the administration because the plan would "cost money" and could be seen as "encouraging promiscuity" even though the administration admitted that it could reduce teen pregnancy and the number of single-parent families (Pear, 7/6/90). This decision was made even though infant mortality rates for teenaged mothers are even higher than for African Americans (Byrd, 8/3/90). In May 1990, roughly half of the states began cutbacks on caseloads for the Special Supplemental Food Program for Women, Infants, and Children (WIC). Vouchers given under this program supplied 4.5 million expectant and new mothers, and children, with supplemental food. Many states began cutting caseloads by eliminating women and young children who, though undernourished, showed no signs of malnutrition. It was expected that these women and children would be put back on the rolls when they did show actual signs of malnutrition. This pathetically short-sighted policy forces women and children to become more unhealthy in order to receive benefits (Pear, 5/29/90). The shortfall in money, which prompted cutbacks in the WIC program, was blamed on unexpected increases in food prices, but these same increases in food prices were forcing even more poor families into malnutrition.

California expected to save $1.2 million by cutting in half the monthly juice allotment for children three to five years of age. A savings of $6 million was expected through the elimination of cheese from the foods that could be secured through a voucher program. Even though the State Department of Health Services argued that these cuts would not affect the minimum daily requirement met by the package, others working in the program pointed out that many of the people they worked with were severely undernourished and needed more than the minimum daily requirement of nutrients. Workers in the program pointed out as well that the relatively modest savings gained by the cuts would be more than offset by subsequent rises in health care that would be the result of the lack of nourishment (Mydans, 6/2/90).

The WIC program was being cut even though it had been one of the most successful government programs in decreasing infant mortality and preventing illness (Pear, 5/29/90). Even critics of the WIC program consider it to be one of the most helpful food programs in existence. Proponents of the program point out that it is more of an investment than an expenditure in that it decreases public spending on programs later on in the life of the women and children it serves (Hey, 7/13/90). Again, if the real concern was with the health and well-being of children, programs such as WIC would not be cut.

In addition, due to administration inaction on the problem of AIDS and its refusal to implement programs (such as providing free needles) because they might encourage drug use, AIDS, which was virtually unknown in 1980, today infects hundreds of children who are abandoned and in need of care.

Another leading cause of children entering the child welfare system in the 1980s was child abuse. Reports of abuse have more than doubled in the past decade, with over 2.2 million cases reported in 1989 (Downey and Miller, 7/10/90). It is estimated that at least 900,000 children were sexually or physically abused in 1989. The U.S. Advisory Board on Child Abuse and Neglect maintains that "child abuse and neglect in the United States now represents a national emergency." Joyce Strom, deputy director of the Child Welfare League of America, noted that a large part of the increase in child abuse was due to "poverty, because of homelessness" (Hey, 6/29/90).

But the administration shows little concern to relieve any of the stress that leads to child abuse. Joblessness, homelessness, and poverty all contribute to child abuse. But in July 1990, Bush even vetoed minimal medical and parental leave legislation that would have affected about 5 percent of all U.S. employers and 44 percent of all workers (*Christian Science Monitor*, 7/2/90).

Nor is the administration really concerned with the youth it claims to be protecting through its drug policies. The federal government estimates that each year there are roughly 500,000 runaways or "throwaways" under the age of eighteen. These children add to the numbers of homeless people in the country. Most of these young people, according to surveys in shelters, are victims of physical abuse or sexual abuse. As Gregory Evans, a deputy counsel for the National Coalition for the Homeless, has noted, "You've got these kids huddling in a dark alley somewhere for shelter. They are preyed upon by pimps, molesters and drug dealers, and those who ran away from sexual abuse often suffer the same type of abuse on the streets" (Barden, 2/5/90).

The refusal to provide an adequate standard of living for the populace (which would help prevent child poverty and abuse) is not cheap. It is estimated that the federal government's share of the annual cost of keeping youths in out-of-home placements is at least $1.8 billion (Barden, 2/5/90). In the state of Alabama alone, there were 10,590 babies born to girls nineteen years of age and younger in 1988. The state spent an estimated $117.5 million taking care of these girls and their babies (Lewis, 5/29/90).

In 1987, 32.5 million people in this country were living in poverty; 13 million of them were below the age of eighteen. Among the numerous factors thought to have brought about this situation are a shortage of affordable day care for young parents and a growing number of jobs for which the young parents are not qualified (Barden, 4/16/90). "We should be outraged and appalled that the country continues to allow this to happen," says James Weill of the Children's Defense Fund. "In the long run it's going to be very damaging to the country" (Keen, 4/16/90).

The Children's Defense Fund recommended that if the cycle of poverty was to be broken the government would have to provide income support for all employed parents and assure child support payments for single parents. Also recommended were provisions for community child care centers; the expansion of Head Start and other preschool programs to serve all children of low-income families, and the expansion of such programs to full day, year-round programs; and the preparation of poor young adults for employment in more technically demanding jobs (Barden, 4/16/90).

The director of the Center for Children in Poverty was quoted as saying:

We pay welfare costs for teen-age mothers rather than the costs of preventive services, education and decent jobs and wages for them and their partners. We pay the high costs of neonatal intensive care for infants rather than offering quality low-cost prenatal care for their mothers. (Barden, 4/16/90)

Secretary of Health and Human Services, Dr. Louis Sullivan, has bemoaned the existence of crack babies, whose "potential to become productive adults has been compromised" (Foster, 6/13/90). There is very little comment from the administration, however, about the thwarting of human potential brought about by cutbacks in social programs. The compromising of human potential is simply not the issue. If it was, every child would have enough to eat, a decent education and adequate health care, as a minimum.

Infant mortality is the clearest case of compromising human potential. In mid–1990, a panel of Bush administration officials concluded (in the words of the *New York Times*) that "the United States could substantially reduce infant deaths without redistributing income, eradicating poverty, or spending billions of dollars" (Paper, 8/12/90). Essentially, the panel was arguing that infant mortality rates could be substantially reduced simply by providing routine clinical care and social services to pregnant women. Dr. Ezra C. Davidson, Jr., president of the American College of Obstetricians and Gynecologists, estimated that such measures could eliminate as much as one-third of infant mortality. Simple measures such as providing easy access to prenatal care could save the lives of many children whose potential is certainly being thwarted.[7]

But, after receiving the recommendations of its own panel, the Bush administration had no intention of disseminating the findings. The Justice Department and the Department of Health and Human Services withheld most of the document from Congress, saying they must "preserve the confidentiality of the deliberative process" in the executive branch of government (Pear, 8/12/90).

In June 1990, a national commission issued a report that stated: "Never before has one generation of American teenagers been less healthy, less cared for, or less prepared for life than their parents were at the same age" (Leary, 6/9/90). The commission recommended that all teenagers be guaranteed access to health care and counseling regardless of their ability to pay. The commission also noted that the problem represented by this new generation was a problem not only for the children involved but for the society as a whole, since undernourished, uneducated, suicidal children will not be able to achieve the educational levels that are necessary "for success in the 21st century" (Leary, 6/9/90). Similarly, a Columbia University report issued in April 1990 recommended universal health insurance, better child care, unemployment insurance, affordable housing, education, and job training reforms. The report also noted that more than half of poor children live outside big cities, over 50 percent have at least one working parent, and only 28 percent live in families totally dependent on public assistance. Nearly half of black children live in poor families, and children in single female households are the hardest hit (Keen, 4/16/90).

The continuing reliance on local taxes to support schools also ensures that children in the more impoverished areas of the country and areas within states will continue to receive substandard education, which will consequently handicap them in the competition for jobs. The "even playing field" that the Reagan administration was so concerned about in Nicaragua does not seem to be important when children in the United States are considered. And at a time when employers are finding it difficult to find skilled workers, Bush, the self-proclaimed "Education President," proposed only a 1 percent increase in federal education spending (Nader and Green, 4/2/90).

In March 1990, the Census Bureau released a study in which various social indicators were compared for children in other industrialized countries. Children in the United States were found to be more likely to die before their first birthday, be killed before they reached the age of twenty-five, or live in poverty than children in eleven other industrialized countries. Representative George Miller (D-Cal.) remarked on the release of the study:

The dead babies, the murders, the child poverty, are a hemorrhage on human resources and the American spirit. We just can't continue to have it go on. It escalates the amount of budget resources that must go in to clean up the mess. And clearly we have the ability to prevent it. (*Atlanta Journal Constitution*, 3/19/90)

Regardless of the focus on the long-term effects of taking care of crack babies, the effects of the poverty ignored by two Republican administrations linger for generations. In a study conducted in Chicago and reported in the *American Journal of Public Health*, researchers found that low birth weight infants were more common in poorer households and that they were more common among blacks than whites, no matter what their present income or educational level. Researchers concluded that it might well take more than one generation of non-poverty and adequate services to bring about an increase in birth weight (*Montgomery Advertiser*, 6/5/90).

This society has operated for too long as if the fate of individuals was an individual problem. This society is built on individualism and it is now suffering the consequences. The fate of individual children is not an individual fate but a collective one. Until people in this country understand that their fate as a collectivity is intimately tied with the fate of other individuals, with each deprived child, this society will be condemned to live with increasing levels of aggression, violence, alienation, and rampant crime. The fate of this nation is intimately tied to the fate of every child living within it.

Widespread social and economic inequalities that so negatively affect children are not inevitable, even though the dominant segments of society would have us believe so. They are matters of choice and priority. In Sweden, parents are entitled to twelve months of paid leave after the birth of a child, and national health insurance covers not only all hospitalization costs but 90 percent of the income an individual loses while ill. Education is almost entirely free, from day care through university, and a pension provides the employee with two-thirds of his average income in the retiree's fifteen best paid years (Pedersen, 3/5/90).

The choice that has been made by those in power in this country, however, is to ignore widespread social and economic inequality and to focus on the use, abuse, and trafficking of illegal drugs as if they were the most severe and damaging social problems the country faces. The War on Drugs is used as a diversion from these other, more serious, social problems. Poverty, homelessness, and lack of equal opportunity, which are actively promoted by administration policy, encourage drug trafficking and abuse; but poverty, homelessness, and lack of equal opportunity virtually disappear as problems beneath the rhetoric of the War on Drugs.

RACE: THE CREATION OF AN ENEMY CLASS

There is no question that the enforcement tactics of the War on Drugs are focused on minority populations. In fact, drug panics have been used historically in this country as part of a larger war against marginalized populations, designed to further marginalize them and legitimate their oppression. As Michael Woodiwiss (1988:3–4) has noted, in the early 1900s Jewish and Italian communities in the Northeast and Midwest were deemed to be leading the slide toward moral degeneracy through drug use. Prejudice against the Chinese was a large factor behind widespread legislation prohibiting opium smoking in the latter nineteenth century. Campaigns to prohibit the use of intoxicants in the South and to disenfranchise and repress blacks were frequently lead by the same people, and they were part of a wider movement to keep blacks in a subordinate position (see also Helmer, 1975).

The rhetoric that accompanied these previous campaigns against drugs and minorities is amazingly similar to that of the present War on Drugs. Minority group drug users were and are portrayed as especially dangerous. During the opium scare, for example, "yellow fiends" or "yellow devils" were portrayed as enslaving white women and children. In 1988, while discussing crack users in an interview with the *Washington Post*, Roger Guevara, DEA spokesman in Los Angeles, remarked: "We frequently hear stories of patrol officers shooting somebody 14 or so times and the guy keeps going at him. . . . They can literally get their arms torn off, and they don't feel a . . . thing. It's really scary" (Lait, 4/17/88). This is so similar to the comments published in the late nineteenth century about blacks and cocaine that it is uncanny. Blacks were argued to be able to achieve immense strength and cunning when using cocaine, a popular and legal ingredient of medicines and soft drinks at the time. It was argued that blacks were capable of withstanding .32-caliber bullets, and because of these stories some police departments in the South switched to .38-caliber bullets (Woodiwiss, 1988:4).

In another similarity to the present War on Drugs, the threat that this minority drug use represented was portrayed in dire terms. The San Jose *Mercury*, for example, editorialized that the practice of opium smoking had to be "rooted out" before it could "decimate our youth, emasculate the coming generation, if not completely destroy the whole population of our coast" (Woodiwiss, 1988:4).

The focus of drug panics on minority populations, therefore, is nothing new. As Courtland Milloy has noted in the *Washington Post*, "It is not that America has a low tolerance for drugs—but no tolerance for blacks who remind her of injustice, racism and hypocrisy" (Milloy, 1/28/90). It is no accident that the Ku Klux Klan in Lakeland, Florida, began a "Krush Krack Kokaine" campaign in the spring of 1989 and began patrolling the streets for evidence against suspected drug dealers (*Time*, 1/8/90).[8]

The siege on minority populations being fueled by the War on Drugs is evident. One out of every ten adult African American males is now living under some kind of correctional supervision (Crittenden, 12/29/

89). The death rate of black men is now seven to eight times that of white men, and violence is the leading cause of that death. In East Palo Alto, California, which is a largely black community of 18,500 people forty miles south of San Francisco, one in five people is unemployed. One in ten is in prison. The homicide rate in East Palo Alto in 1989 was ten times the national homicide rate (Gross, 2/10/90). Administration policies have ensured that drug trafficking will be an attractive alternative to lower-class segments of the population, and then administration rhetoric has blamed the involvement in drug trafficking on supposed criminogenic tendencies. But, as Derrick Bell (1/14/90) has noted, "It is only surprising that, given their exclusion from traditional paths of upward mobility, more black men do not choose crime as their means of 'making it' in a society that equates wealth and power with success."

In an interview with the *Washington Post*, one top DEA official argued that youth trafficking in drugs had to be shown "that it is better to earn a slow honest nickel than to earn a fast, dishonest dime." Judy Mann editorialized with relish in the *Washington Post* that this slogan "ought to be put on bumper stickers and plastered on banners across cafeterias and stuck up on the walls of restrooms in every school and gathering spot for youngsters in the city" (Mann, 12/8/89). But why lower-class youth should aspire to a slow, honest nickel in a society that glorifies the fast buck is not asked, much less answered.

Lower-class involvement in drug trafficking and abuse is not only a matter of rational choice between economic alternatives. There are other, deeper factors involved. Cecil Williams, for example, has noted that after the past decade, there is "an abiding sense of powerlessness, the breakdown of the spirit" in many black communities (Williams, 2/15/90). Because of the persistence of racism, discrimination, and inequality of opportunity, the alienation of minority populations has reached such an extent that many in the black community now argue that drugs were purposefully introduced into ghettos (Williams, 2/15/90; Reeves, 2/14/90; White, 1/22/90). While these charges are called "preposterous" by some commentators (see, for example, White, 1/22/90), the very fact of their existence and widespread belief is highly significant. As Jack White has noted in *Time* magazine (1/22/90), "Fears of a diabolical conspiracy to exterminate blacks have been around for decades, but seldom have they been believed by so many people."

A *New York Times*/WCBS-TV News poll in New York City in June 1990 revealed that roughly 58 percent of black respondents felt it was certainly or possibly true that the "government deliberately makes sure that drugs are easily available in poor black neighborhoods in order to harm black people." This is contrasted with only 16 percent of whites who felt it certainly or possibly true (DeParle, 10/29/90).

The National Urban League published a report in 1989 in which it was stated that "there is at least one concept that must be recognized if one is to see the pervasive and insidious nature of the drug problem for the African-American community. Though difficult to accept, that is the concept of genocide" (White, 1/22/90).

Cecil Williams, pastor of Glide Memorial Church writing in the *New York Times*, has also argued that the crack epidemic "amounts to genocide," a genocide he blames on everyone involved, including "those in our government who have winked and nodded at drug trafficking in the name of 'national security' " (Williams, 2/15/90).

It is not necessary to argue or demonstrate that drugs were purposefully introduced into black and other minority communities in order to perceive the functionality of their pervasive existence there in terms of maintaining the subordination of minorities. Drug trafficking provides an alternate opportunity structure for those who would otherwise be unemployed or underemployed. For example, one drug dealer in Washington, D.C., who was convicted in 1989, was said by prosecutors to have managed a business that provided employment for over 150 people (Mann, 12/8/89). Drug trafficking, therefore, provides a lucrative source of income for those who might otherwise be protesting and organizing to change the conditions of their existence. Those in power are under less pressure to provide full employment when there is a viable alternative to legitimate employment, one that in terms of money and self-determination offers greater rewards than any legitimate job opportunities likely to be offered through government programs.

Black and other marginalized populations have the most to complain about in terms of the distribution of wealth and opportunity in this country. But widespread involvement in drug trafficking and abuse functions to diffuse opposition and political pressure for change. It functions to turn what sociologists refer to as potential "social dynamite" into "social junk."

Focused political mobilization is made difficult by the disorganization of life that is characteristic not of drug use itself but of illegal drug use—surveillance, processing through the criminal justice system, and subsequent labelling. In addition, the violence that surrounds the illegal drug market combines with conditions of poverty to produce high mortality rates that also eliminate large numbers of young men who might otherwise be politically active. In certain parts of New York City that are predominately populated by marginalized segments of the population, life expectancy is lower than in Bangladesh (Prowse, 1990).

Simply put, instead of burning down Washington, D.C., in protest over the conditions of their existence, many minority youth are selling drugs, abusing drugs, sitting in prison, or dead. The latter is certainly preferable to the former from the standpoint of those in power. As Joseph Lowery, head of the Southern Christian Leadership Conference, has commented, "If the powers that be really wanted to deal with this issue, they wouldn't have let it get this far" (White, 1/22/90).

It is difficult to overestimate the role the War on Drugs has played in the hardening of attitudes toward marginalized populations, and therefore in legitimating their abandonment. Williams has noted that the 1970s and 1980s were characterized by a "general acceptance of the attitude that blacks were, at least, expendable" (Williams, 2/15/90).

Derrick Bell, who teaches civil rights law at Harvard, has written the following in the *New York Times*:

Police crackdowns, like the campaign to restore the death penalty in states that abandoned it, and the much publicized war on drugs, are all policies of racial diversion.

Opponents of social reform are able to transform this unconscious Caucasian consensus into policies that undermine civil rights efforts. (Bell, 1/14/90)

The hardening of attitudes has reached such an extent that it has fueled widespread vigilante action. In September 1989, a dozen off-duty soldiers exchanged gunfire with a group of alleged drug dealers. It was reported that hundreds of rounds of ammunition were fired in a thirty-minute gun battle. Police confiscated two semiautomatic rifles, one 12-gauge shotgun, eight semiautomatic hand guns, and one revolver from the soldiers, who were members of the Army Rangers, an elite force of light infantry (*New York Times*, 9/27/89). There have been other instances of citizens burning down suspected crack houses. The administration, abetted by the media, has created the sentiment that if drug use or trafficking are suspected, anything goes.

By focusing on illegal drug use and trafficking by minorities, the administration has abetted a larger process of bifurcating the population, dividing it into good people and bad people, respectable citizens and criminals, the worthy and the unworthy, us and them. The more sharply these divisions are drawn and the more vilification heaped upon the unworthy and the criminal groups, the easier it will become to abandon the poor and minority groups. Within the criminal justice system, this process of bifurcation is reflected in the growing transformation of the legal process from a mechanism of determining guilt or innocence of violating laws to a mechanism for distinguishing certain types of people. The criminal justice system is increasingly only peripherally concerned with law violation. In fact, for certain segments of the population, violation of the law has become irrelevant. To cite but one example, John Poindexter's obstruction of justice was termed by the *Wall Street Journal* (6/8/90) as not an "understandable crime." It was maintained that Poindexter's prosecution was not a matter of law violation but part of "congressional criminalizing of policy differences." The editorial claimed that a sentence of community service was appropriate for Poindexter, as it had been for Oliver North.

The recent hardening in attitudes against crime and criminals is, in fact, only a hardening of attitudes toward certain crimes committed by certain types of offenders. The courts, which are now packed with Reagan appointees, suspended two convictions of Oliver North because of the type of person North is, not because of the crimes he committed. Oliver North is considered to be part of "us." The drug dealer on the street, part of "them." Similarly, presidents of banks who launder drug money are presumed innocent and unwitting. Residents of public housing suspected of drug dealing are considered guilty and knowledgeable.

Even though there is substantial published evidence of organized crime involvement in the looting of the S&Ls, the FBI has simply failed to pursue the information. The attorney general has maintained that there is no evidence of such involvement. The *Houston Post* also published information about the involvement in the S&L scandal of some with CIA affiliations. That "good" people who helped loot the S&Ls were doing so aided by organized crime and the CIA is, however, not considered worthy of investigation (Kwitny, 9/10/90).

Segments of the population whose behavior is being criminalized and so harshly punished are aware to some extent of the unfairness of their victimization. And they are fighting back in the small spaces they have left. There has been considerable discussion, for example, of what syndicated columnist Richard Reeves calls "jury-room vigilantism"—the refusal of juries to convict even when faced with overwhelming evidence of guilt (Reeves, 8/27/90). In one case, jurors revealed that much of the discussion in the jury room before the decision to acquit had centered around the unwillingness of jurors to see another young black male go to prison. The refusal of the jury in Marion Barry's case to convict on more than one count, even when confronted with videotape of Barry smoking crack, is another example of the recognition by some segments of the population that types of people are being prosecuted, not crime.

However, these are isolated instances, and those in power seem oblivious to the level of alienation such instances represent. The determination to abandon minority and poor segments of the society seems fixed. The policy decisions of the past decade have made it clear that the unskilled, the untrained, the uneducated are no longer (in terms of those in power) needed; they are expendable.

To cite but one example, in June 1990 the Commission on the Skills of the American Work Force released a report entitled "America's Choice: High Skills or Low Wages?" in which it was concluded that if the United States wanted to continue to compete on an international scale, it would have to do some serious work to reform the educational system in this country and upgrade the opportunities for training the work force. In comparison with other countries, the report's authors noted, the United States kept its workers in "rote, repetitive tasks unlike many other countries which are training employees to be highly skilled professionals." The report noted that the United States was not changing its educational system to produce trained workers for new kinds of jobs (Foster, 6/19/90).

The response of Congress was to change immigration law to admit more skilled immigrants to compensate for what is predicted to be a labor shortage in the future. Many businesses argued that it was cheaper and easier to import foreign-born professionals than to invest in the education and training of unskilled, poorly educated Americans (Pear, 8/15/90).

What, then, is to be done with this segment of the population that is no longer needed? First, their abandonment must be legitimated to the wider society; second, any resistance to this abandonment must be diluted or stamped out. As has been argued in this section, the War on Drugs has facilitated both. There is scant sympathy for the marginalized since their problems and alienation are now largely perceived to be drug-related, and, therefore, self-induced. Illegal drugs and enforcement tactics against the marginalized have insured their virtual political neutralization. The rhetoric of concern so loudly proclaimed by the administration is quite rightly perceived as a lie by those who claim genocide.

Ronald K. Siegel, a research psychopharmacologist at the UCLA School of Medicine, has argued in his book *Intoxication: Life in Pursuit of Artificial Paradise* that drug use is a natural part of human and animal behavior. Siegel argues that the War on Drugs is doomed to failure because drug taking is part of the nature of man. He further argues that the dangers of the current drugs of fashion suggest that research funds should be invested in manufacturing less dangerous intoxicants. Siegel's proposal was received with predictable hostility from William Bennett's Office of National Drug Control Policy. Drug researcher Andrew Weil of the University of Arizona College of Medicine responded to Siegel's proposal: "There is a real danger in thinking there is a perfect drug that won't interfere with psychological and spiritual growth" (Beaty, 8/21/89). The social conditions under which marginalized segments of the society live certainly interfere with psychological and spiritual growth but do not raise similar concerns. Psychological and spiritual growth is not promoted by creating economic and social conditions that foster drug trafficking and abuse, incarcerating those who engage in it, and then blaming them for their own victimization.

The discussion of minority involvement in drug trafficking and abuse is important because the focus of the criminalization-eradication strategy of the War on Drugs is on minority groups. But contrary to the impression left by the media, drug trafficking, drug use, and drug abuse are not confined to marginal populations. For example, a nationwide drug survey of high school students conducted in 1989 by the Atlanta-based Parents' Resource Institute for Drug Education (PRIDE) found that even though black high school students reported cocaine easier to find than did white students, they reported using cocaine less (Skorneck, 12/19/89). A report by the Greater Washington Research Center in December 1987 also showed high rates of drug usage by whites (Milloy, 1/28/90). Reasons for drug trafficking and abuse among the poor and marginalized are easy enough to find. But what are the explanations for widespread drug abuse by the more fortunate?

THE SOCIAL REALITY THAT LEADS TO DRUG ABUSE

Another major issue masked by the rhetoric of the War on Drugs is the social and cultural reality that makes the U.S. population such a consumer of drugs. The United States composes 5 percent of the world's population but consumes 50 percent of the world's cocaine (Milloy, 1/28/90). Drug use and abuse are pervasive not only among lower-class and minority segments of the population but also among the well-to-do. For example, crack is widely considered to be a problem in urban ghettos, but it is not confined there. Crack use among middle- and upper-class segments of the population has been increasing. Dr. Arnold M. Washton, director of a New York treatment center, noted that 70 percent of his clients were from the middle class and that there were more crack addicts among the white middle class than any other segment of the population (Malcolm, 10/1/89).[9] Bill Coonce, head of the Detroit office of the DEA, has remarked: "It's not just a black or minority drug. We're seeing a rapid expansion of addiction now into suburban and small town America" (Malcolm, 10/1/89). In fact, the use of cocaine in all its forms is greatest among white single men in metropolitan areas of the Northeast and West. An estimated 70 percent of the patients at Horizon Center, a private treatment center in East Lansing, Michigan, for example, are crack users. "They're just average Joes with jobs," remarked a senior therapist at Horizon Center in an interview with the *New York Times* (Malcolm, 10/1/89).

The U.S. population is a mass consumer not just of illegal drugs, but of legal drugs as well. Alcohol, tobacco, and mood-altering prescription drug use is endemic in all classes.

Part of the explanation for the widespread use of so many drugs within the society can be found by examining the social reality of life in advanced capitalist countries, even for the well-off. At first glance it seems strange that the middle and upper classes would be such heavy drug consumers. The standard explanations of alienation due to poverty and racism do not apply. But the reality is that even the affluent in the society experience profound stress and alienation.

Life in post-industrial centers, even for the well-off, requires existence in a highly stressing context. It is stressing partly because it involves the overuse and overexploitation of time. According to one Harris survey, for example, the amount of leisure time enjoyed by the average American has shrunk 37 percent since 1973. The average work week has increased from under 41 hours to 47 hours. Small business people work an average of 57 hours per week; those with incomes over $50,000, over 52 hours per week (Hunnicut, 1/4/90). In some professions such as law, finance, and medicine, the work week is often over 80 hours long (Gibbs, 4/24/89). On average, Americans have 8.5 hours of leisure time per week. The workplace demands for time have decreased the amount of time available for family and social life. One Yale psychologist noted to *Time* magazine that because of the shortage of leisure time the country is "at the breaking point as far as the family is concerned" (Burtless, 1/4/90).

In addition to the increasing amount of time North Americans spend at work, researchers have noted elevated levels of stress in the workplace. Management recruiting firms have noted increased susceptibility to colds and minor infections among management personnel, and complaints of exhaustion, difficulties making decisions, and guilt feelings about work left undone at the office. These symptoms of stress are now being found at an earlier and earlier age.

In addition, even the affluent in this society live with the threat of economic insecurity. The increasing phenomenon of mergers has led to feelings of insecurity on the job and is blamed for much of the stress. Management firms have noted that in the future corporations will need more than exercise programs or "leisure clothes" workdays to manage the stress levels that they are creating (Fowler, 9/12/89).

A 1987 Westinghouse Electric Corporation study of white collar employees makes this apparent. The study was conducted shortly after layoffs and a restructuring were announced. Nine percent of the men and 17 percent of the women reported having had major episodes of depression lasting ten days or longer during the year before the study. Twenty-three percent of the men and 36 percent of the women reported having had such an episode at least once during their lives. The major factors causing depression at work were uncertainties about future employment, lack of rewards, pay cuts, and negative employer evaluations (Bair, 6/13/90).

It should be noted that the increasing interest in and notice of workplace stress for managers come after years of predictions that management life would become easier with new technology (Fowler, 9/12/89). There was an era in which the expansion of leisure time was thought to be a mark of progress and civilization. Futurists predicted an expansion rather than a decrease in leisure time. In fact, Americans have less leisure time than many people in what are considered underdeveloped countries; even that leisure time is so structured that it ceases to be anything that could be considered leisure. Leisure has become work. For example, physical fitness in the United States is not a leisure activity. Leisure has in fact become consumption. The demands of the workplace, therefore, are compounded by the constant consumerism of leisure time.

Children's leisure activity in some families is scheduled as tightly as their parents' work schedule. The incessant activity and the excessive planned consumption of time are having a profound impact on family life. Many middle- and upper-class children are overprogrammed and pressured into rapid achievement (Gibbs, 4/24/89). Even children at the preschool age are pressured for performance (see Goleman, 9/21/89). And there are disturbing indications of the consequences. According to a report issued by the National Association of State Boards of Education and the American Medical Association, the suicide rate for teenagers has doubled since 1968. Other reports show that 10 percent of adolescent boys and 20 percent of girls have attempted suicide (Leary, 6/9/90).

The requirement of constant, excessive action translates into physiological and psychological demands far in excess of what the human animal can withstand. The body must assume these demands. It is argued that one of the reasons why cocaine became the drug of choice for middle- and upper-class communities is that "success" in the post-industrial world demands overactivity. Cocaine stimulates overactivity. Cocaine keeps a person awake, functioning, striving, competing, running with the accelerated rhythms of life in post-industrial centers.

Post-industrial life imposes a permanent state of "organic alarm." The ideological paradigms of the post-industrial society linked to excessive competition and consumption impose on individuals elevated psychological and physical demands. In response to the requirements of success, personal power, and consumption, cocaine is a panacea. If, in the beginning of the development of capitalism, time was money, in the post-industrial centers time has become cocaine.

Every culture provides a particular experience of time. Time as a dimension of life, a dimension of pleasure, work, knowledge, satisfaction, pain. Time as a corporal experience. The post-industrial capitalist society requires bodies that are economically useful, socially efficient, and politically innocuous. Drugs, especially cocaine, ensure such bodies.

Therefore, even for the well-off in this society, life is highly stressful and overly demanding. Not only is the workplace stressful, but social interaction is also increasingly stressful and dangerous. No other society in the world produces more noninstrumental violence. An element of fear is imbedded in every chance encounter. Especially in urban centers, any stranger can become a predator. Every daily newspaper carries examples of growing social pathology.

According to a survey in the *Journal of the American Medical Association* released in mid–1990, the murder rate for young men in the United States is more than four times the murder rate of any other developed country. The murder rate for men fifteen to twenty-four years of age in the United States was twenty-two homicides per 100,000. This compared to 0.3 per 100,000 in Austria (Sperling, 6/27/90). Sampling from but one day of state events from *USA Today* (7/30/90) revealed a raid in Cambridge, Massachusetts, in which 200 handguns, 300 rifles, a machine gun, and an antitank gun were seized from a duplex apartment—more firepower than the city police had; a twenty-two-year-old man who, after barricading himself in a motel for five hours, shot himself; a Missouri state representative arraigned on federal charges of distributing marijuana and amphetamines to persons under age twenty-one (he was awaiting trial on charges of selling cocaine and amphetamines); a fifty-three-year-old man in Aspen, Colorado, holding off police for a fourth day, threatening to kill himself and his wife. In August 1990, a thirty-year-old man set himself afire after pouring a flammable liquid over his body. He was having what were described as marital difficulties. After setting himself afire, he ran into the house of his invalid mother, and the ensuing fire killed her (*Montgomery Advertiser*, 8/9/90). In July 1990, a woman testified against her husband in the death of their son. The husband had used disciplinary techniques on the two-year-old son, including forcing the child to stand in the corner with his hands on his head, forcing him to eat feces, and grinding his fist and cayenne pepper into the child's genitals. The then father dunked the child repeatedly in the toilet, holding him by the ankles. After this, the child was made to take a cold shower and come to the living room where the couple beat him with cushions until he collapsed. The child was pronounced dead the next day. In a taped statement, the father said that he had meant to scare the child and had had "a bad day" (*Montgomery Advertiser*, 7/25/90b).

While these incidents have no direct effect on most people in the society, they create a climate of pervasive social disintegration and anxiety. Drugs, legal and illegal, intervene to perform a dual function. First, drugs provide an escape from stress and anxiety (whether due to fears of losing one's job or being mugged in the street). Second, drugs (used by others) become the convenient explanation for social disintegration. Confronting the violence and corruption of the society without the explanation of drugs is deeply disturbing.

One example of how pervasive the drug excuse is in present explanations of social disintegration can be seen in the Central Park jogger case. For weeks after the event, commentators struggled for an explanation because none of the youths arrested were involved with drugs. Had even one of them been involved with drugs, the media and the public could have rested more easily, satisfied that the brutal event was just another example of a bunch of drug-crazed youths destroying life. The fact that none of those arrested could even be implicated in drug taking left the media and the public deeply anxious. Events such as these force the public to confront the severity of the social breakdown that cannot be attributed to drugs or psychotic disorder. The undercurrent of confused rage and disregard for life displayed so vividly in the Central Park case, which involved violence not only against the woman jogger but against other people in the park as well, is much more complex than people want to admit. This event was an example of the reproduction of the violence that is endemic within the society and that is too deeply disturbing to confront.

The violence and pathology of the social order is written off as caused by either drugs or mental illness, and increasingly the populace retreats into its own drugs of choice, or television. Survey researchers at the University of Michigan and the University of Maryland have found that the amount of time spent watching television has increased faster than the average amount of free time in the past twenty years (Burtless, 1/4/90).

The retreatism is evidenced on many levels. Politically, U.S. citizens are increasingly alienated from the society they live in. They feel increasingly less able to influence or change the course of events. Many Americans do not even bother to vote. At a time when the administration and the media cannot get enough of celebrating participatory democracy in Eastern Europe, Americans participate less and less. After a two-year study of presidential politics, the Markle Commission on the Media and the Electorate concluded that most U.S. citizens are not even well enough informed to recognize manipulative advertising or false campaign claims. The president of the commission remarked: "They act as if they believe that Presidential elections belong to somebody else, most notably Presidential candidates and their handlers." The commission report termed the voters "cynical, passive and uninformed" (Oreskes, 5/6/90). And there is good reason for the alienation. As Anthony Lewis has written, noting the profound changes in the rest of the world, "In the United States, the political system is frozen" (Lewis, 4/13/90).

The failure of the populace to vote in part reflects the fact that many times they have no one to vote for. In the November 1990 congressional elections, sixteen of the thirty-two senators running for reelection were assured of gaining office either because they had no opponent or had finances so in excess of their opponents that there was no question of the outcome. The number of senators who faced no opponent at all (four) was the largest in thirty-four years (Taylor, 8/13–/19/90).

Rather than actively confronting the problems that face society, the populace is increasingly retreating. The profound depression of the American populace can be seen in its reaction to the S&L scandal. Estimates of the costs of the S&L bailout went from $50 billion in October 1988 to $500 billion in April 1990. Some estimates had even reached $1 trillion by the middle of 1990 (Bartlett, 6/10/90). The $500 billion estimate means that each household would eventually pay $5,000 to clean up the mess (Rosenbaum, 6/6/90). The enormous cost of the bailout (much more than the government spends on social programs such as preschool education, aid to the homeless, or even the drug war) and the fact that this enormous burden was generated by graft, the regulatory free-for-all of the Reagan administration, and politics as usual from a Congress that received campaign contributions from the industry[10] should have created a furor. But, as David E. Rosenbaum noted in the *New York Times*, the S&L bailout "has not become a scandal like Watergate or Teapot Dome" (Rosenbaum, 3/18/90). Part of the reason, according to Rosenbaum, is that so many politicians were involved either directly or indirectly that there is no one left to blame them.

Even though Bush promised aggressive pursuit of the officers and directors of the S&Ls, the government largely adopted the position that nothing was to be done. But, as Harvey F. Wachsman, president of the American Board of Professional Liability Attorneys, argued in the *New York Times*, if the government was serious about prosecuting the offenders, the answer was simple: free enterprise. Wachsman proposed that the government make the initial investigations already performed by the Justice Department and the Resolution Trust Corporation available to private law firms around the country, offering them a contingency fee to bring lawsuits on behalf of the government. As Wachsman pointed out, the officers who bilked their depositors should be forced to pay with their own money, and then their liability insurance should be required to pay. Virtually all of those involved carried liability insurance, and Wachsman estimated that they could be held liable for a total of $30 billion. He noted, however, that "the insurance industry will object to this proposal, as it does any time it has to pay off on a claim." Wachsman indicated that some of the cases had been turned over to private law firms, but these firms were being paid on an hourly basis, rather than on a contingency basis in which they would be paid only if they won the cases. The cases farmed out on an hourly basis were moving slowly (Wachsman, 6/21/90).

The Senate Judiciary Committee chairman, Senator Joseph Biden, criticized the administration's efforts at prosecuting S&L officials in mid–

1990. Biden pointed out that FBI statistics showed that the average S&L offender convicted in 1989 received 1.9 years, while the average bank robber is sentenced to 9.4 years (*Montgomery Advertiser*, 7/25/90a). In July 1990, Senator Paul Simon (D-Ill.) noted that the FBI had a backlog of 20,000 tips of fraud and embezzlement in the S&Ls that had not been investigated. Government investigators estimated that of the 700 S&Ls that have failed, fraudulent practices may have been involved in as many as 60 percent of them.

But apparently in the past few decades people have seen so much corruption and experienced so many shocks that they simply don't want to hear anymore. The country has turned off and has tuned in to the television.

SUMMARY

There is evidence that at least some people in the country know there is something desperately wrong. Rushworth M. Kidder, for example, has written in the *Christian Science Monitor* that "the secret of the drug problem is that it isn't most fundamentally a drug problem. It's a values problem. It's about failure of self-worth, respect for others, sense of purpose, and meaningfulness of life" (Kidder, 9/21/89). Kidder finds it necessary to specify that these are not "airy philosophical concepts." The necessity to qualify this says all that needs to be said about the political culture in this country. When did self-worth and meaningfuless of life become airy philosophical concepts? Why is it necessary to apologize for speaking of meaningfulness?

The problem with Kidder's analysis, however (and others like it), is the assumption that these failures came from a movement away from communicating ethics to children. This sounds very much like the Moral Majority argument against what is called secular humanism. The problem, however, is not that we as a society fail to communicate ethics. The problem is that we are communicating the wrong ethics.

This society is characterized by opportunism, greed, and corruption at every level. However, the opportunism, greed, and corruption of the more powerful segments of the society are not being prosecuted with the zeal reserved for minority and lower-class drug traffickers and drug abusers. Opportunism, greed, and corruption have been institutionalized at the upper levels of the social system. Kidder is right that we are living in a sort of "ethical fairyland," but part of what is happening is that the fairyland is disappearing.

Most of the rhetoric surrounding the War on Drugs is about communicating ethics. Kidder argues that the "gravest domestic threat" is not drugs but a "cave-in of values." What we are experiencing, however, is not a cave-in of values. What we are experiencing at all levels of society is the vague, alienated realization that the values supposedly so cherished in this society apply only to certain classes of people. Delay of gratification, honesty, hard work, respectfulness, trustworthiness, and morality are in fact qualities expected of working- and lower-class individuals, certainly not the powerful. The lie, the fiction that these values are cherished for all levels of the society has been and is continually being exposed (such as in the Iran-Contra affair and the S&L crisis). The reaction, however, is not outrage or disappointment, but depression and alienation. This is a depressed culture that can bear to hear no more and spends its time attempting to escape through television and drugs.

Anthony Lewis has summed up the situation well:

The United States . . . seems determined to close its eyes to the realities that menace its future. That is true of the Government and of the public.

American society has problems as serious today as at any time since the Depression. Savings and investment have declined; we rely on foreign capital and then, illogically, sputter when that capital acquires U.S. assets. Our infrastructure of roads and bridges and other public facilities is crumbling.

It is an ill-educated society in a world where education is increasingly essential. The United States, alone among developed countries, has no national system of health insurance; 31 million Americans have no medical insurance.

A vast underclass mocks America's reputation as a just society. Homeless men and women huddle on the fanciest streets of our cities. An expensive restaurant has a notice on the wall headed "We all need food and shelter"; it lists places where people in need can get "a free meal or a place to sleep."

On these and similar problems President Bush offers no leadership worth mentioning. His economic remedy is a cut in the capital gains tax, irrelevant at best. He has nothing of substance to suggest on the country's corrupting social ills. . . .

It takes leadership for a country to face the need for change. This country has no leadership: not in the White House and not in the opposition party. (Lewis, 4/13/90)

NOTES

1. For a discussion of the Nixon administration's blatant manipulation of public sentiment regarding heroin, see Epstein, 1977.

2. It is interesting to note that substantial declines in the use of these legal drugs have been accomplished over the years not by measures such as incarceration or asset seizures, but by education. The methods used to discourage legal drug use have become more and more positive. In mid–1990, for example, the surgeon general released a report on cigarette smoking stressing the positive effects of quitting at any age, no matter how long the user had been smoking. However, these positive methods of persuasion and encouragement are not mobilized to deal with the use of illegal drugs, even though the health effects of using alcohol and tobacco are arguably more serious than the health effects of using the other, illegal drugs.

3. The Partnership for a Drug Free America produced the egg and frying pan commercial with the words: "This is your brain on drugs."

4. It should also be noted that Reagan administration cutbacks severely affected the FDA's ability to adequately supervise drug companies.

5. Economists attribute this growing wagespread in part to a decline in the power of unions, which had kept wages more uniform (Uchitelle, 8/14/90). It should be noted, however, that this decline of unions is largely a result of another concerted war conducted by the Reagan administration to break the unions.

6. It is interesting to note that economists attribute part of the "discouraged worker" phenomenon to the wage spread (unequal wages for the same type of work). Finding themselves paid less than their peers, workers grow discouraged and leave the labor force (Uchitelle, 8/14/90).

7. In the military, universal access to prenatal care has meant that infant mortality rates for military families are lower than the national average.

8. Klan members posed as police officers and detained two black women, one of whom turned out to be an undercover police officer (*Time*, 1/8/90).

9. It is argued that those middle-class users, because they have more to lose, are more secretive about their crack use (Malcolm, 10/1/89). It is interesting to note that crack use can be hidden. If one listened to the public discourse about crack, one would think that crack addiction couldn't be hidden. The fact that large numbers of middle-class crack users can hide their addiction and maintain jobs and family relations belies the administration's rhetoric about the drug.

10. During the 1980s it is estimated that savings and loan directors and others connected to the savings and loans contributed over $11 million to congressional candidates and committees of the two political parties (Hey, 7/9/90).

4

EXPANSION OF DOMESTIC STATE POWER

It is difficult to overemphasize the importance of the War on Drugs in helping to legitimate a vast expansion of domestic state power over the past decade. The war metaphor, in fact, is useful precisely because it promotes extremes. It has been used to generate so great a perception of external threat that there is increasing tolerance for the expansion of state power into all phases of social life and the erosion of democratic freedoms.[1] As Tom Wicker has written, "a war on drugs emphasizing combat, arrests and jailings could produce a wartime mentality—the spirit that anything goes, including the sacrifice of constitutional freedoms in the battle against drugs" (Wicker, 11/28/89). Syndicated columnist Courtland Milloy has also criticized what he has referred to as "the fascist bent" to the War on Drugs. This fascist bent, he argued, "has already fractured the foundation of the Bill of Rights" (Milloy, 1/28/90).

In the name of fighting the War on Drugs, legislators have enacted sweeping new legislation with apparent disdain for constitutional guarantees. In early 1990, for example, the governor of Maryland, responding to criticism from those who questioned the constitutionality of some of the provisions of his anti–drug abuse package, stated: "I can first say the constitution won't allow many of these things. I can say my rights as an individual are being violated. The question is: Are we going to take the drug situation as a serious problem in our state?" (Schneider, 1/28/90).

It is not only public officials who are calling for extreme, and constitutionally dubious, measures. Certain segments of the community are also calling for tougher measures, even the imposition of martial law (Beck et al., 3/13/89). In a *Washington Post/ABC* News poll in 1989, 62 percent of the respondents said that they would be willing to "give up a few of the freedoms" in order to reduce the amount of illegal drug use (Morin, 9/8/89).

As the ideological frenzy about drugs has been heightened, "effective" law enforcement has come to be seen as more important than the protection of civil liberties. Norval Morris wrote long ago that attempts by the courts to restrain the police from illegal enforcement of statutes against victimless crime might be a herald of the erosion of constitutional guarantees, not their protection (Eitzen and Timmer, 1985:234). It is now evident that this was the case.

William Bennett clearly demonstrated his disdain for the protection of civil rights during his tenure as Drug Czar, lecturing "ACLU-types" that the drug war was "not a pillow fight" (*USA Today*, 5/23/90a). Bennett's sweeping federal intervention in Washington, D.C., was characterized by the administration as a "test case," implying that this kind of federal intervention and control could be extended to other cities (Berke, 4/7/89).

In 1989, President Bush stated that he intended to implement a national drug strategy that reached "into every school, every workplace . . . every family" (Berke, 9/6/89). He has, in fact, used the War on Drugs to facilitate creeping state control, which now does reach into every school, workplace, and family.

Examples of the expansion of domestic state power justified by the War on Drugs include the erosion of privacy rights, expanded search and seizure, widespread drug testing, less stringent rules about the introduction of illegally gathered evidence, the erosion of due process guarantees, expansion of the death penalty, and the denial of opportunity for those suspected of drug involvement.

THE RIGHT TO PRIVACY AND SEARCHES

The Supreme Court has validated through numerous decisions the move toward greater and greater intrusions into privacy in the form of increased surveillance and wider toleration for search and seizure. The increasing tolerance of the Court for privacy intrusion can be seen in cases that validate aerial surveillance to find indications of drug possession (*Florida v. Riley*, 1989); searches in airports without probable cause of people who fit a drug-courier profile (*Florida v. Royer*, 1983);[2] warrantless searches of automobiles and inside compartments (*United States v. Ross*, 1982);[3] surveillance of suspects with electronic devices placed inside cars, briefcases, or trunks (*United States v. Knotts*, 1983); the acquisition of warrants to search private homes based on anonymous tips (*Illinois v. Gates;* 1983), police inspection of bank records without customer consent (*United States v. Miller,* 1976); and the reading and inspecting of contents of a person's trash without a warrant or probable cause (*California v. Greenwood,* 1988) (Drug Policy Foundation, 1989).

There are few objections from the public about this increasing encroachment on privacy and erosion of prohibitions against unreasonable search and seizure. In fact, as Joseph Treaster pointed out in the *New York Times,* some citizens seem to take "a kind of patriotic pride in submitting to roadblocks and airport questioning" (Treaster, 5/6/90). In a 1989 *Washington Post*/ABC News poll, 52 percent of respondents said that they were willing to allow searches of their houses, and 67 percent were willing to have warrantless searches of their automobiles to deter drug trafficking and use (Wicker, 11/28/89).

Even though large numbers of respondents in surveys indicate that they are willing to support an expansion of search and seizure, it is arguable that these people are responding to what they perceive of as search and seizure policies that will affect others, not themselves. In the *Washington Post*/ABC News poll, respondents said that they were willing to have their homes searched without a court order even if houses of "people like you were sometimes searched by mistake." However, it is arguable that many people in responding to such polls do not perceive these policies as a direct threat to themselves personally. And this is not an unreasonable perception. As with other law enforcement tactics, expanded search and seizure primarily affects the poor and minorities.

Many have argued that the "profiles" used by local as well as federal authorities to stop and search suspected drug couriers are racially biased. The darker the skin, the more likely the person is to be stopped. In Mississippi, for example, a newspaper reporter examined police files on people stopped on one interstate highway. Fifty-five of the fifty-seven stops were of blacks or Hispanics. In another study conducted by a Rutgers University statistician, 80 percent of the arrests on one stretch of the New Jersey Turnpike were of black males driving late model cars with out-of-state license plates. Only 4.7 percent of the total traffic fit that description (Belkin 3/20/90). In New York, all but two of the over two hundred people arrested in 1989 in a drug-interdiction program at the Port Authority Bus Terminal were Hispanic or black.[4] Critics of drug profiles argue that since the Supreme Court upheld the use of profiles in selecting people to be questioned, the arrests of black and Hispanic suspects have increased.

Supporters of drug profiles argue that the racial disparity in arrests reflects not a policy of racial discrimination but the "reality of the streets." Their argument is that the preponderance of black and Hispanic arrests reflects "the fact" that most people who committed crimes are poor, and black and Hispanic people are poor (Sullivan, 4/26/90). This argument, which is presented repeatedly in the press without clarification, is simply not true. Most people who commit crimes are not poor. Most people who commit *street* crimes are poor. It is important to note that there is no "corporate criminal" profile that allows the police to search and seize corporate records.

The willingness of some segments of the population to support expanded search and seizure in the belief that they are licensing an invasion of privacy for "others" and not themselves is to some extent correct. What many people fail to understand, however, is that even if they are prepared to have others (poor people and minorities) searched, once they are in place these search and seizure provisions can apply to anyone.

Within the climate of increased tolerance for searches, raids have been conducted of businesses when the discovery of drugs was not even an issue. In October 1989, for example, the DEA conducted raids of retail stores specializing in the sale of indoor garden supplies in forty-six states. The rationale for the raids was that the stores were assisting in the production of marijuana. The DEA seized not drugs but books, records, and merchandise from over three dozen stores (Gorman, 12/30/90).

These raids represent a government seizure of records from legitimate businesses not for the purpose of discovering any illegal activity on their part, but for the purpose of investigating their customers who could (the DEA reasoned) be using the equipment to grow marijuana. In conducting these raids, the government went into shops without evidence of wrongdoing, arrested owners, and padlocked doors. It then effectively shut down the businesses by seizing merchandise and records necessary for their operation (Gorman, 12/30/90).

As with many of the policies promoted by the administration to control drugs, the effectiveness of expanded search and seizure to accomplish stated goals is at least questionable. Official records are rarely kept on encounters in which an individual is stopped and questioned (e.g., in an airport). It is, therefore, almost impossible to gauge the effectiveness of drug profiles. Customs officials, however, do keep records on the outcomes of X-ray searches. A sampling of these records from three cities conducted by a reporter for the *New York Times* revealed a 50 percent failure rate (Belkin, 3/20/90).

But even though these measures represent dangerous precedents of erosion of constitutional guarantees, and their effectiveness at controlling drug abuse or trafficking is questionable, many members of the public continue to support them.

Adults have even shown their willingness to accept widespread implementation of searches in schools and of students. In 1989, the *Washington Post*/ABC News poll revealed that 87 percent of the respondents agreed that school officials should be allowed to search student lockers for drugs, including the lockers of students not suspected of drug use (Morin, 9/8/89). Increasingly, high schools are using metal detectors, X-ray machines, and locker searches to detect student drug involvement (Marriott, 1/10/90a). The head of the United Federation of Teachers has advocated the use of metal detectors in schools even though other teachers point out that the presence of metal detectors creates a "jailhouse atmosphere inappropriate to an educational setting" and has resulted in even more disruptions in schools, including increased assaults on teachers (Rabinovitz, 12/29/89).

THE RIGHT TO FREE SPEECH

The effectiveness of the expanded search and seizure provisions to deter drug use or trafficking is questionable to say the least. The ability of the government to abuse its authority through them is not. The indoor gardening supply centers investigated in the 1989 DEA raids, for example, had previously advertised in *High Times* or *Sinsemilla Tips*, pro-marijuana magazines. But the equipment targeted by the operation could have been purchased from thousands of stores nationwide. It seems apparent, therefore, that a part of the intent of the raids was to drive advertisers away from the two magazines.

There is nothing illegal in publishing a pro-marijuana publication, and the harassment of advertisers is an infringement on the First Amendment guarantee of free speech. As Peter Gorman noted in discussing this raid, "The fact that the Government can target publications' advertisers, investigate consumers and disrupt the lives of thousands without evidence of a crime is an obvious misuse of judicial authority" (Gorman, 12/30/90).

But again, not only is there little objection to such tactics, there is even support for further curtailing freedom of speech. In the 1989 *Washington Post*/ABC News poll, for example, a startling 71 percent of the respondents said that they would support making "it against the law to show the use of illegal drugs in entertainment movies" (Morin, 9/8/89).

THE RIGHT TO FINANCIAL PRIVACY

Through a series of formal and informal measures, the right to financial privacy is being eroded in the name of the War on Drugs. Once again, the effectiveness of these actions to deter drug abuse or trafficking is open to question. In April 1990, for example, the Justice Department froze roughly 680 bank accounts mainly in New York and Miami in an action it called Operation Polar Cap. At the time, Treasury Secretary Nicholas Brady called the action "one of the most significant law en-

forcement undertakings involving bank account seizures in U.S. history"
(Barrett, 5/16/90).

Wilmer Parker, an assistant U.S. attorney and lead prosecutor in the
action, predicted that only a "small percentage" of the targeted bank
accounts would contain legitimate assets. By mid-May, however, all but
ninety of the bank accounts had been cleared because they either contained legitimately gained assets or because they were empty. Government officials, however, described themselves as "pleased" and said
they were only seeking information from the bank accounts, not the
recovery of money. Among those cleared were businesses and individuals, including some Colombians, not involved with drug trafficking
(Barrett, 5/16/90).

In the name of stopping money laundering, the Treasury Department
has computerized an enormous amount of information about financial
transactions. Even so, most large money-laundering prosecutions (like
drug-interdiction efforts) begin not with information generated from this
vast computer bank of information but from informant tips (Barrett, 12/
14/89). The Treasury Department has also said that it may in the future
require banks to develop profiles of "suspicious" customers (Isikoff, 11/
6–/12/89).

Many of the expansions of state power legitimated by the War on
Drugs are being accomplished not by government fiat but through voluntary capitulation. The American Bankers Association, for example,
began a series of radio spots in January 1990 aimed at encouraging bank
customers to help in the war against drugs by cooperating when they
were asked for information by their banks (*Wall Street Journal*, 2/1/90). It
has been written that the wise ruler does not govern by force but through
the chains within the minds of his subjects. The government does not
have to pass laws to take away civil and constitutional guarantees if the
populace willingly surrenders them.

ILLEGALLY GATHERED EVIDENCE: THE
EXCLUSIONARY RULE

As the frustration with the drug problem has grown, due to the unwillingness of both the Democratic and Republican parties to come up
with any effective policy, so too has grown the volume of calls to over-
turn the exclusionary rule. This is the case even though the American
Bar Association (ABA) has concluded that police and prosecutors do not
consider the exclusionary rule to be a serious obstacle. In discussing an
ABA report regarding the exclusionary rule, the *New York Times* noted
that the "suspects released or cases dismissed as a result of illegal
searches account for no more than 2.35 percent of all adult felony arrests,
perhaps as little as .6 percent" (10/10/88). The figure may be higher in

drug cases, but violent crime cases are rarely lost because of the exclusion of illegally gathered evidence (Criminal Justice Newsletter, 12/15/88). In addition, the report noted that many credit the exclusionary rule with promoting professional police conduct.

Rather than overturning the exclusionary rule directly, the courts and legislators have adopted a tactic of narrowing its applicability. A provision incorporated into the Anti–Drug Abuse Bill of 1988 and supported by the Reagan-Bush administration (New York Times, 10/10/88) was a codification of a 1984 Supreme Court decision that permitted the admission of flawed evidence obtained with a search warrant in cases in which the police had a "good-faith" belief that they were acting properly. A similar provision in the House version of the drug bill, which was passed in September 1988, allowed good-faith exceptions in searches conducted without a written warrant (Mohr, 10/13/88). By January 1990, Bush was proposing to Congress legislation that would allow such good-faith exceptions in warrantless searches (Rosenthal, 1/24/90).

The reason for the exclusionary rule, however, is that the police cannot be trusted to act in good faith. As Supreme Court Justice Brandeis noted in 1928, doing away with the exclusionary rule makes the Court an accomplice to official misconduct.

DRUG TESTING

The Fourth Amendment prohibition against unreasonable search and seizure is also being assaulted by administration efforts to implement random drug testing in all segments of society. In 1986, the Reagan-Bush administration began asking federal agencies to test employees in "sensitive" positions. By 1988, Attorney General Edwin Meese was calling for virtually all workers in the country to be tested by their employers for the use of illicit drugs (McAllister, 4/25/88).

By 1988, there had been a number of federal court decisions in which judges had declared that random testing violated the Constitution's ban on unreasonable searches and seizures. But the Justice Departments of both the Reagan and Bush administrations simply ignored the constitutional issues that universal drug testing raises.

Alan Adler of the American Civil Liberties Union (ACLU) has remarked that by encouraging drug testing in the private sector, the administration was trying to get "employers to do things that the government could not do itself" (McAllister, 4/25/88). If private industry can effectively monitor the lives of employees, the government has no need to. As Dr. Benway noted in George Orwell's novel, 1984, "A functioning police state needs no police."

The effort to promote drug testing in the private sector has been highly successful. By 1988, 30 to 50 percent of the Fortune 500 companies were testing prospective employees for drug use (McAllister, 4/25/88; Jacoby, 11/14/88), and at the end of 1989, an estimated 21 million employees had employers with drug-testing programs (Freudenheim, 1/3/90).

The courts have largely upheld mandatory random drug testing for employees in occupations that affect the safety of the public. It should be noted, however, that the courts have also in some cases been clear about the existence of an invasion of privacy. The reasoning has been that an invasion of privacy clearly existed but that the interests of the state outweighed this infringement.

In September 1989, for example, the federal appeals court for the District of Columbia upheld a Transportation Department program of mandatory random drug tests for 300,000 employees. The three-judge panel declared that the sensitivity of the jobs of the bulk of the employees justified "the invasions of privacy entailed by conducting" random drug testing (*New York Times*, 9/10/89).

Until the mid–1970s, the Supreme Court had taken the position that reasonable searches required "particularized" suspicion, that is, that a person could be searched or tested only if there was evidence of illegal behavior. The shift that recent decisions represent, however, is that searches can be considered reasonable even if there is no such suspicion. This opens the door for searches that would primarily affect people not involved in illegal behavior, and searches of categories of people, like whole neighborhoods. The Supreme Court has now taken the position that searches need not be based on particularized suspicion to be considered reasonable, when the interests of the state are perceived to outweigh the intrusion into the private lives of citizens. The Court has argued that this balancing test is used "when special needs, beyond the normal need for law enforcement, make the warrant and probable cause requirement impracticable" (*Skinner v. Railway Labor Executives Assn.*, 109 U.S., 1989). But, as Jurg Gerber et al. (1990) point out, the special need may today be drug use. Later it could be child abuse, communism, or flag burning.

The special need for widespread drug testing has certainly not been supported by the evidence of drug use among employees. Random drug testing was scheduled to begin for 4 million transportation workers in December 1989, even though employee groups pointed out that previous random drug tests on Transportation Department employees resulted in a very low number of positive results—approximately 0.5 percent (*Alabama Journal*, 12/18/89b).[5] Companies implementing testing programs even sometimes admit that they have had no drug-related accidents or problems (Roberts, 2/19/90). For example, while maintaining that Johns Hopkins did not have much of a drug problem with its staff, the hospital initiated a random drug and alcohol testing program for doctors who came in contact with patients (Lewin, 2/10/90). Customs maintained that it was "largely drug-free" before it implemented drug testing for employees (Jacoby, 11/14/88). In fact, as Lynn Zimmer (1989) has pointed out, drug testing is primarily being implemented in industries that have the least problem with drug use.

In addition, widely cited studies that are used as evidence of a need for drug testing are often faulty. In February 1990, for example, the National Transportation Safety Board released a study that board members described as the most detailed ever conducted of drug and alcohol abuse in interstate trucking. The *New York Times* ran its report of the study under this headline: "Truck Deaths Linked to Alcohol or Drugs." Reporting the findings that Safety Board members called significant, the *Times* reporter quoted a board member as saying, "I expected to find higher alcohol and drug use than the industry and the regulatory agencies have predicted. But I did not expect to find 33 percent" (Cushman, 2/7/90).

However, if the study is examined, one finds that the results are far from significant; they are utterly useless. The data were collected from autopsies performed on truck drivers who had been killed in accidents in eight states. One-third of them had recently used what was described as "drugs and alcohol" (Cushman, 2/7/90). But there was no control group. Theoretically, 99 percent of truckers who did not have accidents could have recently used drugs or alcohol.

Even the Transportation Department itself has admitted that no reliable studies linked drug use to serious accidents in the trucking industry. After a review of studies designed to determine the relationship between drug use and highway accidents, the National Highway Traffic Safety Administration admitted that "the nature and extent to which drugs, other than alcohol, are a serious highway safety problem cannot be specified with certainty" (Salpukas, 1/27/90).

Figures are frequently cited to indicate that drug and alcohol use is costing industry billions of dollars per year in lost productivity (Bensinger, 4/19/90). Almost never are the methods of determining these figures given. Dr. John Morgan, a professor at the City University of New York Medical School, reviewed the evidence behind these figures and has pointed out that the most widely quoted statistics in this regard come from a 1984 report by the Research Triangle Institute (RTI). Morgan termed the reasoning of the RTI analysis "unclear" and the figures "questionable." He concluded that "zealous advocates of drug use testing have misused data and statistics and quoted 'studies' lacking proper analysis in order to support their own ideology" (Morgan, 1989). And, as Zimmer (1989) has pointed out, the companies most likely to test are large companies, firms that already have mechanisms in place for dealing with unsatisfactory performance. Drug testing does not even detect impairment or unsatisfactory performance, only recent drug use (Jacoby, 11/14/88).

Worker productivity is affected by many factors—job insecurity, job stress, abusive management, low wages, and worker alienation, to mention but a few. Once again, these factors are conveniently ignored and drug use comes to be the scapegoat explanation for low productivity. The federal government is not mandating a stress-free workplace for every worker in the country to improve productivity.

Both the state and private industry have vested interests in widespread drug testing (see Gerber et al., 1990 for an excellent discussion of this point). Drug testing expands the control both the state and private industry have over workers, thus ensuring a controlled and more docile work force.

In addition, as well as masking profound social and economic inequality, the focus on drugs in some cases masks corporate crime and the unwillingness of private industry to spend the money to provide a safe workplace. To give but one example, in March 1990 a motorman on a Philadelphia subway train that crashed was suspended because of alleged cocaine use. However, investigators later focused on the failure of a traction motor assembly on the subway car axle as the cause of the accident, not impairment of the motorman (*Washington Post*, 3/11/90).

In addition, alcohol is the most abused drug in the society and is the most likely to cause impairment of performance. Yet many of the testing programs do not even test for alcohol. As a report by the APT Foundation (headed by David Musto, a professor of psychiatry at Yale) has noted, "Alcohol is by far the most abused substance and the most likely to cause impaired performance. . . . [a]bout 10 percent of the working age population are heavy users of alcohol, abuse alcohol, or are dependent on alcohol" (Wicker, 12/1/89).

In many studies alcohol and illegal drug use are lumped together, as they were in the National Transportation Safety Board study of fatal trucking accidents. By failing to specify what type of drug—illegal or alcohol—is involved with accidents, these studies leave the impression that illegal drugs are causing all the problems.

There are many reasons why widespread private sector drug testing is unlikely to have a significant impact on drug use or accidents thought to be related to drug use. First, some drug users are unemployed. Second, most companies give advance warning of drug testing, which allows those using drugs to either stop use for a while or switch to less detectable drugs. There are even substances on the market that mask the traces of some drugs (e.g., steroids) for the few hours of the test (National Public Radio, 3/5/91). As Zimmer (1989) has noted, folk wisdom is already replete with stories of how to beat the drug tests. There is also some indication that drug testing (like interdiction efforts) often has the effect of merely pushing the problem around. When employers begin to test, workers move to other employers in the area who are not testing (Roberts, 2/19/90). The APT Foundation report noted that testing alone, even of employees in "safety-sensitive" positions, was unlikely to provide adequate protection from accidents (Wicker, 12/1/89).

Even amid the lack of evidence of a need for widespread drug testing and the likelihood that the testing will be ineffective in preventing the drug use that does exist, there are increasing attempts to expand drug testing and to punish those that do not submit. Techniques to detect drug-using drivers, for example, are being used by police departments in Los Angeles and parts of New York, Texas, Virginia, Indiana, Arizona, Illinois, Colorado, and Utah. "Particular reactions" form the basis for an officer to assume probable cause to demand a urine or a blood test. In New York, failure to provide a blood or urine sample can result in the loss of a driver's license for six months (Meier, 9/25/89). The governor of Maryland proposed bills in 1990 that would require drivers to submit to drug tests or lose their licenses (Schneider, 1/28/90). In 1990, a bill was introduced into the Louisiana legislature that would have required first-time driver's license applicants to be tested for drug use (*USA Today*, 5/16/90).

In late 1990, the FBI announced that it would begin field testing kits that would make it possible for police to test for the handling of drugs by wiping the palms of stopped drivers. This method was described as offering the advantage of being "less intrusive" (and therefore presumably more palatable) than other testing methods. The test uses antibodies that detect small amounts of the target substance on skin, desk tops, or other surfaces. It is argued that the tests are so highly calibrated that they do not pick up the tiny amounts of cocaine that are now evidently on virtually all $20 and $50 bills in circulation (*Montgomery Advertiser*, 8/30/90b). Similarly, New Hampshire has been using a chemical that police drop on the driver's licenses of people whom they have stopped. If the chemical indicates the presence of drugs, the police used it as a legal justification for searching the driver and the car. However, the president of the New Hampshire Criminal Defense Lawyers Association, which filed charges against the state for the practice, maintains that licenses may test positive when there is no cocaine present. Laboratory tests conducted by the Lawyers Association showed that thousands of other chemicals, including those in laundry detergents, produced the same reaction (Lewin, 9/13/90).

Widespread drug testing not only of adults but of children is gaining more and more acceptance. One Texas school district has already implemented a random testing program for students and school workers who volunteer (Marriott, 1/10/90a). The reliance on testing and law enforcement to deal with the drug use of children has reached such an extent that various professionals participating in a Public Broadcasting System (PBS) seminar on drugs agreed with a recommendation that doctors conduct routine drug screening on children coming to them for medical examination. Several of the panelists said that they would take their own children to be tested if they had any reason to suspect drug use. Several also said they would phone the police if they suspected drug use by their children. Attorney General Thornburgh, who was on the panel, likened it to the arms race: "Trust but verify" (Public Broadcasting System, 1/6/90).

Predictably, drug testing itself has become a growth industry and the major companies involved, advocates for the practice. Laboratories now charge an average of $30 to $35 per test, but the actual cost to the employer may be as high as $60 to $85 per worker once all the expenses for setting up the program are taken into consideration. A representative of SmithKline Beecham, the company that took in the most revenues from drug testing in 1989, noted that 8 million U.S. citizens were tested for drug use in 1989. He estimated that the figure would be 13 million in 1990 and 22 million in 1992. Five companies took in 75 percent of the revenues from drug testing in 1989, and total testing revenue was $230 million. It is estimated that in 1990 the market will be $340 million, an increase of 48 percent (Freudenheim, 1/3/90).

Again, the ideological work on the part of the administration about drug testing has been highly successful. In a survey of college freshmen in January 1990, the percentage of students who felt that employers should be free to test their employees and applicants for drugs was 77.8 percent. This represented a jump from 71 percent in the same poll in 1988 (Henry, 1/22/90). In a *Washington Post*/ABC News poll conducted in 1989, 55 percent of the respondents advocated mandatory drug tests for all U.S. citizens. Sixty-seven percent agreed that all high school students should be regularly tested for drugs (Morin, 9/8/89). The ACLU has persuaded some states to pass laws prohibiting drug testing unless there is reason to suspect a particular individual. But at least one bill has been introduced in Congress that would override such state laws and allow employer drug testing of virtually any employee (ACLU, 1989).

As was noted earlier, the willingness of citizens to advocate more widespread drug testing may in fact have a great deal to do with a perception that these tests would not affect them. It is interesting to note that while police and corrections officers have not been in the forefront of the struggle to protect constitutional guarantees for others, they have fought to protect them for themselves. In December 1989, a New York State Supreme Court justice in Manhattan upheld a policy of the New York City Police Department to require its uniformed force to submit to random drug tests. The Sergeants Benevolent Association argued that the program violated Fourth Amendment protection against unlawful searches. Similarly, the Correction Officers Benevolent Association in New York appealed a decision to subject officers to random drug testing on the grounds that it would violate constitutional protection against unlawful searches (*New York Times*, 10/13/89).[6]

DUE PROCESS AND THE RIGHTS OF DEFENDANTS

The assault on due process guarantees for those accused or convicted of drug use or trafficking is also wide-ranging. In fact, what is developing is a bifurcated criminal justice system—one track for defendants associated with illegal drugs and another for defendants not so associated. The provisions of the Anti–Drug Abuse Bill of 1988 (HR 5210, passed by Congress in October 1988) demonstrate this clearly. In one version of the bill, the Justice Department would have been permitted to send a person accused of drug use to a civil hearing. The hearing would be conducted by a hearing examiner who could impose a fine against the person if the majority of the presented evidence was against him. In this hearing, the accused would not have to be proven guilty beyond a reasonable doubt, but merely by a "preponderance of evidence." The provision was changed in the Senate, giving the defendant the option of insisting on a criminal trial (Mohr, 10/30/88).[7]

By 1989, Thornburgh submitted what he called this "new alternative to criminal prosecution" in the form of an administrative rule. The measure was geared not toward traffickers but toward those found in possession of small "personal use" amounts of illegal drugs. The administrative judge would be allowed to impose a fine of up to $10,000. In addition, prosecutors would be given increased discretion and power in pressuring defendants to accept the civil fine rather than face criminal prosecution. Because these civil proceedings could add thousands of new drug cases to the court docket, the Justice Department was planning to hire almost 900 new prosecutors.

According to Don Fiedler of the National Organization for Reform of Marijuana Laws, the proposal represents "an end run around the Constitution," specifically because traditional legal protections are not afforded the civil proceedings. For example, there is no authority for a motion to suppress a search on constitutional grounds in civil proceedings (*New York Times*, 12/2/89).

Increasingly, there have been moves to deny rights to individuals *before* they have been convicted on drug charges. This turns the presumption of innocence on its head. In 1989, for example, the police in Lawrence, Massachusetts, began confiscating Medicaid and food stamp identification cards from people arrested but not convicted on drug charges. A legal defense group in Massachusetts challenged the statute allowing this as unlawful search and seizure and denying due process (Mydans, 10/16/89).

Elsewhere, there have also been confiscations of driver's licenses and threats to withdraw federal benefits, including education subsidies, from people involved with drugs. Forfeiture laws allow the confiscation of automobiles, boats, and other property of people accused but yet to be convicted of drug offenses. Seizures are sometimes allowed even when the owner of the property is unaware of the presence of drugs (Mydans, 10/16/89).

Similarly, the Racketeer Influenced and Corrupt Organizations Act (RICO) adopted by Congress in 1970, which has been widely used to prosecute those suspected of drug offenses, allows that targets of RICO prosecution can have their assets temporarily seized before a trial begins. This includes funds that would be used to pay a defense attorney. In April 1988, law enforcement authorities seized two apartments in New York City public housing projects because the tenants were charged with selling drugs from these apartments.

PUBLIC HOUSING

Thanks to the War on Drugs, public housing has been turned into a virtual war zone. To give but one example, in August 1990 police in Montgomery, Alabama, stormed a local housing project using "no-knock" narcotics search warrants and battering rams. The raid by officers using riot gear resulted in eighteen misdemeanor arrests. The Montgomery chief of police described the raid as "psychological warfare" (Morse, 8/25/90).[8] As Richard Rubenstein, a professor of conflict resolution at George Mason University, has commented, such raids make the War on Drugs a war against the poor (Squitieri, 6/25/90).

The Anti–Drug Abuse Bill of 1988 contained provisions under which public housing tenants would lose their housing not only if they engaged in criminal activity, including drug-related activity, but also if members of their households, guests, or other persons said to be under their control engaged in criminal activity, including drug-related activity.

In a memorandum issued to 3,000 public housing authorities in April 1989, Secretary of Housing and Urban Development Jack Kemp asked the housing authorities to submit a report about what they were doing to "evict drug abusers and drug dealers" from their projects. A staff lawyer with the National Housing Law Project was quoted in the *New York Times* as responding: "Does Mr. Kemp have some magic way to find out who these people are? The issue is not whether people should be dealing drugs, but how to decide if someone really is a drug dealer" (Tolchin, 3/8/89).

Under the Kemp policies, those accused of dealing in or abusing drugs would be considered to have broken their lease and the entire family would be subject to eviction. When Kemp was interviewed on the *MacNeil/Lehrer Newshour* (4/17/89), he was asked if a child evicted at one housing project could really be considered as implicated in drugs. His answer was that often children helped their parents deal drugs.

The conventional procedures for eviction from public housing that include an administrative proceeding subject to court review are evidently considered too cumbersome and time-consuming by the Bush administration. One attorney with the ACLU expressed fears that the Kemp policies would lead to "extra-judicial procedures that jeopardize constitutional rights." When told of the remark, Kemp responded that the ACLU was "part of the problem" (Tolchin, 3/8/89).

In Berkeley, California, and Alexandria, Virginia, local authorities have taken action that would terminate federal rent subsidies and evict tenants in whose homes evidence of drug dealing had been found, regardless of whether there was any evidence that the tenant was personally involved. In Chicago, under Operation Clean Sweep, public housing projects were sealed off, house-to-house inspections were carried out under housing regulations, and residents were required to show identification in order to enter. The program was modified after the American Civil Liberties Union charged that it involved illegal searches and seizures. With the typical newsspeak common to the Drug Warriors, Vincent Lane, chairman of the Chicago Housing Authority, remarked: "We are not infringing on rights; we are restoring rights" (Mydans, 10/16/89).

The administration had planned to begin a twenty-city coordinated sweep of public housing units composed of surprise raids and on-the-spot evictions in June 1990. After a suit was brought by several legal aid groups, however, a federal district judge issued a temporary restraining order. The judge made the order permanent in December 1990, noting that evicting tenants without a hearing was clearly unconstitutional.

Under the proposed program, which was a major part of Kemp's campaign to get drugs out of public housing, tenants were to be evicted on the basis of an affidavit signed by a law enforcement official that the leaseholder was involved in illegal drug activity. The eviction could take place even though there had been no formal charge brought against the leaseholder, much less a conviction (Lewis, 12/20/90).

Both the ACLU and the American Bar Association opposed the eviction plan and argued that it violated the constitutional right to due process. Congressional Democrats sent a letter to Kemp in 1990 in which the plan was called "shocking to fundamental notions of justice" and "ill-conceived" (Lewis, 6/25/90).

As with the many other constitutionally dubious measures implemented by two Republican administrations to deal with the drug problem, these draconian measures in public housing cannot even be demonstrated to be effective in decreasing drug trafficking or abuse (see Hayeslip, 1990, for a discussion of the methodological problems of evaluating anti-drug programs in public housing).

But again, there is little protest over these measures. In fact, the situation within public housing projects has been ignored for so long and has become so serious that public housing tenants themselves have not only not opposed these measures, but they have even (in Atlanta, for example) urged that the National Guard be called out and installed in their housing project (Applebome, 12/14/89).

THE FAMILY

The state is expanding its control not only through formal institutions but through informal institutions as well, especially the family. What is being encouraged is an informant culture, a society in which citizens are encouraged to act as informants against each other, and even family members are encouraged (and in some cases expected) to inform on their fathers, husbands, siblings, and children. For example, after one of George Bush's drug war speeches, a small boy responded by turning in his mother and her boyfriend for using drugs. A women from Moultrie, Georgia, whose husband was convicted of growing marijuana, was widely criticized by callers to the *Larry King Live* show for not having turned her husband in to the police. The woman lost her job as a teacher as a result of the case, even though she had never used illegal drugs of any kind (*Montgomery Advertiser*, 12/6/89).

Many states have implemented programs providing free telephone numbers that take reports from citizens on drunk drivers (Johnson, 6/17/90). In Anderson, South Carolina, the county had billboards erected that read: "Need Cash? Turn in a drug dealer." Using a program patterned after one used by the U.S. Customs Service, the county offered not only cash rewards but a percentage of the take, assets seized from a dealer the informant turned in. In Des Moines, the police have initiated a program in which hotel employees are trained to look for drug dealers and maids are asked to keep the trash of suspicious people (Kelley, 5/17/90).

Increasingly, the family is becoming an instrument of social control for the state, conducting searches and gathering evidence that the government cannot. Shertest Corporation, for example, has begun distributing a product called Drug Alert; when sprayed on surfaces—desks or doorknobs, for example—the product will indicate traces of marijuana, hashish, cocaine, or crack. The product is being marketed for home use so that parents can check for suspected drug use by their children (*Time*, 9/10/90).

A number of scientists have made statements to the press about the dubious value of the product, not even considering the invasion of privacy it represents. It was pointed out that even some over-the-counter antihistamines could trigger a positive response. Dr. John Ambre, head of the American Medical Association's department of toxicology, said he considered the product virtually useless.

When several New York television channels refused to run ads for Drug Alert because of their concerns that it encouraged an invasion of privacy, the distributor responded by running a full-page ad in the *New York Times* that named the channels and criticized them for their reluctance to join the War on Drugs by refusing to advertise the product (Lewin, 9/13/90).

To further encourage a society in which parents inform on their children or turn them over to the police, the state is attempting to make parents liable to punishment and sometimes criminally responsible for the behavior of their children in many different areas. In Wisconsin, for example, a program was begin in 1988 that links parents' welfare benefits to their children's school attendance. Several states link adult welfare benefits to things like participation in work programs for the recipient, but Wisconsin goes farther than any other state in making a family's benefits contingent on a child's school attendance. Unexcused absences of children are closely monitored; if there are more than ten unexcused absences in a semester, money is deducted from welfare checks (Wilkerson, 12/11/89).

Programs like this exemplify the increasing use of punitive measures to deal with social problems. Children's educational difficulties are related to poverty. For example, absences can result from having to stay home to sit with a sibling when the family cannot afford a baby sitter. The punitive measures of Wisconsin's Learnfare program, however, have resulted in a number of families ending up in emergency shelters because they cannot make the rent payment. Wisconsin officials have admitted that 70 percent of the families whose benefits are cut under the Learnfare program have their payments reinstated within three months; but for most families, three months is too late to avoid a disaster. To give but one example, a pregnant teenager's benefits were cut by error for three months, and in that time the family lost its housing (Gerharz, 1/29/90).

In Alabama, the mayor of Montgomery and the police chief argued in January 1990 that parents of habitual youthful offenders should be held criminally responsible for their children's behavior by being arrested and charged with contributing to the delinquency of a minor (Harper, 1/17/90). In addition, Mobile County, Alabama, expanded a truancy prevention program in 1990 under which parents could be sent to jail for a year for contributing to the delinquency of a minor if their children had six unexcused absences (*Montgomery Advertiser*, 8/30/90a). Maryland and Illinois have similar provisions for jail sentences for parents with children with unexcused absences (*New York Times*, 11/11/90). All of these laws, in effect, work to transform the family into a social control mechanism of the state.

WOMEN, THE UNBORN, AND DRUGS

The increasing erosions of the rights of women are not driven solely by the drug issue; as with so many other assaults on civil liberties, they have been given new credence and impetus by the War on Drugs rhetoric. The crack baby has become a symbol as evocative as that of Willie Horton. When Bush appears at a hospital cuddling crack babies for the press, the message is clear: The caring state must protect innocent babies from drug-crazed mothers. Once again, the War on Drugs transforms a tragedy into a crime.

Once again, the War on Drugs helps legitimate an expansion of state control, this time over the right of women to control their own bodies. The "life begins at conception" rulings such as the 1989 court decision in Tennessee regarding the custody of frozen embryos[9] spell an expanding infringement on women's rights because of their specific reproductive role. If life begins at conception, it appears that women's rights are going to end there. Women are being subjected to a new array of legal controls, justified by what are called "the rights of the fetus." The courts have opened the door for states to require parental notification, and the notification of the father, in abortion cases. For example, in November 1989 Pennsylvania enacted the most restrictive set of abortion laws in the country: These require women to notify their husbands if they are planning an abortion, and they ban abortions after twenty-four weeks unless the mother faces death or irreversible harm (Blood, 11/15/89). Legislation requiring "permission" from parents or judges for an abortion has been approved by legislatures in South Carolina, Michigan, and Wisconsin (Balz, 2/26–3/4/90). What is being created in these decisions is an adversarial relationship between the woman and her fetus. In one Florida case, for example, the adversarial relationship was considered so central that a lawyer was appointed by the court to represent the fetus in an abortion case (Greenhouse, 5/17/89).

The "life begins at conception" rulings also open the door for prosecuting women more harshly than men for drug use. In 1988, for example, a judge in the District of Columbia sent a woman who pleaded guilty to forgery to jail until the date her baby was due, when tests showed she had used cocaine. The woman was sent to jail even though it was her first offense and she would have normally received a sentence of probation (Lewin, 1/9/89).

Another mechanism for more harshly punishing women who use drugs (thereby extending control over women in general) is to prosecute mothers whose babies show evidence of exposure to illegal substances. The district attorney in Butte County, California, announced in 1989 that such mothers would face a 90-day minimum sentence due to be increased to 180 days. Prosecutors in Butte County maintained that they would defer prosecution for women entering drug rehabilitation programs. Critics pointed out, however, that there were no programs for pregnant women to enter (Lewin, 1/9/89).[10]

The criteria for entering most diversion programs are very narrow. In California, for example, women can be excluded from consideration for diversion programs (1) if they have previous convictions for illegal drug use or any felony conviction in the past five years; (2) if they have previously been diverted to treatment; or (3) if they have ever had probation or parole revoked. In addition, there is a movement in California that seeks to repeal the diversion law entirely in hope of sending more drug users to jail (LaCroix, 5/1/89).

Wendy Chavkin, a physician and Rockefeller Foundation fellow at the Columbia School of Public Health, surveyed seventy-eight drug treatment programs in New York City. She noted that 54 percent of the programs she surveyed refused service to women claiming to be pregnant and addicted to drugs. Sixty-seven percent of the programs denied treatment to pregnant addicts on Medicaid; 87 percent denied treatment to pregnant women on Medicaid who were addicted to crack. Less than half of the drug treatment programs Chavkin surveyed that accepted pregnant women made any arrangements for prenatal care. Only two of the programs provided child care, even though NIDA research has indicated that refusal to provide child care precludes the participation of most women in drug treatment programs (Chavkin, 7/18/89). Research by a House of Representatives committee indicated that of nearly five thousand treatment programs nationwide, only fifty provided child or obstetric care (Shepard, 4/20/90).

In December 1989, the ACLU brought a class action suit against three hospitals and a drug treatment center in New York City for refusing to provide drug and alcohol treatment to pregnant women (*New York Times*, 12/10/89a). As Sue Mahan and Julie Howkins (1990) point out, while the state assumes a responsibility to protect the fetus, it accepts no responsibility to protect the health of the mother.

Even given the lack of treatment facilities for addicted pregnant women, prosecutions continue. By early 1990, forty-four women had been prosecuted for fetal abuse from the use of cocaine alone (Mahan and Hawkins, 1990). Women have been prosecuted for child abuse, criminal failure to provide medical help for a child (Lewin, 1/9/89), involuntary manslaughter, delivery of a dangerous drug to a minor (*New York Times*, 5/10/89), and reckless endangerment (*Fairbanks Daily News*, 12/18/88).[11] Some of these charges carried maximum sentences of thirty years. According to research done by the ACLU, 80 percent of the women prosecuted have been black, Hispanic, or members of other minority groups (Kolata, 7/20/90).

Drug-using mothers are subject not only to criminal prosecution but also to having their children taken away from them. In New York State, for example, the Department of Social Services (DDS) is allowed to petition the court for permission to temporarily take away the baby of a mother who shows through testing at the hospital that she has taken drugs within seventy-two hours of delivery. DSS may also initiate neglect proceedings in such cases and sever the mother's rights entirely (Lewin, 1/9/89).

What these policies and prosecutions represent is the state essentially taking custody of a child before it is born, assuming a knowledge of its "best interests," and making the determination that the best interests of the fetus supercede the rights of the woman. This effectively reduces the pregnant woman to the status of a non-person, a host, or (in the language of the court in a recent surrogacy case) an "environment."

Pamela Rae Stewart, for example, was charged with criminal failure to provide medical help for a child after she ignored her doctor's advice to discontinue taking drugs and to abstain from sexual intercourse during her pregnancy. Stewart was later released when the court ruled that the law did not apply to fetuses, but the case illustrates well a trend that could end in the state prosecuting pregnant women for failing to be an adequate "environment" through faulty diets, lack of exercise, and smoking during pregnancy (Lewin, 1/9/89).

One Bronx family court judge (who dissented in a case that affirmed the Nassau County, New York, social services policy) noted:

By becoming pregnant women do not waive the constitutional protections afforded to other citizens. . . . To carry the law guardian's argument to its logical extension, the state would be able to supercede a mother's custody right to her child if she smoked cigarettes . . . or ate junk food. (Lewin, 1/9/89)

The trend toward state intervention that transforms the mother into a mere host can also be seen in attempts to legally override the right of a pregnant woman to refuse therapy. Medical institutions have obtained court orders for Caesarean sections, intrauterine transfusions, and hospital detention of pregnant women against their will (LaCroix, 5/1/89).[12]

In May 1987, the *New England Journal of Medicine* published the results of a survey regarding state intervention in the rights of pregnant women.

Support for state intervention in the rights of pregnant women was found not only among the medical community but among the general public as well. Even though in other areas the trend is toward an expansion of patients' rights (such as the right to refuse treatment, drugs, surgery, or blood transfusions), the trend is toward narrowing the rights of pregnant women. Nearly half of the respondents in the survey felt that women should be held legally liable if they smoked cigarettes or drank alcohol while pregnant or refused to have a Caesarean birth recommended by a doctor (LaCroix, 5/1/89).

Prosecutions represent a trend in the society in general to criminalize an increasingly wide array of behavior, and such policies have disastrous consequences. Through such policies the medical profession is transformed into another policing and intelligence-gathering arm of the state. Consequently, women who already suffer from lack of prenatal care are further discouraged from seeking medical attention for fear of being reported. The result will be an increasing number of children born without medical attention, at home, on floors, or in toilets. The San Francisco deputy city attorney noted seeing more and more of such "toilet-bowl babies," even in 1989, because their mothers were afraid to go to the hospital (LaCroix, 5/1/89). In addition, incarceration is used as a quick fix to make the society feel that something fundamental is being done about a public health crisis, while incarcerated women are unlikely to receive drug treatment or adequate prenatal care. The stigma of having been prosecuted or imprisoned will further impede the woman's ability to secure employment even if she does manage to stop using drugs. Consequently, the children of many drug-using mothers will end up in what is clearly an inadequate foster care system.

Even though the policy of criminalizing what is essentially a public health issue brings about disastrous consequences, there is little sympathy for the drug-using mother or her children. In 1989, 80 percent of those responding to the *Washington Post*/ABC News poll reported that they would favor imprisoning pregnant drug addicts whose children inherited the addiction to drugs (Morin, 9/8/89). In 1991, there were suggestions that drug-abusing women should be required to use a new birth control implant that would prevent pregnancy for up to five years (Mesce, 1/14/91). As one of the lawyers for a pregnant drug user remarked, "why is it that all these straight white men are telling pregnant women how they should act and feel? The War on Drugs had degenerated into a war on women" (Hoffman, 8/19/90).

EXPANSION OF THE DEATH PENALTY

The Reagan-Bush administration strongly supported the death penalty provisions of the Anti–Drug Abuse Bill of 1988 (*New York Times*, 10/10/

88). These provisions expanded the administration of the death penalty to any person "engaging in a drug-related felony offense, who intentionally kills, or counsels, commands, or causes the intentional killing of an individual and such killing results" (*Congressional Quarterly*, 1988).[13] When the drug bill was being debated in Congress, Senator D'Amato went so far as to suggest that the death penalty should also apply to drug "dealers and traffickers" not guilty of murder (Mohr, 10/14/88). By October 1989, Justice Department officials were telling the *New York Times* that Bush was preparing to ask Congress to expand the use of the death penalty for "drug kingpins" whether or not they were involved with a murder or killing (Mydans, 10/16/89). In January 1990, Bush proposed to Congress new laws that would expand the applicability of the death penalty beyond those applying to drug "kingpins" (Rosenthal, 1/24/90).[14] This was one of the few points on which Democrats and Republicans disagreed in their 1990 drug control plans. The drug control plan distributed by the Senate Judiciary Committee contained no recommendation for the expansion of the application of the death penalty. Senator Joseph Biden called Bush's proposed expansion excessive (*New York Times*, 1/26/90).

By expanding the application of the death penalty in this way, what is created is a new kind of aggravating circumstance. Whereas "aggravating circumstances" have previously referred to the way in which the murder was carried out, (e.g., it was especially brutal) or referred to the crime itself (e.g., treason), this aggravating circumstance depends not on the offense itself but its relation to another activity.

We see in this expansion of the use of the death penalty the eradication strategy in its most palpable form. It is an illustration of the administration's increasing use of violence and repressive strategies to deal with social problems and a characteristic disdain for arguments regarding discrimination and the administration of the death penalty. For example, the Senate killed by a vote of fifty-two to thirty-five a proposal introduced by Senator Kennedy that would have forbidden the death penalty in states in which a disproportionate number of blacks and other minority groups were executed and where most whites customarily escaped the death penalty in capital crimes (Mohr, 10/14/88). Bush later warned that he would veto any legislation containing what he called racial quotas in the administration of the death penalty (Nash, 10/8/90).

There also have been efforts by Republicans to place new limits on death penalty appeals (Greenhouse, 9/22/89). In January 1990, for example, Bush proposed legislation to Congress that would require that any appeal of a death sentence be completed within a year (Rosenthal, 1/24/90). In February 1990, Attorney General Thornburgh, testifying before a congressional committee, endorsed committee recommendations to limit the appeals of death row inmates to two rounds—one to challenge the verdict and one to challenge violations of rights (*New York Times*, 2/1/90).

The administration has also argued before the Supreme Court for the admission of "victim impact" statements in death penalty cases. This move further elaborates the trend toward changing the focus of the legal system from considering particular types of crime to considering particular types of people—in this case, victims. The direct implication (as some justices remarked) is that the life of a model citizen with aggrieved family members is more serious than that of a reprobate with no family to testify to loss (see Greenhouse, 4/25/91, for a summary of the arguments before the Supreme Court).

During the hearings on the nomination of Robert Bork to the Supreme Court, Republicans charged the various groups opposing Bork with attempting to politicize the judiciary. Republican-appointed justices, however, are the most overtly political members of the Court. For example, in May 1990 Chief Justice William H. Rehnquist was publicly campaigning for limits to appeals by death row inmates, noting and criticizing specific proposals before Congress (Greenhouse, 5/16/90).

Even though over half of state court death sentences are overturned through federal court habeas corpus proceedings, Rehnquist called the existence of habeas corpus proceedings in death penalty appeals a "serious malfunction in our legal system" and argued for a limit of only one federal habeas corpus appeal per inmate.

It is interesting to note that the administration portrays drug sellers as crazed individuals, almost animals, but at the same time supports a policy that in some ways suggests they are also coolly calculating individuals who weigh the costs and benefits of their criminal activities and who will desist if only the costs can be made to outweigh the benefits. It seems bizarre (to say the least) to believe that people who are involved in such a life-threatening profession will be deterred by the death penalty. The threat to their lives from competitors is arguably much greater than any threat the state can represent.

HARSHER PUNISHMENT

In addition to fueling efforts to expand the applicability of the death penalty, the War on Drugs has led to an increasing severity of punishment for street crimes in general. William Bennett summed up the administration's position on penalties when he said publicly that he did not see anything wrong with beheading drug offenders (ACLU, 1989). Los Angeles Police Chief Daryl Gates said before a Senate hearing that casual drug users should be "shot" (*In These Times*, 9/19–/25/90a).

State legislatures throughout the country have increased sentences, attached mandatory sentences to certain drug offenses, implemented mandatory sentences for drug "kingpins," mandated sentences for the use of a gun in drug-trafficking offenses, and mandated denial of probation and parole, among other measures. In Georgia, to give but one example, average sentences for drug possession increased almost 30 percent between 1985 and 1988. Sentences for drug sales increased by almost 50 percent (Whitt, 9/5/89). In Arizona, possession of even small amounts of marijuana is a felony (Barrett, 1/31/90). Florida has mandated prison time for possession of small amounts of cocaine as well as other illegal drugs (Isikoff, 1/14–/20/90). In Mississippi, the state legislature considered a bill in 1990 to sentence cocaine dealers to life imprisonment without parole (*USA Today*, 5/21/90). These measures reflect the policy of the administration. Bush has called for "vigorous prosecution" of even minor drug users (Barrett, 1/31/90).

In their zeal to pass legislation mandating draconian penalties for drug use and trafficking, some states have passed laws so broad they have later been declared unconstitutional (Rawls, 5/2/91). In other states, the legislation has simply been foolhardy. From 1979 to 1981, for example, Florida had a law on the books that required defendants to pay for their own incarceration. The law was repealed after the state expended roughly $90,000 a year for three years in administrative costs to recover $7,636 in collections (*Montgomery Advertiser*, 2/2/90).

Federal sentencing guidelines implemented in late 1988 mandated harsher penalties for a wide array of crimes. The sentencing guidelines not only mandated harsher penalties but also gave judges less discretion in imposing those penalties. Federal District Judge William W. Schwarzer found himself in the position of having to sentence a man with no previous criminal convictions to ten years in prison for unknowingly giving a ride to a man making a drug deal. The man who gave the ride was convicted of conspiracy to traffic narcotics. Schwarzer remarked that in this case "the law does anything but serve justice" (Bishop, 6/8/90).

In July 1989, federal judges in the fifteen district courts in the Ninth Circuit asked Congress in a resolution to reconsider the harsh mandatory sentences specified in the guidelines (Bishop, 6/8/90). In November 1990, Federal District Judge J. Lawrence Irving resigned because he felt the sentencing guidelines were too harsh. "I just can't," he remarked, "in good conscience, continue to do this." Irving gave an example of a young man charged with possession and intent to distribute cocaine. Under the old law, the offender was sentenced to six months in prison and five years' probation. Under the mandatory sentencing guidelines, the offender would be sentenced to twenty years in prison with no possibility of parole (*New York Times*, 9/30/90).

It should be noted that after intense lobbying by major companies, the Bush administration withdrew its support for tough mandatory sentences for corporations convicted of crimes (Barrett and Lambert, 4/30/90).

The sentencing guidelines in effect give prosecutors more power to determine punishment, since the prosecution determines the charges taken before the grand jury (Labaton, 12/29/89). This shift toward placing more responsibility in the hands of prosecutors and taking responsibility away from judges reflects the long-held conservative disdain for the judiciary. Conservative attempts to portray the "liberal" judiciary as part of the reason for the crime problem have been dutifully parroted by the press. To cite but one example, Judy Mann (an astute commentator on the War on Drugs) praised the shift toward prosecutors and criticized "weak-minded judge[s] who might go misty-eyed over the prospect of sentencing a young man to spend the rest of his days in the slammer" (Mann, 12/8/89).

The public as well appears to support harsh penalties for street crimes, especially drug offenses. In a 1989 *Washington Post*/ABC News poll, almost three out of ten people questioned favored sentences of life imprisonment or death for those convicted of selling cocaine. Eight out of ten believed that illegal drug use would decline if "we punished drug users more heavily than we do now." Eight out of ten also favored giving drug tests for convicted cocaine users for a year (Morin, 9/8/89). In a poll also released in 1989, citizens in Georgia indicated that they would be willing to pay $50 more in taxes to build more prisons. More than 50 percent of the respondents favored sending first-time users of crack or cocaine to jail for thirty days or more (Whitt, 9/5/89).

Because of the widespread support for harsher and harsher methods of dealing with street crime, politicians compete with each other to appear "toughest" on crime. When Bush was urging Congress to adopt his 1990 anti-crime package, he made a speech in Kansas City evoking the legends of Bat Masterson and Wild Bill Hickok to bolster his arguments that the proposals of the Democrats were "tougher on law enforcement than on criminals." Four months later, when Congress was considering the package, Senator Biden (rather than proposing a different strategy) argued that the new penalties would have little effect if they were not backed up with "new police, new prosecutors, and new prisons" (Shenon, 5/13/90).

While the public in general appears to favor harsher penalties, there are occasions in which harsher mandatory punishments have produced results contrary to those intended. In November 1989, for example, a federal district judge in San Francisco revealed to the jury before their deliberations that the defendant who was charged in a crack case would, if convicted, have to be sentenced to life in prison without parole because of his two prior convictions. The jury consequently acquitted the defendant (Labaton, 12/29/89).

One of the few impediments to further increasing sentences for street crimes is financial. For example, a proposal made by the governor of Alabama to mandate a one-year prison sentence for first-time drug offenders was "put on the back burner" when Alabama lawmakers argued that it would bankrupt the state (Herring, 1/25/90). But even the financial impediment has little sway in what the *Atlanta Journal Constitution* (1/28/90) called a "frenzy of prison-building." In early 1990, the Georgia legislature found money to double the number of prison beds requested by the governor.

The resort to harsher penalties for drug trafficking and abuse holds little promise of decreasing either activity. There has been an explosion of drug activity in prisons, at times abetted by corrupt prison guards, and few prisons offer comprehensive drug treatment. In addition, in some states that have adopted draconian penalties for drug offenses the overload of an already overburdened prison system has meant an increase in early release. In Florida, for example, prisoners served 52 percent of their sentences in 1986. In 1990, they served an average of 33 percent. Many of the new inmates were sent to prison for possession, a felony in Florida. Even Florida officials admitted that the result of increasingly harsh penalties for drugs was that at least some violent offenders were being released to make room for nonviolent drug users. In 1989, one out of every three "early releasees" in Florida committed additional crimes (Isikoff, 1/14–/20/90).

In addition, current laws work to the advantage of big-time drug dealers. Federal sentencing guidelines allow a judge to give a more lenient sentence only if the defendant has rendered "substantial" assistance to the state in convicting other drug suspects. The low-level "mules," who are so harshly prosecuted under the sentencing guidelines, have no such information about other drug dealers to provide (Isikoff and Thompson, 11/4/90). As one federal district judge described them, "a lot of them have severe economic problems. They often have no prior criminal record, just a financial crisis" (Bishop, 6/8/90).

Harsher penalties come not only in the form of longer sentences but also in an increasing harshness of the prison regime. In an article in the *New York Times* entitled "More Prisons Using Iron Hand to Control Inmates," the executive director of the American Correctional Association was quoted as saying that this new harsher treatment for inmates was "the new order" (Johnson, 11/1/90).

DANGEROUSNESS AND PREVENTIVE DETENTION

The War on Drugs has ushered in an era in which the legal system increasingly considers not crimes but types of individuals. Habitual offender statutes and preventive detention on the basis of "dangerousness," by definition, refer not to individual crimes but to types of people. Habitual offender statutes are based on prior convictions, ignoring the nature of the present offense and the racial biases in conviction rates. For example, Alabama's Habitual Offender Act, which was passed in 1977, makes no distinction between prior property offenses and prior violent acts. In 1990, two-thirds of those serving longer sentences under the act were sentenced for property crimes. Determinations of dangerousness on which preventive detention statutes rely are frequently based on several non-legal factors (such as unemployment), which also are disproportionately associated with minorities and the very poor (see Decker and Salert, 1987, for a discussion of scales that predict dangerousness).

Criminology has been notoriously unsuccessful at predicting future criminal behavior, especially in individual cases (see, for example, Wilkins, 1980; Gottfredson and Gottfredson, 1984; Gottfredson, 1985; Radzinowicz and Hood, 1980). As Scott Decker and Barbara Salert (1987) point out, the burden of proof for the use of such predictive scales rests with those who want to implement them.[15] Such scales give "illegitimate reinforcement of past undesirable (and indeed in many cases, illegal) practices." In fact, in a study conducted by Decker and Salert, the most commonly used scale to predict dangerousness was shown to be "biased against women, blacks, and those of lower socioeconomic groups" (1987).

It is also necessary to note that there are no habitual offender statutes or profiles to predict "dangerous" corporations, even though characteristically in corporate crime most corporations prosecuted are repeat offenders.

The Supreme Court in 1987 upheld the constitutionality of preventive detention. Some federal criminal defendants, however, have been held for a year or more based on a determination that they were "dangerous," and then later they have been acquitted (*Criminal Justice Newsletter*, 7/3/89). Again, as with evictions from public housing, this turns the presumption of innocence on its head.

The Bail Reform Act of 1984 created a presumption of dangerousness for those charged with certain drug offenses. But as David A. Reiser, staff attorney with the Public Defender Service for the District of Columbia, pointed out, most of the people to whom this rebuttable presumption is applied are people at a low level in the drug trade. In addition, preventive detention has added to the problem of prison overcrowding (*Criminal Justice Newsletter*, 7/3/89).

Judge Jon O. Newman of the Second Circuit Court, U.S. Court of Appeals, has argued against preventive detention lasting more than six months, but he has pointed out that there is little popular support for limiting preventive detention because of the public's belief that preventive detention gets drug dealers off the street (*Criminal Justice Newsletter*, 7/3/89).

There is very little evidence that preventive detention reduces crime or more effectively utilizes prison space (another argument used by those who advocate preventive detention). The most persuasive argument for the implementation of preventive detention is that it appeals to the public mood; in the words of Decker and Salert (1987), it "appeases the public mind."

STUDENT LOANS AND THE RIGHT TO AN EDUCATION

As has been noted earlier, the War on Drugs has facilitated the expansion of state control not only through the formal policing apparatuses but also by facilitating the transformation of informal institutions (the family, the school) into policing agencies of the state.

In early 1989, the Department of Education began requiring students to sign an oath that while they received financial aid, they would not manufacture, distribute, dispense, or use drugs. This policy drew criticism from the National Association of Student Financial Aid Officers, who resisted being expected to enforce a policy that would require them to turn students over to the government and, in effect, function as law enforcement officers (*New York Times*, 10/8/89).

The requirement that students sign this oath not only means that they can lose their financial aid if they are convicted on a drug-related charge, but it also makes them subject to fraud charges that carry a potential $10,000 fine and a jail sentence (*New York Times*, 10/8/89).

The provision clearly has a disproportionate effect on low-income students, who are the primary recipients of financial aid. It means that these students, if prosecuted, will be left with few alternatives but to continue manufacturing, distributing, dispensing, or using drugs, since by denying them money to continue their education, they are condemned to low-paying jobs that cannot compete with the economic rewards of the drug trade.

In June 1988, a policy board chaired by Edwin Meese approved proposals to deny student loans and other governmental benefits to persons convicted of drug use (Isikoff, 6/8/88). By November 1988, William Bennett was complaining that schools and colleges were not sufficiently enforcing stringent anti-drug policies (Barrett, 11/30/89).

The states have followed suit. Governor Kay Orr of Nebraska, for example, proposed an anti-drug plan in January 1990 that would include expelling students of public colleges and universities upon their conviction for any drug offense, even misdemeanors. Students could re-enter school only after mandatory completion of a drug rehabilitation program. Another part of the plan was to require students entering institutions of higher education to certify that they will be "drug free" (*New York Times*, 1/9/90a).

WORKPLACE SURVEILLANCE

As Alan Alder of the ACLU has noted, the administration is increasingly getting private industry to do what it cannot, that is, conduct surveillance of workers. General Motors, for example, has hired private investigators to pose as workers in order to find drug dealers in its plants (*Wall Street Journal*, 2/5/90). If the trend continues, the United States will have the most highly surveilled work force in the world.

The Anti–Drug Abuse Bill of 1988 contained a provision putting companies and institutions that receive federal contracts and grants at risk of losing their federal funding if they did not make "good-faith efforts" to implement programs to ensure a drug-free workplace. As Stephen Sandherr, director of congressional relations for the Associated General Contractors of America, noted in an interview, this measure makes the employer into "a cop at the workplace" (Berke, 3/18/89).

The Anti–Drug Abuse Bill also provided that contracts awarded by a federal agency were subject to suspension of payments or termination if a federal agency determined that enough of the employees of a contractor had been convicted of violations to indicate that the contractor had failed to make a good-faith effort to provide a drug-free workplace. Within thirty days of receiving notice from an employee of the violation of the drug-free workplace requirements, federal contractors must take appropriate personnel action, up to and including termination, or require that the employee satisfactorily participate in a drug abuse assistance or rehabilitation program.

Peter B. Bensinger, former U.S. drug enforcement administrator and now (interestingly enough) a private consultant on substance abuse in the workplace, advocates the use of "professional, undercover, investigative services" as "an appropriate technique that . . . should be considered and utilized." Bensinger also argues that employees "applaud" such actions (Bensinger, 4/19/90).

ASSET SEIZURES

In the "get tough" atmosphere of the War on Drugs, the public has been encouraged (1) to believe that seizure of the assets of suspected drug dealers and users is what Attorney General Thornburgh has called "poetic justice" and (2) to ignore the troubling aspects of such seizures. The Comprehensive Forfeiture Act of 1984 permitted pretrial seizure of the assets of many criminal defendants, especially in racketeering, narcotics, and money-laundering cases. The seizure of assets before a criminal conviction again turns the presumption of innocence on its head.

In Maryland in 1990, for example, two men were stopped and searched based on drug courier profiles and the fact that police dogs sniffed cocaine on their money. The cash of the men was confiscated. Even though most cash is now tainted with traces of cocaine and the men were never charged with any crime, they were responsible for proving that they were not involved with drugs in order to get their money back (*USA Today*, 5/23/90).

Largely because the fruits of the drug profits revenue program are shared with local law enforcement agencies, seizures from drug cases increased from $27 million in 1985 to $360 million in 1989 (*New York Times*, 3/11/90). Fines collected through the criminal justice system usually go into the general treasury, not to the agencies that track down the offender. They have historically gone to the general treasury for a very good reason—to decrease the bounty-hunting aspects such a connection would generate. But federal law has purposefully set up this connection as an incentive in drug cases. One sheriff in Anderson, South Carolina, for example, set up a program encouraging individuals to make money by buying drugs and turning in drug dealers. The program includes billboards that read: "Need Cash? Turn in a dope dealer," and it promises to reward informants with up to 25 percent of the money or assets seized. Federal authorities have a similar informant program with a 25 percent split (*Montgomery Advertiser*, 1/27/90).

This bounty hunting has predictably led to targeting particular drug dealers for the usefulness of their assets to the department. At a police conference in Michigan, even law enforcement officials admitted that police agencies become so dependent on funds generated from asset seizures that seizures become more important than fighting drug abuse (*USA Today*, 4/11/90). One spokeswoman for the U.S. Marshall's Service in Texas admitted that the service discouraged the seizure of run-down property or property that carried a large bank loan (*New York Times*, 3/11/90). In addition, a General Accounting Office (GAO) report completed in 1991 revealed that the Marshall's Service was mismanaging the more than $1.4 billion in property it had seized from drug dealers, and that at least in one case it had seized property from an innocent third party. The Marshall's Service has in fact seized so much property that in 1991 it was proposing to create a commercial real estate management unit within the service (Margasak, 4/20/91).

The money from such seizures is supposed to be earmarked to fight the War on Drugs, but it is expended on law enforcement, not treatment (*New York Times*, 3/11/90). In fiscal 1989, for example, the Marshall's Service program generated $311 million for new prison construction and the hiring of new prosecutors (Margasak, 4/20/91).

As Jack Katz, a professor of sociology at UCLA, wrote in the *Washington Post*, "While attacking foreign dictators for raking off huge profits from international drug dealers, the new administration seems eager to perfect the criminal justice system's financial exploitation of the drug market" (Katz, 6/5–/11/89).[16]

THE RIGHT TO A DEFENSE ATTORNEY

Two cases decided in 1989 (*Caplin & Drysdale, Chartered v. United States* and *United States v. Monsanto*) made it possible for the state to freeze assets that would be used by a defendant to pay an attorney. In both these decisions the Court majority essentially refused to accept the realities of litigation. In *Caplin & Drysdale*, the majority found that forfeiture did not unduly burden the defendants' right to counsel of choice. The majority reasoned that a lawyer might be persuaded to accept the case on condition that the fees would be paid on acquittal, or based on "means that a defendant might come by in the future." Judge Blackmun, in his dissent, noted the absurdity of the reasoning that a private attorney would be "so foolish ignorant, or beholden or idealistic as to take the business" on such a basis. ABA rules disallow contingency fees, and furthermore, attorneys are unlikely to risk basing their fees on people who are facing possible life imprisonment (Tarlow, 1989).

These cases make it possible for the state to impoverish drug defendants and leave them dependent on court-appointed counsel. The Court has done this even while acknowledging in *Caplin & Drysdale* that "the harsh reality" is that "the quality of a criminal defendant's representation frequently may turn on his ability to retain the best counsel money can buy.[17] As Justices Blackmun, Brennan, Marshall, and Stevens noted in their dissent, "it is unseemly and unjust for the Government to beggar those it prosecutes in order to disable their defense at trial."

In addition, if appointed counsel is adequate and the state has an interest in disallowing the use of "drug merchants" their assets, why are not all criminal defendants forced to rely on appointed attorneys? It is highly doubtful that any of the defendants prosecuted in connection with the S&L scandal have been forced to rely on court-appointed counsel due to asset seizure.

The dissenters in *Caplin & Drysdale* point out that Congress "concluded that crime had become too lucrative for criminals to be deterred by conventional punishments." If this is the case, the resort to "unconventional punishments" like asset seizure should be applied to all criminals. The reality, however, is that they are being applied only to street criminals, most especially defendants in drug cases.

In addition to denying drug defendants the right to counsel of their choice, the state is increasingly eroding the right to confidentiality in the lawyer-client relationship. In 1990, there were major court cases pending in New York, Tulsa, Houston, and Denver regarding whether or not a lawyer in a drug case could be forced to reveal who paid the legal fees. In Tulsa and Houston, lawyers were put in jail for their refusal to answer questions about the sources of their fees (Lewis, 2/9/90).

In 1985, a law was passed that required any business receiving payment of $10,000 or more in cash for goods and services to report that payment to the Internal Revenue Service (IRS). Described by Fred T. Goldberg, Jr., commissioner of the Internal Revenue Service, as "another weapon in fighting the war on drugs," this law contained no exceptions. In the fall of 1989, therefore, the IRS contacted 950 lawyers who had reported cash transactions over $10,000 and had not revealed the names of those paying the fees (Goldberg, 3/13/90).

Neal Sonnett, president of the National Association of Criminal Defense Lawyers, maintained that the action forced "lawyers to become witnesses against clients." Sonnett argued that such laws would discourage clients from consulting lawyers because they could not keep confidential their consultation even though lawyer-client relations are supposed to be protected. Sonnett pointed out that many clients who pay in cash do so because they do not want spouses or employers, for example, to know that they have consulted a criminal attorney. "There must be limits to government power," Sonnett said. He then added:

At a time when people around the globe are casting off authoritarian governments, it is tragic to think that we who inspired their dreams of freedom are, step by step, in our single-minded hysteria over drugs, shrugging off our most cherished rights. (Sonnett, 3/13/90)

Sonnett maintained that the IRS summonses demanded that lawyers "divulge virtually all client records." He added, "I worry about what drugs are doing to America. But I am also worried about what the 'war on drugs' is doing to America; it is becoming a war on the Bill of Rights and on our adversarial system of justice" (Sonnett, 3/13/90).

TREATMENT

During the era of the War on Drugs, treatment itself has become a punishment, something the state does to people rather than for people. In Alabama, for example, a bill was introduced in the 1990 legislative session that would make drug education and treatment mandatory for first-time drug offenders (*Montgomery Advertiser*, 11/15/89). By late 1989, nineteen states had civil commitment laws that enabled parents to commit children for mandatory drug treatment (Malcolm, 11/19/89).

While there has been an increasing willingness to mandate drug treatment as a punishment, there has been an unwillingness to provide drug treatment on demand. In late 1989, in New York City alone there were 3,000 addicts on waiting lists for drug treatment; in Los Angeles there were 1,800. And, it should be remembered, these figures reflect only those on formal waiting lists. Many treatment facilities, already overburdened, do not even bother to keep waiting lists anymore. In addition, many addicts do not put their names on waiting lists, knowing that they are unlikely to receive services. For those who do, the wait for treatment can be a long one, and many who are told to wait do not return (Marriott, 1/10/90b).

The refusal to provide nonpunitive drug treatment outside the criminal justice net for those who want it, and the willingness to mandate treatment within the criminal justice net for those who do not want it, says a great deal about the real intent of the Drug Warriors. Simply put, the state is less concerned with decreasing drug use than in expanding state control.

As James Jacobs and Lynn Zimmer (1991) have pointed out, within the employment realm mandatory drug treatment rather than punitive sanctions such as immediate dismissal have facilitated the widespread implementation of drug testing and a consequent growth of the drug-testing industry. The use of mandatory treatment rather than criminal sanctions or immediate dismissal is more palatable and less challengeable in court. Stronger penalties have the potential of arousing public opposition. Mandatory drug treatment for employees is presented as a benevolent rather than an intrusive or coercive action on the part of employers.

Even though opinion polls show little public support for punitive sanctions in the workplace, there is support for mandatory treatment. In a *Newsweek*/Gallup poll conducted in 1986, 60 percent of the respondents favored requiring detected drug users in the workplace to attend treatment programs (Jacobs and Zimmer, 1991).

While the disease model of drug abuse (the notion that drug abuse is a sickness) is widely (if selectively) accepted by the American public, there is little evidence that mandatory treatment is effective at curing the "sickness." As Jacobs and Zimmer (1991) note, the success rates for privately financed drug treatment programs have never been scientifically established, and the success rates of public treatment programs are low.

Even so, the trend is toward expanding mandatory treatment. In New York there have been proposals for massive drug treatment compounds on state or federal land. The apparent benevolence of treatment facilitates the expansion of control that the state and the business sector have over the lives of individuals. Intrusions into the lives of people in the name of treatment are more easily implemented than intrusions in the form of punitive sanctions. The head of one treatment center called mandatory treatment "humane coercion" (Malcolm, 11/19/89).

THE MILITARIZATION OF CIVIL SOCIETY

The War on Drugs has facilitated the blurring of distinctions between civil and military state power. The military has been used in raids of public housing units, and boot camp treatment programs reflect a growing militarization of punishment. In 1981, Ronald Reagan signed a law that changed policy established after the Civil War to keep the police and the military separate. The 1981 law allowed military cooperation with civilian drug enforcement authorities (Pastor and Castañeda, 1989:267).

In early December 1989, Defense Secretary Cheney approved $70 million in state allotments for an expanded role of the National Guard in the War on Drugs (*New York Times*, 12/10/89a). In 1990, Bush proposed a 50 percent increase in funding for the military to intensify its efforts to stop drug smuggling (Berke, 1/25/90). "Boot camp" centers for drug offenders are being tested in Alabama and are being proposed in Maryland (Gimbel, 12/29/89).

As a result of these and other policies increasing the use of the military in domestic law enforcement, active-duty military units were used in a 1990 raid on clandestine marijuana gardens in a California national conservation area. Guardsmen and agents destroyed 1,200 marijuana plants and equipment said to have been used in cultivation, but no suspects were arrested. The raid generated a storm of protest from California residents over military convoys passing through their towns, Blackhawk helicopters flying over their houses, and camouflaged National Guardsmen complete with M-16 rifles walking through their woods. Protesters carried signs saying "Stop U.S. military terrorism" (Bishop, 8/10/90).

The National Guard alone estimated that their part in the operation had cost $400,000. Many in the area, including law enforcement officials, protested the invasion of civil rights and the costs of the two-week exercise (Bishop, 8/10/90).

A spokeswoman for the Bureau of Land Management, the agency that organized the exercise, said that the government expected that this exercise would be a prototype for similar actions. The spokeswoman stated: "California presented the first opportunity for an operation of this magnitude with the help of the military." The spokeswoman also admitted that there had been no complaints about marijuana growing in the conservation area (Bishop, 8/10/90).

California residents have filed a civil lawsuit seeking to block further use of the military in domestic drug enforcement and to restrict the use of low-flying helicopters over private homes (Bishop, 8/10/90).

Active-duty military personnel and National Guard troops have also been used to conduct reconnaissance in preparation for drug raids in Oregon and Washington (Knickerbocker, 8/27/90). There have been proposals to use the military to establish martial law in some cities (Beck et al., 3/13/89). The military has been used to conduct aerial spraying of paraquat in Hawaii (*ABC Nightly News*, 9/4/90), to search cargo at airports, to board up crack houses, and to search out and destroy marijuana crops (Knickerbocker, 8/27/90). In 1990, the Senate was considering the use of former military bases as boot camps and prisons for drug dealers (*New York Times*, 4/3/90).

But even though many people (including one former member of the U.S. Commission on Civil Rights) argue that the proposed military solutions are worse than the problem, in a *Washington Post*/ABC News poll conducted in 1989, 82 percent of those surveyed said that they favored using the military to control illegal drugs within the United States (Morin, 9/8/89). While initially resisting involvement in the War on Drugs, the Pentagon began (after threats of military cuts) to use participation in the War on Drugs as a rationale for further funding (Engelberg, 1/9/90; Rosenthal, 9/19/90).

ENTRAPMENT

The most celebrated case of increasing official tolerance for entrapment related to the War on Drugs was that of the mayor of Washington, D.C., Marion T. Barry. William Safire, writing on the editorial page of the *New York Times*, characterized the affair—and especially Attorney General Thornburgh's approval of it—"an abomination." Safire noted that in this case "[t]he Federal Government, for the first time . . . used the expectation of sexual intercourse to lure a target into committing an illegal act in front of concealed cameras" (Safire, 1/26/90). As Safire noted, the woman who lured Barry to a D.C. hotel was tracked down by federal prosecutors and flown across the country to contact Barry. Safire criticized what he called the "Thornburgh rule": "Intimidation of informants to engage in federally funded sexual enticement is an acceptable investigative procedure" (Safire, 1/26/90).

The courts have held that charges of entrapment are not valid if the target was "predisposed" to commit the crime. With this decision, Safire argues, "The Court wrongly gave to police the power to dangle temptation in front of everyone with a record" (Safire, 1/26/90). Safire argued that in this case the government had stooped to "acting like a pimp" (8/14/90). Allowing evidence of prior similar conduct to be used as rebutting a claim of entrapment is highly prejudicial. This in effect means that any person who has ever in their past engaged in similar conduct cannot be entrapped.

The jury evidently agreed that the government had overstepped its bounds. It convicted Barry on only one misdemeanor count of drug use.

THE INFORMANT SOCIETY

One of the most disturbing aspects of the War on Drugs is the extent to which it is creating a society of informers. The fact that the state is encouraging citizens to become informants is less disturbing than the relish with which the population is doing so. In a poll conducted by the *Washington Post*/ABC News in 1989, 83 percent of the respondents favored encouraging people to phone the police to report drug users even if it meant turning in "a family member who uses drugs" (Morin, 9/8/89). As was noted earlier, participants in one PBS panel argued that they would turn their own children over to the police if they suspected drug use (Public Broadcasting System, 1/6/90).

Measures in many states that hold parents criminally responsible for the conduct of their children also contribute to the expansion of the informant society, putting parents in the position of having to choose between their own imprisonment or their children's. The mayor of Montgomery, Alabama, for example, proposed in early 1990 to have parents of habitual youthful offenders arrested. He justified this by appealing to fears of "drug gangs" establishing a foothold in the city. Mayor Folmer then followed up by admitting that there was no problem of drug gangs in Montgomery, but that if "some drastic things" weren't done, Montgomery was going to find itself "in that situation" (Harper, 1/17/90).

In 1989, the ACLU newsletter reported that rural utility workers in Pennsylvania had been "organized into a network of drug surveillance informants by the state attorney general's office, with instructions to inform the police of unusual 'signs' of possible drug manufacture, like 'unusually high consumption of water' and 'fans whirring through the night' " (ACLU, 1989). In Des Moines, Iowa, there is a police program in which hotel employees are trained to look for drug dealers and are asked to keep the trash of suspicious people (Kelley, 5/17/90).

OTHER DEVELOPMENTS

The War on Drugs has helped legitimate a number of other measures that expand the state's power over the lives of individuals. Among them are measures that

... *increase the level of surveillance of the population.* In January 1990, Bush proposed increases in federal spending on the War on Drugs that included funds for a center to coordinate the gathering of intelligence on drug trafficking (Rosenthal, 1/24/90). But, as the ACLU reported in 1989, the Drug Enforcement Agency had already been maintaining computer files on more than 1.5 million people, including members of Congress, entertainers, clergy, industry leaders, and foreign dignitaries. The DEA admitted that many of the files had been created on the basis of "unsubstantiated allegations." Only 5 percent of the people on whom files had been created were actually under investigation as suspected narcotics traffickers (ACLU, 1989).

. . . *restrict freedom of movement.* In reaction to a rising homicide rate, the City Council of Washington, D.C., approved a curfew (later found to be unconstitutional) for those under age eighteen, even though the average age of homicide victims in the District of Columbia was thirty years and the average age of the killers was over eighteen (*New York Times*, 3/1/89).

. . . *restrict freedom of association.* District of Columbia police sought to expand an anti-loitering law that allowed them to cordon off streets, order people out of an area, and arrest those who gathered in a group of two or more people. There are similar anti-loitering laws in Florida, Ohio, Michigan, Virginia, and elsewhere, some of which have been challenged as infringements on the First Amendment guarantee of freedom of association. Even so, City Attorney Robert H. Cinabro of Kalamazoo, Michigan, defended the anti-loitering law there by saying, "We don't feel there is a constitutional right to associate with drug dealers" (Mydans, 10/16/89).

. . . *deny due process.* The City Council of Miami Beach, Florida, approved an ordinance in early 1991 directing the police to notify the employers of defendants arrested on drug charges, even if the charge was possession of small amounts of illegal substances. The law was limited specifically to drug cases and did not cover drunk driving or other crimes (*New York Times*, 1/25/91a). Similarly, in New Bedford, Massachusetts, one daily newspaper has begun publishing photographs of defendants going into district court on drug charges (Treaster, 2/23/91).

. . . *deny the right to an education.* In June 1988, a policy board chaired by Edwin Meese approved proposals to deny driver's licenses and student loans to people convicted of drug use (Isikoff, 6/8/88). By 1990, there was a proposal in Nebraska to expel students from colleges and universities for drug convictions (*New York Times*, 1/9/90a).

The mayor of Miami Beach, referring to the ordinance passed by the City Council directing police to notify the employers of those arrested in drug cases, made a statement that sums up well the implications of this increasing expansion of state power over the lives of individuals. Mayor Alex Daoud remarked in one hearing that "I hate to equate it with what occurred in Nazi Germany, but that's how I see it. Totalitarian government begins slowly and moves first against the rights of those least able to defend themselves" (Treaster, 2/23/91).

SUMMARY

The expansion of state power that has been detailed in this chapter is certain to continue. There is little to stop it. The mainstream media, dominated by corporate interests and riddled with the fear of being negative, has virtually abdicated its critical and investigative role. While sensationalizing the drug problem by presenting innumerable variations of "Midnight on Crack Street," the media does very little questioning of the strategies being employed by the state in the War on Drugs, and it offers almost no useful analysis of the drug issue. The Democratic party has ceased to be a party of opposition. The intellectual poverty of the party is demonstrated clearly in its failure to mobilize any response to the new proposals of the Drug Warriors except more funds for treatment and more money for the War on Drugs in general. The Supreme Court is following and is likely to follow for years to come what Linda Greenhouse referred to in the *New York Times* as a "path of constitutional disengagement" (3/11/90). The shift in the Court, which some have termed the "massive undermining of an entire approach to civil rights and civil liberties" (Kamen, 7/10–/16/89), has affected not only the population of this country but the populations of other countries (especially in Latin America) as well. This was compounded by a conscious effort by the Reagan administration to pack the federal courts with young, "right-thinking" justices. As the ACLU has pointed out, the courts have abdicated their role as the "safety net for failures of criminal justice in the states" (Greenhouse, 3/11/90).

What is in place, then, is not only a radically more right-wing Supreme Court and, to some extent, federal judiciary, but a more punitive dominant ideology regarding street crime in general and the protection of civil rights and liberties in particular. The country has a conservative executive policy, a party of political "opposition" that has been "Reaganized" during the past decade, and an established cadre of "new right" media pundits who continually elaborate the new right world view and are in the forefront of the new right battle for the vocabulary and the construction of the societal thesaurus.

The courts have shown increased tolerance for the expansion of state power, domestically and internationally, in the name of fighting the War on Drugs. After almost a decade of ideological work on the part of the state and almost complete neglect of the problems of marginalized elements in the society, the populace is more willing to accept these state infringements, at times openly calling for and inviting them.

The resentment of the working and middle classes has been nurtured and fed by the movement to the right that has been evident now for over ten years. The civil rights gains of the 1960s that were fought for so hard have been transformed in the minds of many from being necessary redresses of injustice to advantage taking. Conditions in the inner cities have been neglected to the point that life is so dangerous that the marginalized now invite the military into their neighborhoods and do not mind being forced to carry identification cards in order to enter their own homes.

Since the ascension of Justice Anthony M. Kennedy to replace Justice Lewis F. Powell, Jr., several decisions clearly signal the Supreme Court's abandonment of civil rights. For example, in *Patterson v. McLean Credit Union*, the Supreme Court held that federal law prohibiting racial discrimination in private contracts did not cover discrimination after that contract was made. *Wards Cove Packing Company v. Atonio* placed the burden of proving justifiable business interest in a practice that had discriminatory effect on the plaintiffs bringing suits under Title VII of the Civil Rights Act. *Martin v. Wilks* allowed whites to bring suits against affirmative action plans that they did not contest originally. Other decisions have expanded the applicability of the death penalty to the mentally retarded and those under age eighteen at the time of the crime. Still other decisions chip away at the general right to abortion and virtually eliminate it for poor women. These cases are only the more visible examples of a pattern of civil rights erosion, the foundation for which was laid during the Reagan era.

The Supreme Court has served notice that the future will be marked by a far different approach from that of the Warren Court. It is impossible to overstate the usefulness of the War on Drugs as a tool in justifying this expansion of state control and the subsequent erosion of civil rights, both domestically and internationally.

But, as Supreme Court Justice Thurgood Marshall has written:

Precisely because the need for action against the drug scourge is manifest, the need for vigilance against unconstitutional excess is great. History teaches that grave threats to liberty often come in times of urgency, when constitutional rights seem too extravagant to endure. (Lewis, 2/9/90)

Marshall's warning, however, is unlikely to be heeded. Whether we like it or not, the supports are in place for increasing expansions of state control into the lives of individuals, and increasing disregard for civil rights and international law.

NOTES

1. It is interesting to note that during the war in the Persian Gulf, the War on Drugs all but disappeared from public discourse. A real war functioned to

generate a sentiment of great external threat and, therefore, the necessity to rely on the state for protection. After the cease-fire, however, the administration returned immediately to the War on Drugs.

2. The U.S. Customs Service even has a "drug swallower" profile (Belkin, 3/20/90).

3. In Volusia County, Florida, Sheriff Robert L. Vogel, Jr., regularly stops cars that fit his profile of a drug courier and searches them without a warrant in a procedure that he said has so far been upheld by the courts. If large amounts of cash but no drugs are found, his deputies confiscate the cash as possible evidence of drug dealing (Mydans, 10/16/89).

4. The discriminatory nature of the Port Authority's interdiction campaign caused a Manhattan judge to throw out crucial evidence in a drug arrest case at the Port Authority Bus Terminal (Sullivan, 4/25/90).

5. A truckers' group filed suit against the new regulations before they took effect (Salpukas, 1/27/90).

6. The Supreme Court refused to hear the challenge to New York City's random drug testing program for guards in the city's jails (*New York Times*, 10/2/90).

7. The use of civil proceedings (with less stringent burden of proof and specificity requirements) to secure indefinite confinement of repeat sexual offenders has already been implemented in Washington State.

8. In a previous raid of a public housing unit in Montgomery, many police officers wore Ninja masks to hide their identity (Morse, 6/1/90).

9. This decision raises many more issues that bode ill for the rights of women. See Raspberry (9/26/89).

10. In Butte County, as in many areas of the United States, there are few support services or treatment programs for pregnant drug users. Women in Butte County who are addicted to heroin must travel eighty-five miles and pay $200 a month for treatment in a private outpatient clinic. Withdrawal from heroin without methadone can be deadly, but in Butte County the treatment is so expensive that even many middle-income women cannot afford it (LaCroix, 5/1/89:588).

11. The Alaska "reckless endangerment" prosecution was brought even though state law specifies that life begins at birth. The district attorney maintained that after the baby was born it was a person and that previous drug use had damaged it. He also argued that if the baby died, the woman could be charged with manslaughter (*Fairbanks Daily News*, 12/18/88).

12. A large proportion (81 percent) of court-ordered Caesareans were performed on black, Hispanic, and Asian women (Dixler, 5/15/89).

13. By early 1991 there were three cases pending in which the death penalty was being sought for a "drug-related" killing (Richissin, 2/3/91).

14. State governors (for example, in Alabama; see *Montgomery Advertiser*, 1/10/90) have followed the administration's lead and proposed that similar death penalty statutes be adopted into state law.

15. With the most commonly used scale to predict dangerousness, researchers have demonstrated a false-positive rate as high as 56 percent (von Hirsch and Gottfredson, 1984).

16. It is alarming, but not surprising, that even the conservative majority in

the Supreme Court has used as a rationale for upholding forfeiture statutes the amount of money such forfeitures provide law enforcement. As the dissenters in *Caplin & Drysdale* point out, this view implies that forfeiture provisions are sought "to maximize the amount of money the Government collects."

17. In fact, the majority in *Caplin & Drysdale* seems to be indulging in a strange form of convoluted logic regarding this issue. The majority acknowledges that the quality of legal representation often depends on having the money to hire the best defense. The majority even notes this as a reason for denying to "drug merchants" the ability to pay a lawyer with his or her assets. But at the same time, the majority rejects the notion that forcing the defendant to rely on appointed counsel creates an imbalance between the defendant and the state. Defensively, the majority adds that to admit such an imbalance would "bar the trial of indigents" since they must rely on appointed counsel. This is an argument of practicality, not an addressing of whether or not appointed counsel provides adequate representation.

5

LATIN AMERICAN "DEMOCRACIES IN JEOPARDY"

The reasons why the state continues to pursue the War on Drugs domestically, despite its failure as a strategy to accomplish manifest goals, were discussed in Chapters 3 and 4. In this chapter, the reasons for pursuing a drug war against Latin America (despite similar failure) will be explored. As with the domestic War on Drugs, the international War on Drugs (specifically as it pertains to Latin America) accomplishes two goals. First, it diverts attention away from structural inequalities and injustice. Second, it assists in legitimating a vast expansion of U.S. control over and intervention in Latin America.

DEMOCRACY IN JEOPARDY

Reagan and Bush administration officials have been fond of talking about Latin American "democracies in jeopardy" due to drug trafficking and "narco-terrorism." In doing so, they have attempted to legitimate the War on Drugs by claiming that part of the goal of fighting the war is to protect democracy in Latin America. However, the "democracies" referred to are only those designated as such by the administration, and the designation of particular countries as democracies has little to do with political reality.

Functioning healthy democracies in Latin America are few and far between. "Democracy" means something more than the holding of regular elections. This is a point that the Reagan and Bush administrations have categorically refused to acknowledge. The Reagan administration, in fact, conducted a concerted campaign to define democracy and human rights as almost exclusively the holding of regular elections. But it is easy to see the emptiness of show elections characterized by massive fraud in repressive countries considered by the Reagan and Bush administrations as budding democracies—countries such as El Salvador, Guatemala, and Honduras.

In a democracy, ordinary people have the opportunity to participate in the political process and to organize, free of fear for their lives or their jobs. The predominance of strong oligarchic control, however, in most of Latin America (oligarchic control that is essential to U.S. strategy in the region) means that popular participation in the political process has always been considered dangerous by both the oligarchy and U.S. administrations. In fact, the very factors that could provide a basis for the development of democracy—unions, peasant associations, and other popular organizations—have provoked a violent response from the oligarchies in Latin American countries and in Washington. As Noam Chomsky (1/29/90) has noted, early efforts by the Sandinistas to provide resources to the impoverished minority in Nicaragua, which would allow them to have genuine political participation, "led Washington to initiate economic and ideological warfare, and outright terrorism, to punish these transgressions by reducing life to the zero grade." Democracy also means the elimination of repression. It means freedom of speech and organization. It means an independent judiciary and civilian control of the military. There are few countries in Latin America where these conditions exist. Even though civilian governments have replaced the generals in some Latin American countries such as Honduras, El Salvador, and Guatemala, these nominal governments exercise only marginal power (Fagan, 1987:9, 52–53).

In Guatemala, for example, the elected civilian government has no power over the military and therefore no power to investigate past human rights abuses or to prevent future ones. The police and security forces also remain under military control. Before surrendering official control of the government, the Guatemalan military enacted a series of laws that included a blanket amnesty for themselves. In addition, they received a pledge from President Cerezo that he would make no land, commercial, or banking reforms and would pursue no prosecutions for human rights abuses (Fagan, 1987:94–95). Therefore, Guatemala must still be regarded as a military dictatorship, not a democracy.

In Honduras, a civilian government was elected in 1981 mainly because the Carter administration put pressure on Honduras in the wake of the Sandinista revolution. The United States offered increased military aid in return. Before the election, however, the Honduran military forced the two traditional parties to agree that the military would remain independent and exempt from investigation (primarily into corruption), that the military would continue to control foreign policy, and that the military would have a veto over cabinet appointments (Fagan, 1987:103).

In El Salvador, the situation is much the same. "Centrist" governments (such as that of Duarte) have been unable to wrest real power away from the military, and therefore they have consistently failed to make any significant land reforms, failed to stop repression, and failed to bring about the incorporation of the left into the political process (Diskin and Sharpe, 1986:50–87).

In fact, those countries in Latin America considered by the administration and publicly touted as democracies are, in reality, client states that go along with administration policies in the region. The Tegucigalpa group, for example (Honduras, El Salvador, and Costa Rica), joined in supporting U.S. efforts to isolate Nicaragua. The Honduran military became deeply involved in the effort to overthrow the Sandinista government. Honduras and El Salvador were instrumental in delaying or blocking negotiated settlements to conflict in the region. Pressure was applied to the Contadora countries to do the same (Fagan, 1987:40, 94).[1]

The Reagan administration essentially kept the Costa Rican economy afloat in exchange for hostility toward Nicaragua. As President Oscar Arias commented, "As long as there are nine *comandantes* in Nicaragua, we'll get $200 million a year from Washington aid" (Fagan, 1987:114).

Human Rights Watch released a report in December 1989 regarding the increasing number of murders of human rights monitors around the world. Most of those murders occurred in what are considered by the administration to be democratic countries—Colombia, Brazil, Peru, and Guatemala (*New York Times*, 12/30/89).

The absence of democracy in a Latin American country has never in and of itself determined U.S. foreign policy toward a government, nor has the existence of democracy ensured U.S. support. Guatemala had a democratically elected government in 1954, but because the United Fruit Company perceived its interests to be threatened, the United States installed a military regime in its place. That military regime displayed an appalling human rights record. In fact, in Guatemala under Jacobo Arbenz Guzmán[2] and in Nicaragua under the Sandinistas, pluralist bourgeois democracy provided a level of political freedom rare in Central America (Herman, 1987:10). The Sandinistas, for example, held an election in 1985 (six years after coming to power) in which seven political parties participated. There was a 75 percent turnout, and the Sandinistas won 67 percent of the vote in an election deemed by international observers to be valid (Pfost, 1987:80). However, Ronald Reagan responded to the election by saying in a televised speech: "There seems to be no crime to which the Sandinistas will not stoop." He also called Nicaragua an "outlaw regime" (Black, 1988:164). In Chile, Salvador Allende was democratically elected. But with the aid of the U.S. security establishment, Allende was deposed and killed.

The redefinition of democracy is part of a wider battle for the vocabulary that has been conducted by both the Reagan and Bush administrations.[3] The sham U.S.-inspired elections in countries such as Honduras and El Salvador create the appearance of democracy without any of the substance of democracy. They have been called "the most sophisticated weapon in the U.S. diplomatic arsenal" (Nelson-Pallmeyer, 1989:48). In these countries, civilian governments are superimposed over a terror apparatus through elections. James Petras has written:

The challenge is to recompose the terror network by coopting a new strata of pliable civilian politicians willing to legitimate a newly reformed and more professionally efficient state terror regime. . . . Operating under the mantle of elected civilians, the reconstituted and more efficient terror apparatus, heavily funded by the imperial state, will increase the level of terror. (1987:92).

It is not really possible, therefore, to argue that democracy in Latin America is in jeopardy due to drug trafficking or narco-terrorism. It is more accurate to talk about obstacles to democratic development.

OBSTACLES TO DEMOCRATIC DEVELOPMENT

The administration presents drug trafficking or narco-terrorism as the major threat to the development of democracy in Latin America. But drug trafficking and narco-terrorism are not the only threats to the development of democracy in Latin America, and they are certainly not the most important threats.

The major threats to the development of democratic institutions in Latin America are poverty, widening disparities between the rich and the poor, the external debt, oligarchic control, reliance on export agriculture, and U.S. foreign policy.

Poverty

It is certainly not possible to develop democracy in countries where the poor have limited access not only to the political process but to existence itself. The U.N. Economic Commission for Latin America, for example, has estimated that one-third of the people in South America live in poverty and that another 16 percent live in extreme poverty. This is an increase of 70 million people since 1970, and it means that 183 million people are struggling in South America every day just to find enough to eat. In Bolivia alone, 51,000 children die every year from preventable diseases (McFarren, 5/19/91). During the 1980s per capita income in Central America fell by 17.5 percent. The economic output of the six Central American countries fell from 4.1 percent of Latin America's total in the 1970s to 3.5 percent by the end of the 1980s (Scott, 4/17/91).

These conditions exist even though the U.N. Development Program has estimated that serious malnutrition could be eliminated and universal primary education, primary health care, family planning, and safe water could be provided by the year 2000 in the entire Third World for only $20 billion per year. However, U.S. aid to Latin America is expected to decline in 1992 (Scott, 4/17/91). Representative government, or democracy, depends on the active participation of the people. However, if merely surviving occupies all the time of a majority of the inhabitants of the region, there is little chance of active participation in the political process.

The External Debt

The plight of the poor in Latin America, and their subsequent inability to play a meaningful role in political life, is exacerbated by the external debt. Foreign debt payments cut into what little money there is to pay for social services like health care (McFarren, 5/19/91). The external debt and the austerity measures imposed on Latin American countries through international monetary agencies also represent a barrier to development. As Richard Fagan (1987:54) has noted, "development and debt repayment simply cannot be made compatible." In part because of the weight of this external debt, per capita output fell off 7 percent during the 1980s. Even though Treasury Secretary Nicholas Brady introduced a plan for debt reduction in March 1989, in January 1990 not a single debt reduction package had been concluded.

The debt reduction packages were all tied to reforms designed to foster market-oriented economies (Farnsworth, 1/9/90). But the forced move to market-oriented economies that benefit the First World more than the Third will not solve the social and economic problems of Latin America. Austerity measures required by the monetary agencies further impoverish an already impoverished population.

Oligarchic Control

The third threat to democratic development in Latin America is the existence of entrenched indigenous oligarchies that have profited from their relationship with the advanced capitalist countries and have refused to allow fundamental social change, land redistribution, or tax reforms in their own countries. In Guatemala, for example, the economic elite rejects even the most modest reforms, fearing that they will bring about further land distribution (Fagan, 1987:95). Political parties controlled by the landed elite combined with police repression have stifled the development of civic and nongovernmental organizations. The traditional parties lack a coherent program and are usually merely vehicles for the distribution of patronage (*Christian Science Monitor*, 1/10/91).

The only country in Latin America that successfully broke the relationship between the landed elite and political power was Nicaragua under the Sandinistas (Fagan, 1987:48) This accomplishment was met with a decade of economic and military warfare conducted by the Nicaraguan elite and the United States. After a decade of pressure, this accomplishment is being rolled back by the Chomorro government.

It should be noted that the governments in Latin America that have provoked the most violent response from the U.S. policy elite (Guatemala in 1954, Cuba, and Nicaragua) have been created by revolutions from below. They have been governments that unseated the oligarchy and addressed the basic needs of a formerly depressed and repressed majority. As Edward Herman (1987:10) has noted, "This process of social democratization has been consistently horrifying and intolerable to the U.S. elite." The United States pays lip service to democracy but has consistently sided with the dominant military and economic elites who openly discourage or actively repress democratic expressions of mobilization and protest. Any expression of political aspiration from below is characterized as the provocation of "communists" or "radicals" (Fagan, 1987:123). The refusal of these oligarchies (backed up by the United States) to allow real democratic development in Latin America is, in fact, what makes drug trafficking so appealing. It is simply the only means of social mobility for a large segment of the population.

Export Agriculture

Most Latin American economies have been and still are dependent on the export of a few agricultural products. Coffee and bananas, for example, accounted for more than 70 percent of the export earnings of all five Central American republics in the 1920s. They accounted for more than 90 percent of export earnings in Costa Rica, El Salvador, and Guatemala. When the economic elite began to realize in the 1950s that their future was not guaranteed by coffee and bananas, they began to expand cash crop production into sugar, cotton, and beef. But all these commodities are best produced on extensive holdings. Tens of thousands of small farmers, therefore, were pushed off the land, which reduced the production of food crops for domestic consumption. By the 1970s the region was importing large quantities of corn, beans, and other grains that previously had been produced domestically. These imported food products were more expensive than home-grown products, and this meant that more people had difficulty buying enough food (Fagan, 1987:19).

Despite the addition of sugar, cotton, and cattle during the export diversification drive of the 1960s, the same two products (coffee and bananas) accounted for more than half of all exports in every country except Nicaragua in the mid–1980s (Fagan, 1987:18).

The agro-export model has generated (1) an extremely unequal distribution of income and wealth in Latin America, and (2) repression to maintain the inequality. Profitable agricultural export relies on wresting land from the local inhabitants and suppressing subsequent revolts. Plantation owners financed private armies and used the government to keep the poor majority under control. By the 1930s Nicaragua, El Salvador, Honduras, and Guatemala had succumbed to military rule characterized by the wholesale abuse of human rights and a total lack of political freedom. In addition, the concentration of land and wealth has generated a neglect of industry. Peasants and landless workers without incomes to meet even their most basic needs do not consume manufactured products. Thus, the development of industry to meet domestic demand has been minimal (Fagan, 1987:19).

The agro-export model makes Latin American economies dependent on a small number of agricultural exports, and therefore they are extremely vulnerable to fluctuations in international demand and prices. If, for example, there were a 25 percent drop in the world price of coffee, it would cost Central America $330 million in a typical year—a loss of 8 percent in total export earnings. Even though Central America would be greatly affected by such a market fluctuation, the region accounts for so little of the total world coffee exports that it exerts no major influence on world markets. This means that economic crises in the region are inevitable (Fagan, 1987:19).

While the agro-export model produced overall economic growth from 1950 to 1970, the growth primarily enriched the members of the oligarchies and left the majority of the Latin American people impoverished (Fagan, 1987:5). In recent years, this economic growth has not only come to a halt, but it has actually deteriorated. Per capita income for the region as a whole dropped by almost one-third between 1978 and 1985 (Feinberg and Bagley, 1986:5).

U.S. Foreign Policy

The fifth major threat to the development of democratic institutions in Latin America is the aggressive U.S. campaign of low-intensity conflict in the region. Low-intensity conflict is a creative response to the reluctance of the U.S. populace, until very recently, to support direct military intervention in Latin America. It involves a broad-based strategy of subversion coordinated through various government agencies, private conservative groups, arms merchants, assassins and drug runners (Nelson-Pallmeyer, 1989:2–4). It is as much a pyschological war as a military war, employing experts in psychological operations and civil affairs. The goal is to maintain the inequalities and injustices that characterize Latin American societies and the relationship between the First World and the Third World to maintain a certain amount of "deniability" and to smother the real intent beneath positive rhetoric.

George Kennan, head of the State Department, wrote the following as early as 1948 in outlining the future policy of the United States:

We have about 50% of the world's wealth, but only 6.3% of its populations. . . . Our real task in the coming period is to devise a pattern of relationships which will permit us to maintain this position of disparity without positive detriment to our national security. (quoted in Nelson-Pallmeyer, 1989:5)

This policy of low-intensity conflict has, among other things, exacerbated the economic crisis of the region (Fagan, 1987:31). Martha Huggins (1987:149) has called it "the worst possible antidote for the development crisis that plagues Central America." Furthermore, opposition to political solutions to the region's conflicts has strengthened the far right (Diskin and Sharpe, 1986:71).

In 1980, almost two-thirds of Central Americans were living in poverty. War and political instability directly contributed to that poverty. By 1982, an estimated $3 billion of private capital had been taken out of Central America due to instability. Much more followed in subsequent years (Fagan, 1987:9). U.S. participation in low-intensity conflict has meant that over half of the aid sent to Latin America in the 1980s went to three countries—Costa Rica, Honduras, and El Salvador. These three countries have less than 4 percent of the total population of Latin America. Even U.S. allies in the region consider this to be a gross distortion of priorities. While development needs go unmet, hundreds of millions of dollars are spent on military programs. As Belisario Betancur, president of Colombia in 1984, remarked, "Without peace there can be no development, and without development there can be no peace. We must break this vicious circle" (Fagan, 1987:3, 12).

But there seems little liklihood that there will be a decrease in low-intensity conflict in Latin America. A statement by Neil C. Livingston, Pentagon consultant on low-intensity conflict, sums up well the attitude of the Bush and Reagan administrations: "The security of the United States requires a restructuring of our warmaking capabilities, placing new emphasis on the ability to fight a succession of limited wars, and to project power into the Third World" (quoted in Nelson-Pallmeyer, 1989:1).

Faced with the decreased Soviet threat after the developments in Eastern Europe in late 1989 and 1990, military planners began to stress the anticipated importance for the military of special operations forces such as those deployed in the invasion of Panama (Trainor, 12/31/89).

An essential part of the low-intensity conflict strategy is the training and funding of the police and the military in Latin America, which are essentially anti-democratic forces. Most Latin American countries are characterized by corrupt and brutal police and military institutions whose association with death squads is well documented (Fagan, 1987:23; Huggins, 1987). U.S. officials, however, generally accept the claims of client states that death squads are unconnected with the government. This is the deniability that is so fundamental to low-intensity conflict. Blaming violence on the death squads, which are usually made up of off-duty and irregular official forces, allows the oligarchy to deny that they are actually under state direction. But as Herman (1987:18) has noted, "the acceptance of these claims by U.S. officials shows the essentially collective and supportive relations between the United States and clients employing this mode of terror." In fact, U.S. aid and training is closely connected to the growth of death squads in Latin America (Herman, 1987:18).

The Honduran military forces, for example, have benefited from U.S. funding, training, and hardware. In 1979 Honduras had 14,000 troops. By 1984 the number of troops had almost doubled. This unleashed a repressive campaign against trade union, church, student, and opposition leaders. A clandestine network of prisons was established with the financial assistance of wealthy right-wing businessmen; into these over a hundred Hondurans disappeared. There were over 150 assassinations and hundreds of people tortured, imprisoned, and forced into exile between 1982 and 1983. Before 1981, the "disappearances" and repression on this scale were almost unknown in Honduras (Fagan, 1987:105).

In fact, Herman has noted the following:

U.S. aid has moved fairly consistently in an inverse relationship to democratic and human rights conditions. . . . [A]s democratic conditions deteriorate . . . there is a distinct tendency for total U.S. aid and multinational credits to increase markedly. In a more elaborate quantitative analysis of this relationship, Lars Schoultz found that the correlations between U.S. aid and human rights violations "are uniformly positive." (1987:15)

U.S. policymakers frequently argue that the funding of repressive military and police institutions is geared toward "reforming" them, making them more professional. But even though such training may decrease the rampant brutality of some units, U.S. funding generally increases military control of the levers of power (see, for example, Fagan, 1987:28). In many cases as well, training and funding merely make the repression more sophisticated.

There is no question that training, hardware, and funding has been used in U.S. client states in Latin America to repress popular dissent. For example, in an interview in 1986, a Salvadoran death squad officer related that Salvadoran police and intelligence services officials had received U.S. training in interrogation methods, including advice on the use of torture (Nairn, 1986, cited in Herman, 1987:17).

In the past, military dictatorships have provided a positive investment climate for multinational corporations, ensuring lax tax laws and labor repression. Military dictators in effect formed a tacit joint venture arrangement in which they kept the masses quiet, maintained an open door to multinational investment, and provided bases (Herman, 1987:16).

The preference, however, is no longer for military dictatorships but for the new technocrats such as Salinas (in Mexico) who will provide the proper investment climate for corporate interests without military uniforms or blatant repression. Structural inequalities and injustice remain, but they are now presided over by more palatable figures, men in suits.

WHY THE ADMINISTRATION CONTINUES TO PURSUE THE WAR ON DRUGS IN LATIN AMERICA

The War on Drugs has been useful in helping to legitimate what Thomas Bodenheimer and Robert Gould (1989) have referred to as the global rollback strategy. Although it was present in U.S. foreign policy during the entire postwar period, this strategy emerged as an especially potent force during the Reagan years. As defined by Bodenheimer and Gould, rollback is essentially the determination of U.S. policy elites to return to a pre-communist world with the final goal of eliminating communism in the Soviet Union and establishing free market capitalism worldwide.

Because the dangers of confronting the Soviet Union directly in the past were so great, however, rollback strategy has focused on the Third World. Bodenheimer and Gould (1989:25–34) cite rollbacks or rollback attempts in China (1950–1961), Iran (1953), Guatemala (1954), the Belgian Congo (1960), Cuba (1961–1968), Brazil (1964), the Dominican Republic (1965), Indonesia (1958–1965), Greece (1967), Southeast Asia (1958–1970), Chile (1970–1973), and Jamaica (1974–1980).

More recently, rollback strategy has focused on Nicaragua, Libya,

Grenada, and Afghanistan. Panama as well can now be added to the list. In fact, Panama is an especially good example of how the rollback strategy involves subverting or overthrowing the government of any country that seeks "full independence from the economic, political, or military influence of the United States," not only governments that are socialist or left wing (Bodenheimer and Gould, 1989:3). The "new world order" the Bush administration is touting is nothing more than a vision of successful rollback with the United States in control.[4]

While the far right within the global rollback network[5] publicly proclaims its intentions, the more traditional conservative elite has always preferred to keep rollback efforts covert. Proclaiming peaceful coexistence and pursuing an aggressive rollback strategy have necessitated secrecy and a powerful legitimating mythology. As the Iran Contra affair well illustrated, proclaiming respect for law and the constitution while subverting them both requires covert action backed up by a strong legitimating ideology.

"Global communist expansion" has historically been the most important part of the mythology that has legitimated U.S. expansionism. In order to justify heightened interventionism, the rollback network has continually kept before the public the supposed menace of communist expansion. For example, nationalist revolutionary movements (such as that in Nicaragua) had to be presented as (and in some instances were probably believed to be) Soviet-communist inspired.

Narco-terrorism is now being presented in the same way, that is, as a grave external threat that the United States has a moral imperative to fight, a moral imperative that legitimates intervening in some Latin American countries and propping up puppet or reactionary governments in others. It has been said that war, the joining together to repel the foe, is both profitable and restorative. The War on Drugs has been both in the United States. The administration as well as other members of the political elite continually define drugs and drug trafficking as a threat to U.S. security interests. The examples are legion:

• The mayor of Toledo, Ohio, in hearings before Congress in 1988: "America has been invaded by an enemy as cruel and powerful as any foreign enemy we have faced" (Rasky, 6/10/88).

• Mayor Koch at a meeting called to discuss the drug issue by the U.S. Conference of Mayors: "Wake up America: We are being destroyed" (*Washington Post*, 4/27/88).

• Robert M. Morgenthau, district attorney of New York City, writing in the *New York Times*: "We cannot wait for long-run palliatives because in the long run we are all dead" (9/27/89).

• There is talk of an "international battle plan."

Jeane Kirkpatrick, with her arguments about the values of authoritarian governments over revolutionary autocracies, helped to solve the problem for the right of how to legitimate, on the one hand, support of repressive rightist dictators and, on the other, attempts to overthrow more democratic left-wing governments. Similarly, through charges of drug trafficking levelled against Latin American countries outside U.S. domination (Sandinista Nicaragua and Cuba), the War on Drugs has been used to help legitimate intervention. More clearly proven government complicity in drug trafficking in cooperative countries (Honduras or Mexico, for example) is conveniently ignored. The War on Drugs, therefore, has been used to supplement so-called communist expansion as a legitimation for intervention in some countries and as an excuse for funding repressive governments and militaries in others.

In *War against the Poor* (1989:1), Jack Nelson-Pallmeyer characterized the United States as a "counterrevolutionary super-power in a world of massive structural inequalities." The United States, he argued, "is actively engaged in a global war against the poor." Nelson-Pallmeyer cites General Maxwell Taylor's warning at the close of the Vietnam War that the "haves" will have to fight against the demands of the jealous "have-nots" in order to perpetuate themselves and their standard of living (1989:2).

Central to this fight against the have-nots is the legitimating ideology, the rhetoric. As Nelson-Pallmeyer has noted:

The acceptability of empire is the guiding principle that shapes U.S. foreign policy.... [W]hatever moral ambivalence might accompany this conflict between empire and the well-being of the poor is smothered under a landslide of rhetoric about "fighting communism" and promoting "freedom and democracy," or is quickly passed over as a superpower's unavoidable dilemma. (1989:4)

The War on Drugs has simply become another part of the rhetoric justifying the expansion of U.S. dominance and control in Latin America. And the War on Drugs is likely to become even more important, especially with the events in Eastern Europe and the increasing inability or unwillingness of the Soviets to deter U.S. actions in Latin America. With the decline in usefulness of the myth of communist expansion as a legitimation for U.S. aggression, the myth of narco-terrorism may well take on even more importance. Daniel Shore, for example, has characterized the drug cartels as the new "evil empire" (National Public Radio, 1/27/90).

In terms of its manifest intent, the War on Drugs in Latin America has been just as ineffective as the domestic war on drugs; and like the domestic War on Drugs, it has brought about additional social costs. But, as in the domestic War on Drugs, the Reagan and Bush administrations have pursued a war for other, more important reasons. Domestically, the War on Drugs targets and blames an enemy group for social problems and therefore obscures the real relations of inequality and exploitation. Internationally, the War on Drugs does much the same thing: It targets and blames enemy countries (Colombia, Peru, and Bolivia, for example) to mask the failure to even approximate international social and economic justice.

The Center and the Periphery: Social and Economic Injustice

It is no surprise that urban inner-city ghettos are filled with drug dealers. Nor is it a surprise that people in countries like Peru, Bolivia, and Colombia grow, distribute, process, and traffic in illegal drugs. The question for both the poor in the United States and the poor in Latin America becomes this: Why be poor forever? And why not use any means, however violent, to gain wealth in a world where violence and exploitation are the means to wealth and power?

The relationship between the dominant culture and the ghetto in the United States is similar to the relationship between the developed Western capitalist countries and Latin America. Both have historically been relationships of structural dependence and exploitation. The economic relationship between the central capitalist countries and Latin America has historically been based on an unequal exchange. Until very recently, the outline of this exchange has been that Latin America primarily exported cheap raw materials (cheap only because their price was based on the overexploitation of land, labor, and natural resources) and imported expensive manufactured goods from the center. This exchange was violent in itself and it ensured the continued poverty of a majority of the Latin American people, underdevelopment of Latin American economies, and a sharpening of conflict between the powerful indigenous oligarchies benefiting from the relationship and the less powerful masses who did not.

The new outline of the exchange relationship between Latin America and the advanced capitalist countries is no less violent. Corporations are closing plants in the First World where hard-fought struggles have won a certain modicum of advantages for workers and environmental quality; they are moving plant operations to the Third World where wages are lower, environmental restrictions are almost nonexistent, and the work force is more desperate and therefore more compliant.

To cite but two examples, General Motors has closed eight plants in Michigan and has opened eleven in Mexico (Schwartz, 1989:9). Green Giant frozen foods laid off 300 workers in its plant in Watsonville, California, and moved the operation to Irapuato, Mexico (Cockburn, 7/30–8/6/90). During the past decade, the border area with Mexico has been transformed by the influx of assembly plants.[6]

Wages and benefits in Latin America and other parts of the developing world are far below what they are in the United States. In 1988, for example, wages in Mexico were approximately 10 percent of those of workers in the United States.[7] A policy statement issued by the American Federation of Labor–Congress of Industrial Organizations (AFL-CIO) in mid–1990 noted that some 400,000 Mexican workers, making goods entirely for the U.S. market, were being paid wages of less than $1 per hour. According to figures from the U.S. and Mexican governments, manufacturing wages in Mexico average $1.90 per hour, while in the United States they average $14.50 (Farnsworth, 6/15/90).

More Reason to Control

Even though the economic relationship between the center and the periphery is changing, this change does not decrease; in fact, it increases the vested interests of the United States in maintaining control over Latin America. And it increases the investment the First World elite has in maintaining Third World oligarchies. Oligarchic control functions to ensure the existing structure of unequal social and economic conditions so that there continues to exist a large pool of impoverished laborers willing to work for little or nothing, and in dangerous conditions. The oligarchy and its managers, the police and the military, ensure that pressures for fundamental change will be kept under control.

An additional factor contributing to the necessity of maintaining control in Latin America has to do with maintaining and expanding what Seymour Melman (5/20/91) has referred to as military state capitalism, that is, the expanding focus of government on arms exports and the establishment of permanent military bases—in short, the management of the military-industrial empire.[8] This military-industrial empire thrives on conflict, violence, and war. Oligarchic control in Latin America depends on a military that can contain the conflict it engenders, and containment requires a constant supply of arms. Maintaining oligarchic control in Latin America, which is friendly to the U.S. military, therefore becomes a vested interest.

But perpetuating an economy of war depends on controlling the outcome. As Melman (5/20/91) has noted, Hussein's invasion of Kuwait would not have been possible without the arming of Iraq by the U.S. and Soviet security establishments. However, when Iraq threatened Western control over Kuwait, discipline had to be reestablished. In Panama, full implementation of the Panama Canal Treaty would have eliminated one of the largest army bases in Latin America, and Noriega was no longer under the control of the U.S. security establishment. Control had to be reestablished.

International violence, whether through economic boycott, military invasion, or international kidnapping, has been elevated during the Reagan and Bush administrations to the status of a positive good—a sign of restored confidence in America, an indication that Americans on the international scene and "responsible conservatives" on the domestic scene are showing the world "who is boss." The bombing of the civilian population of another country need not even require an apology or be presented as a necessary evil. It instead has become an open celebration of "restored" American confidence. Interventionist foreign policy has become a celebration of patriotism.

Historical Moment of Cocaine in Latin America

In the context of sharp inequalities in the international terms of commercial interchange, the radical fall in the prices of the traditionally exported raw materials (at present Latin American countries must sell three times more of their raw materials to obtain the same income they obtained twenty years ago), and the external debt, cocaine as an exportable raw material emerged on the national scene in countries like Colombia. None of the raw materials traditionally sold in the international market by Colombia provided enough surplus value to ensure the dynamic accumulation of capital in Latin America. In perhaps all of Latin American history, in fact, cocaine has been the unique raw material able to generate reasonable surplus value to producers and merchants. As Hobsbawm (11/20/86) has noted, cocaine "has no competition as a profit maker. . . . It is basically an ordinary business that had been criminalized."

In Bolivia, for example, it is estimated that coca production brings in $500 million a year (Kerr, 4/17/88). Penny Lernoux (2/13/89) has estimated the earnings in Bolivia at $3 billion a year. This figure is six times the total value of Bolivia's legal exports. Lernoux, in fact, has maintained that the economy of Bolivia would "collapse without cocaine income." In Bolivia, Colombia, and Peru, money earned through drug exports that is returned to the country is greater than money returned from any of the legal exports like coffee, tin, oil, and sugar (MacDonald, 1988:5).

Given this state of affairs it is simply impossible to believe that cocaine exports will cease without massive economic aid—economic aid that the U.S. elite is unwilling to give. Latin American leaders have always seen the drug problem as fundamentally economic. U.S. elites, however, persist in presenting the problem as one of law enforcement. Even after the much-touted Andean summit in February 1990, Bush walked away having increased military aid much more than economic aid. Even though there were some grudging admissions regarding the effects of trade restrictions such as those regarding coffee and flowers for Colombia, no significant progress on this front was made. However, Andean leaders argued that trade policies were hurting their economies much more than economic assistance was helping (Public Broadcasting System, 2/14/90).

After the publicity surrounding the Cartagena summit in February, which was widely hailed by Democrats and Republicans alike, Secretary of State James Baker was back before the U.N. General Assembly by the end of the month attacking production. Speakers from Latin America and Asia accused the industrial countries of not bearing their fair share of the burden by turning attention once again to production and away from demand and economic assistance. Foreign Minister Julio Londono Paredes of Colombia accused the United States of "sneaking away from the dock." Attorney General Enrique Alvarez del Castillo of Mexico called on industrialized countries to control the availability of chemicals used in drug manufacturing and arms supplies used by the drug cartels. Alvarez also criticized once again the U.S. plan to establish a "radar net" for drug flights by placing aircraft carriers off the coast of Colombia. "Unilateral measures, positions that slander and intimidate, threats that offend the sovereignty of peoples and the dignity of individuals," he said, "must not be tolerated" (Lewis, 2/21/90).

Cartagena, then, accomplished little except creating a show of cooperation. Latin American countries found themselves fighting the same battle—that of repeatedly pointing out the economic nature of the drug problem. The Jamaican foreign minister argued that Third World producers were "engulfed in a multiplicity of development problems and did not have access to the necessary financial, technical, and human resources to actively confront the onslaught of drug trafficking and transshipment" (Lewis, 2/21/90). No one, it seemed, in the U.S. administration was listening.[9]

The cocaine boom occurred in countries like Colombia at a moment of deep and pervasive social conflict. The concentration of power and wealth by the economic and political elites had systematically closed the possibilities of advancement and social mobility to a majority of the people. Unable to manage the ensuing social conflicts, the hegemonic classes began exercising a policy of state terror in a strategy of social control that effectively silenced the Colombian people. These policies of terror were intensified by the proliferation of right-wing death squads whose bloody activities were and still are intimately connected to army commanders and police forces.

In this moment of deep social and political conflict characterized by abject poverty, a growing external debt, widening economic distance between social classes, unemployment, political chaos, growing systematic violation of human and civil rights, and the exercise of military and paramilitary violence against citizens, the enormous amounts of "dirty money" provided by the cocaine boom arrived in Colombia as a new and powerful element of the conflict. In this climate the question in Colombia and in the other underdeveloped countries of Latin America was the same as the question in the urban ghetto: Why not use every tool available to gain the money that means power within a context in which money and power are the only protection against exploitation?

History of Exploitation

The people in Latin American countries have a long history of exploitation through the international market. The history of Latin America has been one of spoilation and pillaging of its natural resources exercised by the wealthy countries of the center. Latin Americans have witnessed the methods through which these countries have maintained this fundamentally unequal relationship, including violent military intervention and the promotion and at times the installation of governments that systematically deny civil and human rights to the population (in Guatemala and Chile, for example).

And the lessons of exploitation have been well learned. The process of capital accumulation is violent and always involves benefits to the few at the expense of the many. The accumulation of domestic capital in Colombia through coffee and other products of exportation was obtained through the overexploitation of the Colombian labor force, expropriation and robbing of the fertile lands of farmers and peasants, and the bloodiest political violence during a historical period known simply as "La Violencia." The accumulation of capital that landowners, merchants of coffee, and bankers obtained as a result of expropriation and domestic violence represented elevated social, political, and economic costs to the Colombian people. These costs were only a reproduction of the violence that characterized the international arena.

The only difference between cocaine accumulation and previous processes of accumulation is that social, economic, and political costs of cocaine accumulation are affecting the countries of the center. The First World countries prefer to define the economy of the relationships of exploitation in such a manner that they reap all the benefits and distribute all the costs to the Third World. The War on Drugs is at least in part a rebellion against the position of the United States in this new process of capital accumulation. The more powerful segments of the U.S. population do not want to face their own complicity in setting the pattern for such violent accumulation, and they do not want to change a world economy set up on the basis of one-way exploitative exchange.

Drugs and the Economy: Benefits

The relationship between drug money and the economy is complex. Economists and policymakers want to argue at one and the same time enormous profits and negative economic effects. Robert B. Reich, a political economist at the John F. Kennedy School of Government at Harvard University, has argued: "Unlike our other major industries . . . the narcotics industry doesn't have a net effect of creating wealth. It makes us all substantially poorer. In fact, it is like a reverse industry, tearing things down rather than producing anything" (Labaton, 12/6/89). But the international drug trade is presently estimated to be worth $500 billion per year. This is more than the international trade in oil and less only than the worth of the international arms trade (Lewis, 2/21/90).

It seems unlikely that drug profits are different economically from any other profits. The argument that most of the profits from drug trafficking do not return to producing countries begs the point that some of the profit does return. For countries in which a majority of the population lives in abject poverty, any profit is better than none.

The arguments of the economists about the negative effects of drug profits do not bear scrutiny. Economists have noted as an example of the negative effects of drug money that there are new patterns of capital flight in producer countries such as Colombia, Peru, and Bolivia (Labaton, 12/6/89); but capital flight characterizes most of Latin America. In Mexico, for example, interest rates are kept artificially high to encourage investors to keep their money in pesos. It is estimated that Mexicans hold some $80 billion abroad (Moffett, 5/14/90). In addition, capital flight in producer countries can be attributed to political instability and U.S. seizure policies. If these policies were not in place, or if drugs were decriminalized, more of the profits would return and they would more than likely be invested more productively.

U.S. FOREIGN POLICY AND THE WAR ON DRUGS AS A THREAT TO THE DEVELOPMENT OF DEMOCRACY

Thomas Bodenheimer and Robert Gould note the following in *Rollback!* with reference to the United States:

Never before in history has a great imperial power been as self-deluded about its political identity. . . . The essence of this self-delusion is the insistence of American leadership on portraying this country as playing an essentially defensive and selfless role in world affairs during a period when the reality was one of unprecedented ambition and global commitment. (1989:ix)

Both Democratic and Republican administrations have pursued a rollback strategy in the Third World (at times more overtly than at others). This has involved the rollback (or attempted rollback) of any government that sought economic, political, or social independence from the United States. Again, Bodenheimer and Gould note:

The political culture of the United States lends itself to this kind of disguised aggressiveness. Many Americans want to nurture an image of innocence and decency, and yet most Americans want most of all to stay on top and continue to applaud clear victories in the Third World however achieved. (1989:xiv)

The administration obviously did not create drug trafficking in order to assist in the global rollback strategy in Latin America. The War on Drugs, however, has certainly come in handy, and the administration has made the most of the situation by choosing a strategy of dealing with drug trafficking that focuses on criminalization and enforcement. The threat of narco-terrorism has been used to legitimate U.S. support of certain "friendly" regimes and increased funding of their militaries. The War on Drugs has been used to legitimate military buildup in the region. The drug involvement of members of the government and military is ignored in friendly countries and is used as an excuse to discredit and intervene in the affairs of others.

In fact, the shallowness of drug war rhetoric and the way in which it is used to advance rollback goals in Latin America can be seen nowhere more clearly than in the selectivity of its application. If the evidence and administration pronouncements are examined, drug production and trafficking evidently constitute a threat to U.S. security interests only when they are engaged in by selected people and countries.[10] As noted in the recently issued report by the Senate Foreign Relations Subcommittee on Narcotics, Terrorism and International Relations, the administration has been entirely willing to ignore drug involvement by friendly military and political leaders as long as these leaders support the administration's agenda. This has been the case in Panama, Antigua, the Bahamas, Colombia, El Salvador, Haiti, Honduras, Jamaica, Mexico, and Paraguay.

A law passed by Congress in 1982 required that countries that are not determined by the president to be making sufficient progress in reducing their role as drug producers or transshipment points will lose aid and loans from the United States, tariff benefits, and air travel agreements. The administration has avoided invoking these measures on friendly regimes by having the president stipulate that to impose such penalties would be against the national interests of the United States. Both Reagan and Bush have used this loophole in the law to certify client states. The argument the administration makes is that countries such as Colombia, Peru, Bolivia, and Mexico would be destabilized if they lost U.S. assistance. This policy has not gone without opposition. Senator Dennis DeConcini of Arizona, for example, has maintained that the certification of major drug-producing countries is a circumvention of the law. DeConcini has at least threatened to vote against the certification of Mexico. Charles Rangel, chairman of a House committee on drug control, has noted that the State Department does not even use the threat of sanctions seriously in negotiations with drug-producing nations (Rosenthal, 3/3/89). This is obviously the case.

Consider Honduras. State Department reports have previously cited Honduras as an important transit point for drugs, and key lawmakers have maintained that they have evidence of connections between political, governmental, and/or military forces in Honduras and drugs. But the Reagan administration protected high-level military officials in Honduras because the Honduran military provided support for the Contras. The 1989 report by the State Department's Bureau of International Narcotics contained no recommendations for a censure of Honduras (Sciolino, 3/1/89). However, even Reagan administration officials finally admitted that Honduran military officers were involved in drug trafficking (Collett, 4/11/88). But U.S. military aid to Honduras grew from $4 million in 1980 to an average of $64 million a year between 1983 and 1988 (Uhlig, 12/28/89). Meanwhile, Reagan administration officials sought a reduced sentence for at least one Honduran general with ties to drug trafficking (Berke, 4/14/89).

Consider Mexico. Mexico has been termed by the State Department as "the largest single-country source of the heroin and marijuana imported into the United States" and an "important transshipment point for cocaine" (Rohter, 12/12/88). In 1987, a State Department report criticized "endemic" corruption extending into the highest levels of the Mexican government (Sciolino, 3/2/89). The report characterized this corruption as the "single most important factor undermining meaningful narcotics cooperation" (Sciolino, 3/1/89). In recent large drug busts in Mexico, a number of those arrested were members of the Mexican Federal Judicial Police, the state police, and the customs service (Branigin, 2/26/88).

The complicity of the Mexican police in the death of DEA agent Enrique Camarena has been detailed in Elaine Shannon's book, *Desperados*. Notwithstanding these events, Mexican president Carlos Salinas de Gortari appointed as his attorney general the governor of the state of Jalisco, who U.S. officials complain dragged his feet on the Camarena investigation (Rohter, 12/12/88).[11] But the Mexican president is praised for his few symbolic drug busts.

In January 1990, a federal grand jury in Los Angeles was still exploring the slaying of Enrique Camarena, the DEA agent killed in Mexico. Rafael Caro Quintero and Ernesto Fonseca Carillo were convicted of the murder in December 1989, but federal prosecutors were skeptical that the two drug "kingpins" acted alone. They suspect that Quintero and Fonseca were the fall guys in a plot involving high-level Mexican officials including José Antonio Zorilla Peréz, ex-head of the federal security directorate; Manual Ibarra Herrera, former chief of the federal police; and

Miguel Aldana Ibarra, former head of Mexico's anti-drug program (*Time*, 1/22/90). DEA agents in Mexico are reportedly as afraid of the Mexican police they work with as of the drug traffickers they are supposed to arrest.

Similarly, a close associate of Prime Minister Lynden Pindling of the Bahamas was indicted in 1989 on charges of taking part in smuggling more than $1 billion worth of cocaine into the United States. Another associate was indicted in Florida for receiving bribes in exchange for allowing the Bahamas to be used for drug trafficking (Efron, 2/1/89). Witnesses at the trial of Carlos Lehder Rivas testified that Prime Minister Pindling himself was involved (*New York Times*, 3/23/89).

But neither Mexico nor Honduras nor the Bahamas are rollback targets, so there are no attempts to topple these governments.

Consider the Contras. Members of the Reagan and Bush administration's as well as members of the Iran Contra congressional investigation refused to confront the drug involvement of the Contras. The scope of the congressional investigation was extremely limited and superficial.[12] Recent evidence makes it clear, however, that some U.S. officials looked the other way on Contra drug involvement; others abetted this drug trafficking because it generated funds for themselves or the Contras (Bleifuss, 5/8-/14/91).[13]

The administration has even considered drug involvement by friendly military and political leaders to be a useful form of political leverage. If these officials cease to be cooperative (as in the case of Noriega), threats of public exposure can be brought to bear. When cooperation is not forthcoming, the charge of narco-military control can always be trotted out. As Peter Bourne (3/25/88) has written, "the cooperation of tainted leaders in the hemisphere on a host of political issues ultimately transcends our concern about drugs exported to this country."

Noriega was vilified, toppled, and kidnapped in part because of his anti-democratic tendencies. There is little doubt that rampant vote fraud occurred in the 1989 election. But there was fraud in the 1984 election as well. According to a recently published book by a former Panamanian colonel,[14] the president of the Panamanian Electoral Tribunal participated in rigging results of the 1984 elections (Branigin, 2/26/88). In 1984, however, the Pentagon and the CIA considered Noriega to be an important asset. George P. Shultz gave his blessing to the 1984 election, which the State Department knew was rigged, by attending the inauguration of the new president. For years, even as Noriega consolidated his power and corruption became rampant in his government, "the Reagan Administration chose not to criticize the regimes controlled by Noriega" (Sciolino, 10/28/88).

While ignoring the involvement of government and military officials in drug trafficking in client states, the administration has continually attempted to create the appearance of an alliance between the left and the drug cartels. The drug cartels, however, have nothing to gain and everything to lose by a triumph of left-wing power in any Latin American country. The drug business is the epitome of private enterprise capitalism. And its natural alliance is with the right, not with the left. The administration repeatedly justifies funding the military in Latin America to fight so-called narco-trafficking, but it refuses to acknowledge the intimate connection between the military, right-wing violence, and drugs.

A recently released report from Americas Watch states that Colombian cocaine dealers financed and trained right-wing death squads, which committed most of the political killings and massacres in Colombia in 1987 and 1988. Colombia's drug dealers wage a war against leftist politicians and labor leaders. The military, says the Americas Watch report, at times looks the other way and at other times actively collaborates. The threat in Colombia (and in Latin America in general) is not narco-guerrillas but "narco-repression" (Brooke, 4/6/89)—a commonality of interests between the members of the oligarchy, the right, and the drug traffickers.[15]

Ignoring this symbiotic relationship between the drug traffickers and the right, the administration continually attempts to use the narco-terrorism charge to legitimate the subversion or rollback of left-wing governments. In Reagan's first term, Michael Ledeen, a counterterrorism expert, sought to generate public support for the assassination of terrorists. He made the charge (which was repeated by the American Security Council) that the Sandinistas had organized "a vast drugs and arms-smuggling network to finance their terrorists and guerrillas, flooding our country with narcotics." Reagan administration operatives evidently at one time planned to fake a drug shipment to El Salvador that would be seized. Inside would be evidence, planted by the United States, that would have implicated Nicaragua (see Cockburn, 1987:222). In 1986, Reagan went on television with props and photographs (including a map of Latin America with a spreading red stain) and charged that the Nicaraguan government was tied to the international cocaine trade. "I know," he said, "that every American parent concerned about the drug problem will be outraged to learn that top Nicaraguan government officials are deeply involved in drug trafficking." A day after the speech the DEA admitted that there was no evidence to back up the charge (Black, 1988:165).

Similarly, there have been repeated attempts to implicate Cuba (another rollback target) in drug trafficking.[16] One *Washington Post* foreign correspondent noted "allegations" by a former cartel money launderer that "Cuba's involvement may be a part of some master plan aimed eventually at killing off cartel leaders and taking control of an organization with tentacles reaching into many of the region's governments and with a hold over millions of drug addicts in the United States."

Whatever one believes about Fidel Castro, he is not a stupid man, and the notion that he would attempt to organize a subversive movement in the United States by mobilizing a bunch of junkies is farfetched to say the least. Professional criminals don't even like to work with junkies.

In any event, the intent is clear. If the American people can be convinced that Cuba or Nicaragua (or any other Latin American country that becomes a rollback target) are involved in drug trafficking, intervention in those countries will be, to some extent, legitimated.

JUSTIFICATION OF SUPPORT FOR REACTIONARY ELEMENTS

The War on Drugs is also being used to mask the real nature of political oppression in countries whose governments the United States supports. Political violence, terror, and repression can continually be laid at the door of the drug cartels and their reputed left-wing cohorts. This is particularly evident in the case of Colombia. For example, the assassination of every newspaper editor who has ever written or published an article against drug trafficking becomes "mafia-inspired." Conveniently ignored are articles critical of the government or the military and their interest in (and history of) silencing political opposition through assassination.

A case that illustrates this well is the 1985 attack on the Colombia Supreme Court in which eleven of the twenty-four justices were killed. This complicated event has been reinterpreted by the administration and within the U.S. mainstream media as mafia-financed left-wing terrorism. In fact, the Colombian military drove a tank through the door of the Supreme Court and was responsible for most if not all of the deaths. In the words of the *Washington Post*, however, "the *guerrilla attack*, which U.S. and Colombian officials believe was financed by traffickers, killed 11 of the 24 justices" (Collett, 4/11/88; emphasis added).

The Colombian military has been closely linked with right-wing death squads (as have the militaries in a number of Latin American countries). However, the U.S. administration continues to fund the Colombian military even though large parts of Colombia are essentially under military control, with only formal national government sovereignty. And these areas are among the most violent in the country. In them the military can do what it likes. In January 1989, for example, a right-wing paramilitary group ambushed and assassinated twelve members of a judicial commission that had uncovered evidence on previous right-wing massacres (*New York Times*, 1/22/89).

While the United States funds and trains police and the military to fight the drug war, gross violations of human rights are commonplace in many Latin American countries, and many of these violations are committed by the military and the police. The Colombian general staff has been accused of covering up human rights abuses by the military. An international human rights panel headed by a Nobel Peace Prize laureate[17] concluded that Colombian military officers were involved in death squad activity (Collett, 4/11/88). But the United States is not fighting or funding a "War against Human Rights Abuses." In fact, the War on Drugs is funding those abuses.

In short, the War on Drugs has been used to expand control in Latin America and assist the rollback effort.

SUMMARY

The War on Drugs, in all its glorious failure, is not only likely to continue in its present form, but it is likely to be expanded. We are likely (especially with George Bush in the White House) to see an escalation in the rhetoric, an escalation in U.S. interventionism in Latin America, and an increasing tolerance of right-wing terror in the name of fighting communism and drugs. As Americas Watch notes in its report on human rights and U.S. policy in Latin America, referring to the Reagan and Bush administrations' attitude, "the end justifies any means at all, and certainly nothing so trivial as law—U.S. or international—should be a constraint" (Brown, 1985:39).

In Latin America, the War on Drugs is being used as a tool in a larger war. And this war is against, not for, fundamental social change and popular empowerment in Latin America. The War on Drugs is threatening, not helping to ensure, democratic development in Latin America.

NOTES

1. It should be remembered that Panama was considered a democracy before Noriega became uncooperative with the administration. The popular joke about Honduras is that it is a country that needs to nationalize its own government.

2. The United Fruit Company owned 2 percent of Guatemala's land and kept most of it idle. Arbenz initiated a program that would have redistributed 234,000 of the company's 550,000 acres and would have paid the company exactly the value that it had declared on the land for its taxes to the Guatemalan government (Fagan, 1987:89).

3. This battle for the vocabulary can be seen in the redefinition of the Contras as "freedom fighters" and the confining of the use of the terrorism label to non-state actors; in other words, the Guatemalan or South African governments cannot, in the new right dictionary, be considered terrorist (see Herman, 1987:3, for a further discussion of the semantic manipulation of terrorism).

4. An indication of the agreement of some segments of the Latin American

population with this analysis is a political cartoon that appeared in the Mexican newspaper *UNOMáSUNO*. Over the caption "New World Order" was a drawing of a U.S. flag with a hundred stars.

5. Bodenheimer and Gould (1989:2) include the following in the global roll-back network: the CIA; ex-CIA operatives; representatives of the military-industrial complex; foreign governments such as those of South Korea, South Africa, and Taiwan; anti-communist groups such as the World Anti-Communist League; Third World death squad organizers; international narcotics and arms dealers; and counter-revolutionaries left over from Cuba, Nicaragua, and China.

6. It is estimated that there are now 470,000 jobs being provided for Mexican workers who assemble products that are imported from the United States and then re-exported to the United States. The proposed free trade agreement between Mexico and the Unites States could shift even more labor-intensive jobs to Mexico. The AFL-CIO has opposed the free trade agreement for this reason (Johns and Graham, 1990).

7. The export success of countries such as Korea, Taiwan, Brazil, and Mexico is based in part on their low wages. But low wages do not help many developing countries; in fact, most of the world's poorer countries run trade deficits.

8. The mobilizing and renewal of public support for military state capitalism could be easily seen after the war in the Persian Gulf. Within five months after the end of the war, the state was conducting massive military parades complete with military hardware, which made Washington, D.C., look like Moscow on May Day. In addition, the Persian Gulf military hardware was swiftly transferred to use in detecting airborne drug smuggling (Davis, 6/7/91).

9. The hypocrisy of the U.S. position is evident. While widely criticizing the export by "producing countries" of a highly profitable and supposedly dangerous drug, in mid–1990 Dr. James O. Mason, assistant secretary for health in the Department of Health and Human Services, was forced to cancel his scheduled testimony before a congressional hearing on the health effects of tobacco exports. Dr. Mason had previously been extrememly critical of efforts by tobacco companies to develop Third World markets (which he publicly called "peddling their poison abroad") with government complicity. One Democratic representative said Mason had been "silenced" by the administration. Administration officials attempted to explain away the affair by noting that the pressuring by the administration of Third World countries (such as Thailand) to accept U.S.-made cigarettes was "a trade issue" and that decisions about which trade barriers to fight did not involve health issues (Hilts, 5/18/90).

10. This selectivity does not only apply to Latin America. Myanmar (formerly Burma) supplies half the heroin imported into the United States and has an abysmal human rights record. However, Myanmar has not received attention as an enemy in the War on Drugs, and the U.S. corporations operating there do so with impunity (Saul, 4/18/90).

11. Later this attorney general, Enrique Alvarez del Castillo, was abruptly replaced after an uprising in a Matamoras prison that resulted in the arrest of six high-ranking law enforcement officials, including two regional commanders of the Judicial Police (Uhlig, 6/5/91).

12. As Bodenheimer and Gould (1989:7) note, "The inquiry into the numerous allegations of contra drug-running was superficial, attributable to the involve-

ment of the Senate panel's chief investigator, Thomas Polgar. This was not surprising given that Polgar, a 30-year CIA veteran, had been station chief in Saigon during the Vietnam war."

13. Bodenheimer and Gould (1989) have detailed the history of covert governmental involvement in drug trafficking to generate funds and political alliances that help in the rollback effort. The recent Kerry investigation report cited numerous examples of governmental decisions in which political concerns outweighed concern about the drug problem. Between January and August 1986, for example, the State Department paid $806,401 to four companies owned and operated by drug traffickers for distributing Contra "humanitarian" aid (Berke, 4/14/89). For reports of Contra involvement in drug trafficking, see Cockburn, 1987.

14. Colonel Roberto Diaz Herrera.

15. And, as Hobsbawm notes, the real increase in violence is on the right. Hobsbawm describes the situation in Colombia:

The real growth sector is right-wing terror. This takes the form of threats against and murders of labor leaders and activists of the UP, who during September 1986 were falling at the rate of about one a day—an apparent rise in the rate of attacks on the left, which is said to have lost about three hundred during the last two years of the Betancur era. Even more sinister are "unknown" death squads which, in defense of morality and social order, have taken to making weekend forays through cities like Cali and Medellín, killing "antisocial" elements such as petty criminals, homosexuals, prostitutes, or just plain beggars and bums indiscriminately. (Hobsbawm, 11/20/86)

16. The press, for example, has noted allegations of Cuban involvement with the Colombian drug mafia and included Cuba in a list of five countries (Panama, Honduras, the Bahamas, Haiti, and Cuba) in which there have been allegations of links between Colombian traffickers and government officials.

17. Adolfo Perez Esquivel.

6

EXPANSION OF U.S. STATE POWER IN LATIN AMERICA

Just as the War on Drugs has helped to legitimate an expansion of state power domestically, in Latin America it has helped legitimate the further projection of U.S. power into the region. In the name of fighting the War on Drugs the U.S. population seems willing to tolerate (if not enthusiastically support) assassinations, electoral interference, extradition, violations of international law such as refusal to recognize diplomatic immunity, invasions, and foreign searches. In a political culture in which government officials liken casual domestic drug use to treason, tolerance for the infringement of the rights of citizens of other countries and the eroding of the sovereignty of other countries is very high.

ASSASSINATION

The usefulness of the War on Drugs in creating a climate in which previously prohibited actions will be tolerated is well demonstrated by the changing attitude toward U.S.-sponsored assassinations.[1] U.S. policy elites have long been concerned with the "Vietnam syndrome" and restrictions placed on covert operations after revelations of CIA participation in assassination plots. The War on Drugs has provided a vehicle for breaking down the squeamishness of the U.S. population over the targeting of foreign nationals for assassination.

Before the buildup of the frenzy over Noriega's reputed involvement in drug trafficking and corruption, several trial balloons had been floated about the advisability of targeting "drug kingpins" for assassination, or "neutralization" (Isikoff, 6/5–/11/89). The administration then used a failed coup attempt in Panama in 1989 as an excuse to begin a campaign to ease the 1976 restrictions on CIA involvement in operations that might result in the assassination of foreign leaders. Congress dutifully went along and entered into an agreement with the administration in November 1989 that gave the administration much more latitude in engaging in such operations. One government official quoted in the *New York Times* remarked: "This is obviously not a plan to assassinate Noriega. But if there is loss of life, that's not constrained" (Wines, 11/17/89).

Daniel Patrick Moynihan and others were appalled by this turn of events. Moynihan concluded on the Senate floor: "It may be we just don't believe in law anymore. Fair enough. But shouldn't we have the integrity to say so? Or, rather, the nerve" (Moynihan, 10/20/89).

The administration had neither. Bush authorized the Central Intelligence Agency to spend up to $3 million to recruit Panamanian army officers and exiles to depose Noriega (Friedman, 12/18/89). As Moynihan pointed out, government participation (in assassinations or coups) not only violated executive orders but also violated Article VI, Paragraph 2 of the U.S. Constitution, the U.N. charter, and the charter of the Organization of American States (Moynihan, 10/20/89).

As Richard Reeves, a syndicated columnist, editorialized after the invasion of Panama,

killing Manuel Noriega, which was the obvious plan, would have accomplished nothing more than . . . preventing him from telling what he knows about the relationships between President Reagan's White House and the international drug business. (Reeves, 12/29/89)

The changed agreement between Congress and the administration regarding assassinations was an important signal of official tolerance for overtly and publicly admitted violent intervention into the affairs of other countries; but perhaps more important was that for the first time in over a decade, assassination was publicly discussed as an alternative political strategy. Assassination had become an acceptable option for debate, no longer inconceivable in an open discussion as an official political strategy.

The debate about assassination began over Noriega in the context of the War on Drugs, but by the time of the Persian Gulf war, public acceptance had become so great that newspapers were carrying entire articles discussing whether it would be a good idea to assassinate Saddam Hussein (see, for example, Turner 11/11/90).

Another strategy for fighting the War on Drugs, short of assassination but still encouraging it, has been the offering of large ransoms for the capture of drug kingpins. In December 1989, for example, Colombia's War on Drugs by and large became a manhunt (assisted by U.S. spy planes tracking beeper signals of U.S. agents on the ground) for Jose Gonzalo Rodríguez Gacha and Pablo Escobar Gaviria. A ransom of $625,000 was offered for the capture of either man. The result was a shootout that claimed the life of Gacha, his seventeen-year-old son, and fifteen bodyguards (Treaster, 12/16/89). This action was widely hailed as a "success" by the U.S. mainstream media.

ELECTORAL INTERFERENCE

As was noted in Chapter 5, sham elections have been characterized as the most important weapon in the U.S. arsenal. The holding of elections in client states, however unfair, is hailed as evidence of democracy. Elections in countries not subservient to Washington's will (such as Nicaragua before the defeat of the Sandinistas) are deemed unfair.[2] The massive infusion of money to support factions of which the administration approves is a palatable way of ensuring a result satisfactory to the United States. In the new right dictionary, this is termed "leveling the playing field."

Interference in the electoral process of Latin American countries is nothing new and is not justified solely on the basis of the War on Drugs, but allegations of the drug involvement of various governments (in Panama and Nicaragua, for example) have helped legitimate such intervention.

MILITARY INTERVENTION

The rhetoric of the War on Drugs has served as a rationale for flagrant abuse of international law. Increased calls for the use of the military to halt drug trafficking culminated in December 1989 with the invasion of Panama. There has, however, been a U.S. military presence in Latin America for years, ostensibly to fight the War on Drugs. In 1984, for example, sea checkpoints were set up off the coast of Colombia by the U.S. Navy in Operation Hat Trick in an effort to stop drug trafficking (Magnuson, 1/22/90). In 1986, the Pentagon was involved in Operation Blast Furnace in Bolivia. U.S. Special Forces trainers have been in Bolivia working with Bolivia's drug police ever since (Kawell, 10/25–/31/89). Operation Snowcap was a once-secret effort launched in 1988 to use DEA agents and the military in the Andean region in paramilitary operations to stop coca paste production, refining, and export (Klare, 1/1/90; Karel, 1990).

Reagan formally began the drive to involve the military in the drug war when he signed a national security decision directive in April 1986 declaring that drug trafficking was a threat to national security that could warrant a military response (Shank, 1987:40). Early in 1988, federal Drug

Czar William Bennett renewed the call for military involvement (Kristol, 3/28/88). In 1988, Congress declared the Defense Department the head agency in charge of detecting and monitoring drug smuggling (Magnuson, 1/22/90).

There seemed to be little opposition to these moves to more deeply involve the military in drug operations. Irving Kristol, co-editor of *The Public Interest*, even called for the United States to follow the nineteenth-century British example of stopping and searching boats on the high seas and searching ships in foreign ports to stop the flow of drugs into the United States. Forget education, Kristol argued, it doesn't work. Forget international law as well. Only the pansies at the State Department worry about such things. According to Kristol, the United States had a moral imperative to break the law. "If we are at all serious about a war on drugs," he argued, "let's begin by taking appropriate military action" (Kristol, 3/28/88).

At a meeting in April 1988 to discuss the drug issue, the U.S. Conference of Mayors included in its resolution a call on the federal government to use the military to stop narcotics coming into the country (*Washington Post*, 4/27/88). Secretary of Defense Cheney made it plain from the outset that he viewed drug trafficking as a threat to national security (Trainor, 12/16/89) and therefore an appropriate field for military activity.

In response to critics who objected to involving the military in the War on Drugs, Mayor Ed Koch, testifying before Congress in 1988, voiced an attitude that characterized the debate: "I get so fed up with people . . . complaining about totalitarian measures," he said. "What's totalitarian about using the military to stop a foreign invasion?" The use of the foreign invasion metaphor was widespread and reproduced over and over in the political debate that degenerated into Democrats and Republicans trying to out-tough each other. For example, Representative Steven Solarz, a Democrat, compared the drugs coming from Latin America to "intercontinental ballistic missiles" being "fired at American cities from Peru and Bolivia," and he scolded the administration for not coming up with a plan to "knock out the enemy" (Isikoff, 6/5–/11/89).

During late 1989, the pace stepped up. In September 1989, Bush ordered the major military commands to develop plans for decreasing the flow of drugs from source countries (Trainor, 12/16/89). He also signed a directive that allowed U.S. forces to train military forces in Colombia, Peru, and Bolivia outside of their secure bases (Lewis, 12/29/89). In October 1989, the Defense Department announced plans to use marines to help halt drug smuggling across the Mexican border (Trainor, 12/16/89). In December 1989, marines who were part of a Defense Department program for the U.S. Army, the Marine Corps, and the National Guard to support civilian drug enforcement efforts exchanged gunfire with drug smugglers on the Arizona border.[3]

The Defense Department was reported in December 1989 to be moving ahead with plans for greater military involvement in the War on Drugs. These plans were reported to include the expanded use of planes to detect aircraft carrying drugs and the use of naval combat ships. CBS News reported in mid-December that military units had been authorized by Cheney to capture fugitives wanted on drug charges in foreign countries (Trainor, 12/16/89). By the end of December, troops had invaded Panama.

The Pentagon, while initially reluctant to become involved in the War on Drugs (which it considered a law enforcement problem and a quagmire), changed its strategy when it became apparent that declining East-West tensions would mean military cutbacks. One Capitol Hill source, who was described as a "cynic" by a *Time* reporter, commented: "The military sneered at drug interdiction—until they saw the budget crunch coming." By January 1990, military officials were arguing that in the 1990s a portion of the military budget must be devoted to combating drugs and preparing for intervention in the Third World (Engelberg, 1/9/90).

In January 1990, in proposing an additional $1.2 billion to fight the War on Drugs, Bush proposed a 50 percent increase in funds for the military to increase its anti-drug activities. The Pentagon's budget for anti-drug activities would increase from roughly $800 million to $1.2 billion in the fiscal year beginning in October 1990 (Berke, 1/25/90).

By early 1990, U.S. spy planes were flying missions near Colombia tracking beeper signals from agents on the ground in an attempt to assist in the manhunt for Pablo Escobar, and the Pentagon was engaged in developing sophisticated surveillance technology for further participation in the War on Drugs (Kelley and Meddis, 5/3/90).

By mid–1990, however, Congress was expressing concern over the management of some of the anti-drug military programs. In one program initiated in 1987, the State Department organized a private airforce to support paramilitary operations designed to target the illegal drug industry in Latin America. Private pilots, who were hired to fly military helicopters, transport planes, and crop dusters, and who were being paid as much as $150,000 per year, went on strike for higher pay. Other personnel involved in the program were caught pilfering from the government, and one chief operations officer was indicted for conspiracy to smuggle drugs to Mexico before he had begun working for the State Department (Gerth, 6/13/90).

Military involvement in the War on Drugs is likely to increase. In 1989, the Supreme Court refused to hear and therefore let stand a lower court ruling that a federal law mandating that governors had no power to block the use of the National Guard in overseas training missions was constitutional (Greenhouse, 4/18/89). The National Guard, therefore, will play an even more important role in Latin America than in the past. In May 1990, Attorney General Thornburgh nominated as deputy attorney general William Barr, well known for his advocacy of (1) using the military to conduct U.S. law enforcement missions in other countries, and (2) authorizing U.S. agents to kidnap fugitives in other countries without the approval of the host country (Barrett and Wermiel, 5/14/90).[4]

While the use of the military in Latin America ostensibly to fight the War on Drugs has assisted Latin American oligarchies in repressing opposition groups, Latin American leaders are keenly aware of the resentment of large segments of the Latin American population to U.S. intervention in national affairs. After the extradition, or kidnapping, of Juan Ramon Matta in Honduras, for example, there were widespread riots (Ring, 2/26/88). These riots were not solely over the kidnapping of a Honduran citizen; they were also over resentment of the use of Honduras as a staging base for the Contras.

Even though the administration and the mainstream media portray drug kingpins as international outlaws who are uniformly evil, these outlaws provoke grudging respect and often outright support from segments of the Latin American population. In December 1989, for example, a *New York Times* reporter maintained that attitudes had turned bitter toward Rodríguez Gacha and Pablo Escobar after the bombing of a Colombian airline and intelligence headquarters in Bogotá (Treaster, 12/16/89). However, thousands of villagers attended the reburial of Gacha in his home town (*Alabama Journal*, 12/18/89a). In addition, candidates backed by Escobar and Gacha had been elected as mayors in five towns in the Magdelena Valley shortly before the Rodríguez Gacha assassination (Treaster, 12/16/89). In Mexico, ballads of the rise of cocaine traffickers Ernesto Fonseca Carrillo and Rafael Caro Quintero are played on local radio stations (Rohter, 4/16/89b). During the Cartagena summit, students at several Colombian universities protested Bush's presence in the country. The National Liberation Army, one of Colombia's guerrilla groups, kidnapped an American priest and announced after Bush's visit that it considered every "American interest" in Colombia to be a "military target" (Treaster, 2/16/90).

While the U.S. administration and the mainstream media presented the Panama invasion as benign "big-power intervention" and as "a positive force wielded on behalf of democracy and human rights" (Sesser, 1/17/90), Latin Americans were not so sanguine about the prospect of big-power intervention to "restore democracy."

The president of Peru, Alan Garcia, recalled his ambassador in Washington after the invasion, initially refused to take part in the drug summit scheduled to take place in Colombia, and temporarily halted the joint U.S.-Peruvian anti-drug effort. Garcia characterized the Panama invasion as "an illegal search of an entire nation," and he argued that the

Endara government was illegitimate (Treaster, 1/1/90; Brooke, 1/14/90). The Peruvian ambassador in Panama resigned in response to the invasion. The Organization of American States (OAS) voted to condemn the invasion, as did the United Nations (Cole, 1/20/90). Colombia (and other Latin American countries) reacted vehemently to a U.S. action, which was taken in the flush of victory after the Panama invasion, to send an aircraft carrier to the coast of Colombia (Rosenthal, 2/16/90).

But, in the Panama afterglow, Cheney was reported to be expected to approve a wide array of military actions related to the drug war. Among them were the following:

- mobile ground radar stations for Bolivia, Peru, and Colombia;

- increased training of regional anti-drug teams in jungle combat, night operations, map reading, and intelligence;

- Air Force AWACS planes to surveil drug routes along the Gulf of Mexico;

- the use of ground and air radar stations of the North American Aerospace Defense Command (NORAD) near Colorado Springs to relay intelligence on drug movements to law enforcement agencies;

- military exercises on the U.S. side of the Mexican border designed to intimidate drug traffickers; and

- expanded military support of the U.S. Border Patrol, Customs, and local police (Magnuson, 1/22/90).

The chairman of the House Armed Services Committee, Les Aspin, observed after the Panama invasion: "It was a success. But before our Panama experience becomes a model for more intervention, we should note that it almost surely won't be as easy elsewhere" (Oakes, 1/26/90). Intervention may not be as easy elsewhere, but it is obvious that it is on the drawing board.

The increasing use of the military in the War on Drugs comes at a time of general increase in reliance on military force and violence to resolve problems and impose U.S. will. In May 1990, a presidential commission urged the Bush administration to plan for and train for "preemptive or retaliatory military strikes" against "terrorists" even though a 1990 State Department report indicated that terrorist attacks against the United States had declined (McGinley, 5/16/90). And military involvement in the War on Drugs in Latin America has the potential of developing into another Vietnam, even though administration officials deny this. White House press secretary Marlin Fitzwater, objecting to the "another Vietnam" analogy, said the administration was going to go "to some lengths to knock that down" (Kawell, 10/25–/31/89). They will have to. The similarities are striking. Among them are the following:

- the further funding and strengthening of morally corrupt indigenous military and police institutions;
- widespread popular support for the "enemy";
- class (and, in Latin America, race) differences that translate into little support for the established governments;
- the underground and guerrilla nature of the combat; and
- the fact that the capacity of the military is already stretched to the limit and that an effective counterinsurgency campaign will necessitate more and more U.S. involvement (Klare, 1/1/90).

In addition to the use of the U.S. military, the projection of U.S. power into Latin America involves the funding and training of Latin American military and police establishments. Bush's anti-drug strategy in the Andean region, announced in September 1989, included almost $261 million in aid to the police and the military in Peru, Bolivia, and Colombia (Treaster, 1/1/90).

The lure of U.S. funds and equipment is great. In Peru, for example, the military was initially wary of drug operations in the Upper Huallaga Valley; but after being offered as much as $40 million in military hardware, it began contending that its battle against guerrillas should be considered an anti-cocaine effort (Treaster, 1/1/90).

The use of what are essentially mercenary armies in Latin America has several advantages. First, as was demonstrated in the Contra war against the Sandinista government, the objections of the U.S. population to U.S. interference are much less when people of other cultures (especially people of color) are doing the fighting and dying. Second, because the militaries of other countries are used, U.S. intervention can be presented as autonomous action, the will of Latin Americans themselves. Third, U.S. funding and training of the militaries in Latin America helps to facilitate alliances that can be called upon to control political events in Latin America.

The United States essentially becomes the high command, coordinating and directing activities for which it takes little public responsibility. In July 1990, for example, briefing papers obtained from the U.S. Southern Command headquarters in Panama detailed plans for a hemispheric drug raid to be carried out by the armies of Colombia, Peru, and Bolivia, coordinated by the Southern Command. Press reports noted that the author of the plan, General Max Thurman, head of the Southern Command, was prepared to use U.S. troops in the raid if necessary (*Christian Science Monitor*, 7/9/90).

EXTRADITION

Violation of the national sovereignty of Latin American countries through the pressure to extradite suspected drug traffickers is another example of the expansion of U.S. control. U.S. pressure is so great, through the threat of economic boycott and through influence within international monetary agencies, that the United States is allowed to maintain a virtual stranglehold on the domestic policies of some Latin American countries.

U.S. pressure can clearly be seen in the treaty forced on Colombia that involved a commitment to extradite suspected Colombian drug traffickers. President Virgilio Barco revoked the appointment of Justice Minister Jaime Bernal for even expressing his opposition to such extraditions. The Supreme Court of Colombia finally declared such extraditions unconstitutional. The Supreme Court decision, however, was presented by the administration and the mainstream media as a result of Mafia pressure. The fact that the justices of the Colombian Supreme Court might actually believe that Colombia had a right to national sovereignty was not considered by the Reagan administration, nor was it discussed in the media.

In the case of Juan Ramon Matta in Honduras, what was officially called extradition ended up being the virtual kidnapping of a Honduran citizen. The United States arranged Matta's arrest and deportation with Honduran military officials and security forces rather than through judicial channels. Numerous Honduran judges, legislators, and intellectuals denounced the so-called extradition as unjustifiable under Honduran law. The Honduran constitution specifically prohibits the extradition of citizens of Honduras. This was, in addition, not the first attempt to extradite Matta. In an interview with the *Washington Post* (Ring, 2/26/88), Matta charged in February 1988 that U.S. agents had tried unsuccessfully four times to kidnap him before the final extradition.

The most celebrated extradition was that of Noriega. The Bush administration was preparing to seize Noriega even before the failed coup attempt in October 1989. Secretary of State James A. Baker III said in an interview on NBC's *Meet the Press*: "The message that was sent [to the plotters] was that if there were an opportunity to do this [seize Noriega], without risking bloodshed and significant loss of American life, and to do so without open military involvement... the commander on the ground was free to go ahead."

Secretary of Defense Cheney echoed this on CBS's *Face the Nation*:

After the Panamanians had contacted us and told us... that they had Noriega but that they would not give him to us, I made it clear that our commander on the scene was authorized to get him if he could... and that he should develop an option or get a plan to use military force to get him.

The United States finally did get him. And thereafter a number of legal scholars noted that there was little legal justification for the unprecedented action of seizing Noriega and flying him back to the United States. A senior lawyer at the World Court commented: "It was like the Romans leading back defeated leaders and taking them to the circus to be displayed" (Lewis, 1/10/90).

As several legal scholars have noted, the invasion and seizure of Noriega received after-the-fact legal justification. Officially the administration maintained that Noriega was not seized but had surrendered voluntarily. It strains credulity, however, to argue that Noriega's surrender was voluntary. As was noted in the *New York Times*, "no United States official seriously argues in private that the General was not coerced into surrendering to American military authorities" (Lewis, 1/10/90).

The administration also maintained that Noriega was not arrested until he was aboard a U.S. aircraft. The chairman of the American Bar Association, however, argued that Noriega's arrest occurred when he was taken into custody. Alfred Rubin, a professor of international law at the Fletcher School of Law and Diplomacy, pointed out that the seizure of Noriega was no more legal than if the Ayatollah Khomeini seized Salman Rushdie on British soil and took him back to Iran to face blasphemy charges (Lewis, 1/10/90).

When it came time for a bond hearing for Noriega at the end of January 1990, while publicly maintaining that Noriega had voluntarily surrendered, the government objected to his release on bail, arguing that Noriega was not "a willing fugitive." The U.S. attorney argued that "[i]n a technical sense he surrendered, but he was captured by an invading Army. That's the reality" (Pear 5/27/90). Some reality.

Aside from the illegality of the extradition, U.S. courts have been traditionally unconcerned with the way in which foreign nationals are brought before them. In 1952, the Supreme Court declared that "the power of a court to try a person for a crime is not impaired by the fact that he has been brought within the court's jurisdiction by reason of a 'forcible abduction.' " (Pear, 5/27/90). However, this question of the tolerance for extradition is completely one-sided. In September 1990, the Colombian government issued a warrant for the arrest of Yair Klein, a reserve lieutenant colonel in the Israeli army, for training the guards of drug traffickers. The Israeli government, an ally of the United States, refused to extradite Klein (*New York Times*, 1/26/90). Klein was later linked to a shipment of arms that were found at the ranch of Jose Rodríguez Gacha, a Colombian drug trafficker (Gerth, 5/6/90).

The extraditions and kidnappings represent the determination of the U.S. administration to expand the control of the U.S. legal system over all of Latin America. But even though the desire is to expand the control, none of the rights inherent in that legal system are extended. For example, the Supreme Court ruled in the 1989–1990 session that foreign nationals were not entitled to protection from illegal searches and seizures in their own countries.

By April 1990, the administration had ceased even pretending to extradite suspects. On April 2, 1990, a Mexican doctor, Humberto Alvarez Machain, was captured at gunpoint in Gaudalajara, Mexico, and turned over to authorities in the United States. Alvarez had been accused of participation in the torture-killing of DEA agent Enrique Camarena. After first denying participation in the kidnapping, a federal drug agent testified in California that top DEA officials had authorized the offering of a $50,000 reward for the capture of Alvarez. The DEA then admitted paying $20,000 to the people who abducted Alvarez for "expenses" (Pear, 5/27/90).

After the capture of Alvarez, Mexican newspapers reported that the Mexican government had announced that it would seek the extradition of Hector Berrellez, a supervisor in the DEA, for his role in abducting Alvarez (Wright, 5/27/90). Berrellez, however, will never be extradited.

In this case, contrary to previous court opinion, a federal judge (U.S. District Judge Edward Rafeedie) in August 1990 held that Alvarez had been illegally kidnapped and ordered his return to Mexico. Judge Rafeedie ruled that the case could not be tried in the United States. He rejected the government's argument that the DEA was not responsible for the kidnapping of Alvarez since its agents were not direct participants. "The U.S. is responsible," ruled the judge, "for the actions of its paid agents."

The Mexican government objected strenuously to the invasion of Mexico's sovereignty. President Salinas stated: "If the doctor faces criminal charges, it should be in Mexico, in accordance with Mexican law" (Pear, 5/27/90). Judge Rafeedie ruled that when a protest is made (such as that of the Mexican government, in this case) and a treaty has been violated (the extradition treaty), the defendant had to be returned. The judge further warned the DEA that violations of another nation's sovereignty would not be tolerated even in attempts to stop international drug trafficking (Deutsch, 8/11/90).

DIPLOMATIC IMMUNITY

Even though it is a violation of international law to enter foreign embassies, the administration showed flagrant disregard for international law regarding diplomatic immunity after the invasion of Panama. In their search for Noriega after the invasion, U.S. military forces surrounded the embassies of Cuba, Nicaragua, and Libya (Garcia, 1/3/90). U.S. forces also raided the residence of the Nicaraguan ambassador. Bush attempted to dismiss the raid with his usual eloquence as a "screw up" and then went on to attempt to justify the raid retrospectively because the troops found arms (*New York Times*, 1/1/90). Bush maintained that the ambassador was "up to his eyeballs" in weapons (Friedman, 12/31/89). But, as Justice Cardoza wrote in *People v. Defore* (Court of Appeals of New York, 1926, 242 N.Y.13, 150 N.E. 585): "Means unlawful in their inception do not become lawful by relation when suspicion ripens to discovery."

The Nicaraguan ambassador to Panama characterized the search as a "deliberate and open violation" and maintained that administration officials were lying about key details of the incident. Two telephones had been ripped from the wall inside the residence and a cabinet rifled (Rohter, 12/31/89). The ambassador said that one of the phones had been ripped out of the wall when his sister attempted to phone Managua (Hockstader and Omang, 12/31/91). Family members maintained that money had also been stolen (Rohter, 12/31/89). The State Department accused the Nicaraguans of "irresponsible overreaction" to the incident (Friedman, 12/31/89; Price and Lippman, 12/31/89). In January 1990, the OAS passed a resolution declaring that the U.S. action of invading and searching the residence of the Nicaraguan ambassador in Panama was a violation of international law (*New York Times*, 1/10/90). This was, of course, ignored.

Nicaraguan officials argued that the action was intended to provoke similar searches of homes and offices of U.S. personnel in Nicaragua, thereby justifying U.S. military intervention in Nicaragua (Uhlig, 1/1/90). Toward the end of January 1990, the United States vetoed a U.N. Security Council resolution censuring the action. Thirteen other members of the Security Council supported the resolution, and only Britain abstained (*Wall Street Journal*, 1/18/90).

The Vienna Convention of 1961 guarantees diplomats immunity from search and seizure and arrest, but by January 15, there had been three additional incidents in Panama between Cuban diplomats and U.S. troops. One involved heavily armed U.S. forces halting and attempting to search the car of the Cuban ambassador (Pitt, 1/16/90). And the violations were directed not only at Cuba and Nicaragua. When Peru granted diplomatic asylum to a Noriega aide wanted by the United States, the U.S. military surrounded the Peruvian embassy in Panama (*Wall Street Journal*, 1/10/90).

FOREIGN SEARCHES

In March 1990, the Supreme Court handed down a 6 to 3 decision in *United States v. Verdugo-Urquidez*, 110 S. Ct. 1056 (1991), in which warrantless searches in foreign countries were declared constitutional. The District Court in California and the Court of Appeals for the Ninth Circuit had ruled that the evidence discovered in a search of the home of a Mexican accused of drug smuggling was inadmissible in court. However, the Justice Department in its appeal of the case argued that requiring a warrant for searches outside the country would be impractical and that in any event, "the right against unreasonable searches and seizures" did not "extend to all persons throughout the world" (Greenhouse, 3/1/90, 4/18/89).

The Supreme Court overturned the lower court decisions and agreed with the Justice Department argument that the wording of the Fourth Amendment (particularly the phrase "the people") was probably intended by the framers to refer to people who were "part of a national community or who have otherwise developed sufficient connection with this country to be considered part of that community." The accused man was brought to the U.S.-Mexican border in 1986 after the United States issued a warrant for his arrest. He was then placed in a federal prison in San Diego. Several days later, Mexican officials granted permission for U.S. federal drug enforcement agents to search two of the suspect's homes (Greenhouse, 3/1/90). After the invasion of Panama, U.S. soldiers searched the offices of the Spanish news agency in Panama City. They also entered the offices of Iberia Airlines and the Banco Exterior, a government bank (New York Times, 12/31/89).

The decision in Verdugo-Vrquidez in effect broadens the power of the United States to not only expand its legal system throughout the hemisphere but to expand it while setting up a different standard of rights for foreign nationals. While Justice Rehnquist made a distinction between "the people" used in the Fourth Amendment and "any person" or "the accused" in other amendments, Justice Kennedy wrote a concurring but separate opinion in which he stated: "I cannot place any weight on the reference to 'the people' in the Fourth Amendment as a source of restricting its protections" (Greenhouse, 3/1/90). This kind of judicial nit-picking used as a rationale to restrict rights is likely to be the pattern for the future. And if the intent of the framers is to be slavishly followed, rights are in deep trouble indeed.

SUMMARY

The evidence clearly indicates that the real agenda of the War on Drugs in Latin America is not stopping the drug trade but projecting and expanding U.S. power into the region. It is not possible to continue to accept an argument that the actions of the U.S. policy elite are merely irrational. For example, the administration's pressure on Colombia to do something about the processing and trafficking of drugs goes on while the U.S. administration allows the international coffee agreement with Colombia to be suspended (in July 1989). Coffee is the main legal source of foreign currency for Colombia, and it is estimated that Colombia will lose $500 million a year unless the agreement is restored (Treaster, 1/1/90, 9/24/89). Without economic assistance it will be impossible to stop the drug trade. Jack Weatherford, an anthropologist who studied coca cultivation in Bolivia, has argued that eradication programs such as Operation Blast Furnace in Bolivia actually helped to increase coca production by clearing exhausted coca bushes and improving roads (Weatherford, 9/27/89). It is not credible that the U.S. administration is unaware of these (and innumerable other) facts.

William Bennett said in a speech in 1989 that the drug crisis was "a crisis of authority" (Morley, 10/2/89). This applies not only to the authority of the state domestically but to U.S. authority in relation to Latin America. The U.S. policy elite is using the drug crisis to facilitate the expansion of power into Latin America. And there is very little to stop them. As long as the interventionism is couched in terms of the War on Drugs, the U.S. public seems completely willing to accept it. In a *Wall Street Journal*/NBC poll conducted in 1989, 58 percent of respondents favored sending U.S. troops to Colombia if the Colombian government asked for them (Kawell, 10/25–/31/89). In a similar poll done for the *New York Times* and CBS, 61 percent of respondents approved (Berke, 9/12/89).

Because the United States is the only remaining superpower, media commentators now advocate "a policing role" for the United States when it is in "our national interest" (*In These Times*, 9/19–/25/90a). In a report on human rights and U.S. policy in Latin America, Americas Watch has noted (referring to the attitude of the Reagan and Bush administrations) that "the end justifies any means at all, and certainly nothing so trivial as law—U.S. or international—should be a constraint" (Brown, 1985:39).

In September 1989, the Soviet Union publicly criticized U.S. proposals to send troops to fight the War on Drugs in other countries (*Montgomery Advertiser*, 9/7/89). But the Soviet Union is no longer able or willing to deter U.S. expansionism in Latin America. There is also little likelihood that international tribunals like the United Nations, the World Court, or the OAS will have much influence in stopping expanded U.S. intervention in Latin America. No matter how much the Bush administration praises the United Nations for its actions in relation to the invasion of Kuwait, the U.S. military and political elite simply ignore the international tribunals when they oppose U.S. actions. In 1984, for example, after the World Court ruled in favor of Nicaragua in a dispute with the United States, the United States simply renounced the court's jurisdiction (Lewis, 1/30/90). As the new right media pundits argue, when international law conflicts with U.S. interests, it should be ignored (*In These Times*, 9/19–/25/90a).

The U.S. administration pays attention to U.N. and other international organizations when they can be pressured into serving U.S. interests. Britain and the United States, for example, tried to involve the U.N. Security Council in supporting the War on Drugs by declaring drug trafficking a "threat to international peace and security" and a proper sphere of U.N. activity. As several Third World governments (including Colombia and Brazil) pointed out, however, such an action would encourage the Security Council (dominated by the five permanent members) to intervene in problems that did not involve a direct threat to peace (Lewis, 10/11/90).

In the end, the negative effects of the War on Drugs are largely irrelevant. The battles are likely to go on and on, escalating the attendant crime and violence, increasing the inequality between the center and the periphery, increasing the exploitation and control of the periphery by the center. The War on Drugs is simply too useful a legitimation of state crime to abandon.

NOTES

1. State-sponsored assassination is known as "state-sponsored terrorism" if carried out by states outside U.S. domination (Libya, for example).

2. A memo written by Robert Owen to Oliver North on March 17, 1986, characterizes the true nature of the "opposition" party UNO in Nicaragua:

UNO is a creation of the USG [U.S. government]. . . . [A]lmost anything it has accomplished is because the hand of the USG has been there. . . . [I]f USG agencies actually believe that UNO is a strong and functioning body that truly represents all factions of the Democratic Resistance, they are fooling themselves. (Hackel and Siegel, 1987:19)

3. Details of this program were classified (Trainor, 12/16/89).

4. William Barr should not be confused with another Thornburgh appointee, Henry G. Barr, who was convicted in early 1991 of charges related to cocaine use. Henry Barr served as special assistant to Thornburgh and was Thornburgh's liaison to the FBI and the DEA. In addition, he oversaw counterintelligence operations such as undercover drug operations (Lewis, 2/24/91).

In October 1991, President Bush nominated William Barr to replace Thornburgh as attorney general.

7

THE ROAD FORWARD

A journalist remarked to me at a conference conducted by the Drug Policy Foundation that he believed that at some point the gap between what the Drug Warriors were promising and what they were achieving would become so apparent that the U.S. citizenry would be forced to seriously consider decriminalization. Unfortunately, I do not share his optimism.

The gap between what the prison system has promised and what it has achieved has been apparent for over a century, but few people (in this country at least) are calling for the abolition of prisons. On the contrary, the administration is building more and more prisons and a large segment of the public seems to support this extravagant, useless, and destructive expense.

The logic behind continued prison construction and the continuation of the War on Drugs seems to be something like this: Prisons have been a failure, so more prisons will be a success; punishment has been a failure, so more punishment will be a success; criminalization and enforcement have been a failure, so more criminalization and enforcement will be a success. It's not the kind of logic that appeals to every intellect, but it is apparently sufficient for many.

In fact, the political climate of the past decade has produced an increasing willingness to mobilize repressive strategies to deal with many social problems, especially those that most affect the poor and marginalized. The zeal for repression seems to be absent in, for example, sentencing guidelines for corporate criminals and the prosecution of S&L racketeers and subverters of the Constitution. We seem a very long way from any turnaround in the basic preference for repressive tactics concerning drugs. In state after state, city after city, more and more repressive means are being proposed to deal with the drug problem.

The trend is not toward decriminalization of drugs or their legalization, but away from it. And one of the beauties of the War on Drugs is that both success and failure can be used to justify doing more of the same.

In 1988, for example, Reagan was calling the War on Drugs "an untold American success story." In 1988 as well, Reagan was bemoaning the spending of "16 billion in a futile effort to roll back the flood tide of cocaine entering this country" (Hamm, 1988).

The road forward, the real road forward, is not more of the same. The real road forward must involve a fundamental change in the way we perceive the world and ourselves. We must move away from a cultural predisposition to confront the world and our own problems not as gardeners or teachers but as policemen. We simply cannot continue to confront the world as policemen.

THE WAR ON DRUGS IS TOO BENEFICIAL TO GIVE UP

As I have argued, the primary intent of the War on Drugs is not to stop drug trafficking or drug use. The War on Drugs is a tool in a larger war that is about increased authority and social control. William Bennett, the Drug Czar (or as some say, the Drug Bizarre), said himself that the issue was one of authority and control. The *Wall Street Journal* (12/29/89) echoed Bennett when it editorialized: "This nation is suffering a drug epidemic today because of the loosening of societal control in general." The real agenda, as the Drug Warriors have so plainly stated, is increased social control.

The *Wall Street Journal* editorial continued by arguing that the remedy to the drug epidemic should include maintaining and increasing the stigma of drug use. Drug users, it was reasoned, should be stigmatized more, not less, so that they may be controlled more effectively.

Both domestically and internationally, the War on Drugs has been used as a mechanism for vast expansions of state power and state control. This can be seen domestically in moves to allow warrantless searches, the introduction of illegally seized evidence, asset seizures, random drug testing, the militarization of housing projects, and the incarceration of pregnant women for drug use, among other measures. Internationally, it can be seen in a disdain for international law, increased use of the military in the drug war, assassinations, kidnapping, and invasions.

Because the War on Drugs functions as such an effective tool for the expansion of state power, is too useful to be given up, and I do not see legalization being seriously considered (much less coming about) in the near future.

Be that as it may, it is necessary that we continue arguing for legalization if for no other reason than to point out the hypocrisy of the administration's position and to unpack the lies that are being used to justify this expansion of state power.

THE HOLES IN THE LEGALIZATION ARGUMENT

There are, as I see it, a number of serious holes within the legalization argument, and these holes have been and continue to be used to discredit the legalization movement. Briefly, I see three major holes in the legalization argument that must be addressed. First, the legalization of drugs will not solve the fundamental social problems that exist in this society or the fundamental problems that exist in relation to the Third World. Second, legalization cannot be perceived as, and cannot afford to be, a middle-class movement. Third, most of those in the legalization movement are not considering carefully the terms of any legalization deal that may eventually be offered.

Legalization Must Be Accompanied by a Call for Social Justice

The legalization of drugs will not solve the fundamental social problems that exist in this society or the fundamental problems that exist in relation to the Third World. Therefore, those of us arguing for legalization must constantly stress that even though legalization will alleviate some of the social problems we are now experiencing, the fundamental problems of social and economic inequality and injustice will remain after legalization. Calls for legalization therefore must include a call for fundamental social and economic change—a call for social justice.

The road forward must include measures to decrease social and economic inequality and a serious consideration of the quality of life in a society characterized by rampant drug abuse, both legal and illegal. Doing something about social and economic injustice means more than making speeches about a "kinder and gentler" America, (or a kinder and gentler Panamanian Defense Forces, for that matter), or photo-ops in housing projects, or token social programs.

George Bush received praise for proposing to add $500 million to the budget for Head Start in 1990, the largest budget increase in the program's history. But one-year preschool programs for impoverished children will not solve the problems of inequality, of poverty. They will not even solve the problems of a few Head Start children. Several studies have indicated that the gains children make in such programs do not last throughout their school careers. Part of the reason for this includes other problems such as the dismal quality of schools Head Start children eventually attend, family disintegration, and the disintegration of neighborhoods due to the economic and social policies of the past decade (Chira, 1/14/90).

Legalization of drugs would decrease many of the problems we now see in the inner cities—the violence of competition for turf, uncontrolled dosages of drugs, uncontrolled prices, organized crime involvement— but it would not eliminate the problems of poverty, unemployment, underemployment, and despair, all of which are associated with crime.

The Legalization Movement Must Take into Consideration the Concerns of the Black and Hispanic Communities

Legalization cannot be perceived as, and cannot afford to be, a middle-class movement. Legalization is (or should be) a human rights issue, an issue of the right of people to determine their own lives. Legalization cannot be a movement focused on decriminalizing the drugs of preference of the middle class while condemning the users and sellers of other drugs to harsher and harsher police control, surveillance, and punishment. The legalization movement must be a movement for the legalization of all drugs, not just soft end drugs like marijuana.

Another hole in the legalization argument, which has been seized on recently by the right, lies in its failure to draw the black and Hispanic communities into the movement and the movement's failure to adequately speak to the concerns of these communities. Some leaders in the black community have joined in charges that legalization is a frivolous issue discussed by intellectuals at cocktail parties. Some have gone as far as charging that legalization would be a form of genocide.

I respectfully submit the following reasons why this unholy alliance over the drug issue between some segments of the black community and the likes of Orin Hatch and William Bennett has come about.

First, some segments of the legalization movement feed the charge of class-based advocacy by working for the legalization of some drugs off the backs of other types of drugs; they argue that the drug they want to legalize is safe, unlike all the rest of the "dangerous" drugs that should remain illegal. This leaves the impression (perhaps not false) that the middle class essentially is seeking to decriminalize its drugs of choice while abandoning the users and sellers of other drugs. The *Wall Street Journal* expressed this argument forcefully in an article about decriminalization (12/29/89): "The unspoken thought behind many of the calls for surrender is that the middle classes can take care of themselves and the ghettos are hopeless."

Second, after a decade of social service cuts and neglect of marginalized groups, the situation of despair and hopelessness, anger, and alienation in the inner cities is so great that any attempt at any solution (especially to the violence that is associated with illegal drug trafficking) is welcomed. This is why we see residents of housing projects inviting the National Guard into their neighborhoods. In addition, the drugs that are the cheapest at the moment are also the most damaging; and the black and Hispanic communities are seeing a destruction of their members that is even more serious than that traditionally experienced as the result of racism and discrimination.

Third, administration propaganda has influenced the black and Hispanic communities as well as the general population. Because of this, the problems in inner-city neighborhoods are seen by many not as primarily problems of social and economic injustice or problems caused by the illegality of drugs but as problems caused by the drugs themselves. This is the case even though much of the violence that is associated with drugs is violence over turf and violence that is always associated with the control of an illegal work force; it is not violence committed by those solely under the influence of drugs.

The fourth major reason for this unholy alliance over the drug issue, I would suggest, is political exhaustion. The black community fought a heroic struggle in the 1960s only to see many of the gains they had fought for, and indeed died for, eroded. The prospect of once again taking on the real enemy, the state, is more threatening than fighting the drug dealers. The drug dealers are on the street; George Bush, Ronald Reagan, and the Supreme Court are not.

The legalization movement is not effectively taking on the issues of social and economic exploitation of the marginalized segments of the populace that are related to the legalization issue, and consequently the movement is not receiving the support it should from these segments of society. This fact leaves the legalization movement open to charges of triviality. In an editorial at the end of 1989, the *Wall Street Journal* stated that "these otherwise illustrious citizens are essentially frivolous in their advocacy" (12/29/89).

Legalization Must Not be Accepted at Any Cost

Those in the legalization movement must consider carefully the terms of any legalization deal that may eventually be offered. For example, we cannot and must not accept the legalization of drugs at the cost of even greater erosions of civil and constitutional guarantees. And this is the outline of any legalization deal I can envision, given the present political context.

The establishment of the prison system holds a great many lessons that should be heeded by the legalization movement. The prison system was established by reformers, people who wanted to leave behind the barbarity of corporal punishment. However laudable their intentions, their efforts brought about unintended consequences—the establishment of an even more coercive and insidious form of social control. The reforms that eventually led to the establishment of the prison system were not designed to punish less, but to punish more effectively. What is likely to happen with the legalization of drugs is similar, only worse. The measures currently being proposed and implemented seem to be designed to both punish more and punish more effectively. The present trend in the criminal justice system and in the society in general is a bifurcation of the population—a dividing of the population into manageable, tractable individuals on the one hand and "social dynamite" or "social junk" on the other. The social dynamite will be increasingly repressed and social junk will be increasingly abandoned, and the repression and the abandonment will be justified by drugs.

One of the real dangers of the decriminalization movement is that advocates, in their zeal for decriminalization, will be willing to accept decriminalization at any cost—the further erosion of civil and constitutional guarantees, the abandonment and destruction of marginalized populations, the acceptance of increased state surveillance and control.

An increasing part of the drug war rhetoric is this bifurcation of the population—the innocent and the guilty, the law-abiding citizen and the criminal, us and them. It is a dangerous trend that can lead to the demonizing of a whole segment of the population and a consequent license to take any measure desired to deal with them.

POLITICAL AWARENESS

It is evident that we have a severe problem with political awareness in this country, a disturbing problem of a populace that seems increasingly willing to accept easy answers to complex problems. In a *Washington Post* poll conducted at the end of 1989, less than half of the adults interviewed were aware of the fact that the government's role in the Iran Contra affair had been to sell arms to Iran and divert part of the proceeds to the Contras. Twenty-eight percent thought that it was the reverse—that the government sold arms to the Contras and diverted money to Iran. In comparison, in the same poll, 75 percent of adults could name a football team that had played in the Superbowl in the 1980s (Morin, 1/1/90). Tom Wicker, writing in the *New York Times*, asserted: "Nothing so damages government credibility and public trust as the exposed lie of a formerly trusted leader" (Wicker, 10/10/89). But, as was clearly demonstrated by the Iran Contra affair, this is obviously not true. Perhaps this is because there are no trusted leaders anymore, former or otherwise, or because the population in general seems not to know or care that a lie has been exposed.

This is not a culture that encourages intellectual activity or communicates the joy of a conflict in ideas. Robert W. Pittman, the creator of MTV, has noted that in developing the cable network he and others were merely capitalizing on a profound difference between how younger people receive and process information and how the pre-TV generation did. He has argued that the "TV babies" do many things at once—watch TV, do their homework, talk on the telephone (Pittman, 1/24/90). Although he has argued that this is characteristic of the TV babies, it is increasingly characteristic of the population as a whole. The pace of life has increased to such an extent that people want information quickly and in the least complicated form possible. This may be why Ronald Reagan was considered "the great communicator."

Increasingly, people want images; people communicate not through discourse but through images. There is a kind of impatience with discourse, with anything that cannot be absorbed immediately with the least amount of work possible. MTV and politicians are well aware of this. It has become apparent that one image of Willie Horton is worth fifty well-reasoned arguments. This also explains the media frustration with Jimmy Carter, who insulted the country by holding to the notion that the world was a complicated place, by failing to reduce every issue to black and white, the good guys and the bad.

The right has become very adept at capitalizing on this tendency. It has, for example, attempted to reduce the legalization argument to several images—professors at cocktail parties, surrender, crack babies, distributing "crack in the Pablum," and "putting heroin in milk," to mention but a few.

The legalization movement has a great deal of work to do. It must refine its arguments, close the holes, create its own images, and embark on an endeavor of aggressive education. Most important, however, the legalization movement must develop a political coherence that will give its arguments increased credibility in what has become a desperate struggle for the hegemony of ideas.

REFERENCES

ABC Nightly News. (9/4/90).

Alabama Journal. (12/18/89a). Family Reburies Body of Medellín Cartel Leader:5A.

———. (12/18/89b). 4 Million Transportation Employees Face Prospect of Random Drug Tests:2B.

American Bar Association. (1988). Criminal Justice in Crisis. Washington, D.C.: American Bar Association.

American Civil Liberties Union. (1989). Letter. New York.

Anchorage Daily News. (4/11/89a). Mexico Arrests Top Drug Dealer in Crackdown:15.

———. (4/11/89b). Undercover Sting Nets Ex-Officer:10.

Anderson, John W., and Nancy Lewis. (10/16/87). D.C. Police Allegedly Protected Drug Dealers. *Washington Post*:15.

Applebome, Peter. (4/17/89). On North-South Line, Violence Grows. *New York Times*:5.

———. (12/14/89). Drugs in Atlanta: A Lost Generation. *New York Times*:16.

Atlanta Journal Constitution. (1/28/90). More Prisons Won't Make Us Safer:G6.

———. (3/19/90). U.S. a Leader in Death Risk for Children:A3.

———. (8/11/90). Atlantan among 19 Indicted in Cocaine Ring:A5.

Bair, Jeffrey. (6/13/90). Middle Managers Suffer High-Level Depression. *Montgomery Advertiser*:1E.

Ball, Karen. (2/4/90). "Discouraged Workers" Part of Unemployment. *Montgomery Advertiser*:5A.

Balz, Dan. (2/26–3/4/90). A New Arena for the Abortion Debate. *Washington Post National Weekly Edition*:13.

Barden, J. C. (2/5/90). Toll of Troubled Families: Flood of Homeless Youths. *New York Times*:1.

———. (4/16/90). Poverty Rate Is Up Sharply for Very Young, Study Says. *New York Times*:A7.

Barrett, Paul M. (11/30/89). Drug Czar Bennett, Once Supreme in His Realm, Is Himself in Revolt over Obstacles in His Path. *Wall Street Journal*:A16.

————. (12/14/89). Other Agencies Say No Soap to Treasury's Push for High-Tech Tracking of Money Laundering. *Wall Street Journal*:A24.

————. (1/30/90). Bush Budget Seeks Reduction of 4% in FBI Agent Staff. *Wall Street Journal*:B11.

————. (1/31/90). Program to Prosecute the Casual Drug User Is Casting Wider Net. *Wall Street Journal*:1.

————. (2/9/90). Senate Panel Says Treasury Has Failed to Curb Non-Bank Money Laundering. *Wall Street Journal*:A12.

————. (5/16/90). Ninety Accounts Thought to Hold Illegal Drug Funds. *Wall Street Journal*:A12.

Barrett, Paul M., and Martha Brannigan. (4/3/90). House Panel Says FBI Manpower Isn't Enough for S&L Fraud Cases. *Wall Street Journal*:B8.

Barrett, Paul M., and Wade Lambert. (4/30/90). Justice Department Withdraws Support on Sentencing. *Wall Street Journal*:B5.

Barrett, Paul M., and Stephen Wermiel. (5/14/90). Thornburgh Suffers One More Setback: Aide Quits after Dispute on Sentencing. *Wall Street Journal*:A5A.

Bartlett, Sarah. (6/10/90). Getting a Mental Grip on the Dimensions of the Savings Disaster. *New York Times*:1E.

Beale, Sara Sun. (2/8/90). Get Drug Cases Out of Federal Courts. *Wall Street Journal*:A16.

Beaty, Jonathan. (8/21/89). Do Humans Need to Get High? *Time*:58.

Beck, Melinda, Ann McDaniel, Patricia King, and Lynda Wright. (3/13/89). We Need Drastic Measures. *Newsweek*:50.

Belkin, Lisa. (12/10/89). Houston Police Department in New Turmoil. *New York Times*:20.

————. (3/20/90). Airport Anti-Drug Nets Snare Many People Fitting "Profiles." *New York Times*:1.

Bell, Derrick. (1/14/90). Stuart's Lie: An American Tradition. *New York Times*:23.

Belsie, Laurent. (8/1/90). Concern Grows over Heroin Use. *Christian Science Monitor*:6.

Bensinger, Peter B. (4/19/90). Fighting Drugs Won't Abuse Workers. *USA Today*:12A.

Berke, Richard L. (3/18/89). Anti-Drug Steps Imposed on U.S. Contractors. *New York Times*:1.

————. (4/7/89). Capital's War on Drugs. *New York Times*:1.

————. (4/14/89). Foreign Policy Said to Hinder Drug War. *New York Times*:14.

————. (6/9/89). U.S. Attack on Airborne Drug Smuggling Called Ineffective. *New York Times*:A10.

————. (9/6/89). New Stress on Old Ideas. *New York Times*:1A.

————. (9/12/89). Poll Finds Many in U.S. Back Bush Strategy. *New York Times*:A8.

————. (10/20/89). Reality Intrudes on Drug Crusade in Capital. *New York Times*:1.

————. (12/17/89). Corruption in Drug Agency Called Crippler of Inquiries and Morale. *New York Times*:1A.

————. (1/25/90). Bush to Seek $1.2 Billion for a Bigger Drug War. *New York Times*:A12.

————. (2/3/90). Bennett Doubts Value of Drug Education. *New York Times*:1.

————. (2/18/90). Drugs: Has the Tide Changed, or Only the Spin? *New York Times*:5E.

Bishop, Jerry E. (12/28/89). Cocaine: A Puckish Science. *Wall Street Journal*:A7.

Bishop, Katherine. (6/8/90). Mandatory Sentences in Drug Cases: Is the Law Defeating Its Purpose? *New York Times*:B10.

————. (8/10/90). Military Takes Part in Drug Sweep and Reaps Criticism and a Lawsuit. *New York Times*:A11.

Black, George. (1988). *The Good Neighbor: How the United States Wrote the History of Central America and the Caribbean*. New York: Pantheon Books.

Blair, William G. (11/21/88). Jury in the Bronx Acquits Larry Davis of Attempted Murder in a Police Raid. *New York Times*:1.

Bleifuss, Joel. (5/8–/14/91). You Can Run But You Can't Hide. *In These Times*:4.

Blood, Michael. (11/15/89). Pa. Tightens Abortion Restrictions. *New York Times*:1A.

Bodenheimer, Thomas, and Robert Gould. (1989). *Rollback! Right-Wing Power in U.S. Foreign Policy*. Boston: South End Press.

Bourne, Peter. (3/25/88). U.S. Schizophrenia on Drug Runners. *New York Times*:39.

Branigin, William. (2/26/88). Mexico Cracks Major Arms, Drug Trafficking Ring. *Washington Post*:E16.

Brooke, James. (4/6/89). Colombia Drug Cartels Tied to Terror in Rights Report. *New York Times*:1.

————. (1/14/90). Peruvian Still Outraged by Invasion of Panama. *New York Times*:11.

————. (12/18/90). Drug Peace Pact in Colombia Would Spare the Traffickers. *New York Times*:1.

————. (12/24/90). Was the Beautiful Agent Cartel Spy? *New York Times*:10.

————. (1/9/91). Colombia's Tortured City. *New York Times*:A8.

————. (1/28/91). Colombian Kidnappings Are Gagging the Press. *New York Times*:A2.

Brown, Cynthia (Ed.). (1985). *With Friends Like These: The Americas Watch Report on Human Rights and U.S. Policy in Latin America*. New York: Pantheon Books.

Browne, Malcolm W. (10/24/89). Problems Loom in Effort to Control Use of Chemicals for Illicit Drugs. *New York Times*:17.

Burtless, Gary. (1/4/90). Are We All Working Too Hard? *Wall Street Journal*:A12.

Byrd, Robert. (4/13/90). Study: 7.5 Percent of Mothers Used Drugs Shortly before Birth. *Montgomery Advertiser*:A1.

————. (8/3/90). 24 Percent of Infants Born to Single Women. *Montgomery Advertiser*:1.

Chavkin, Wendy. (7/18/89). Help, Don't Jail, Addicted Mothers. *New York Times*:15A.

Chira, Susan. (1/14/90). Preschool Aid for the Poor: How Big a Head Start? *New York Times*:1.

Chomsky, Noam. (1/29/90). The Dawn, So Far, Is in the East. *The Nation*:130–133.

Christian Science Monitor. (7/2/90). New Currents:2.

————. (7/9/90). U.S. Military Said To Be Planning Drug Strike:9.

————. (7/24/90). Latin America:2.

————. (9/7/90). Progress Cited in War on Drugs:7.

————. (1/10/91). Latin America Democracy:18.

Cockburn, Alexander. (6/26/89). Beat the Devil. The Nation:45.

————. (7/30–8/6/90). Beat the Devil. The Nation:118.

Cockburn, Leslie. (1987). Out of Control. New York: Atlantic Monthly Press.

Cohn, Victor. (8/13–/19/90). Rationing Our Medical Care. Washington Post National Weekly Edition:11.

Cole, David. (1/20/90). Why Noriega Can't Get a Fair Trial. New York Times:19.

Collett, Merrill. (4/11/88). Colombia's Drug Cartel Said to Aim at Military. Washington Post:E15.

Congressional Quarterly. (1988). October 20.

Corn, David. (5/14/90). Justice's War on Drug Treatment. The Nation:659–662.

Corn, David, and Jefferson Morley. (4/17/89a). CIA for the Defense. The Nation:559.

————. (4/17/89b). Winners and Losers in Drug Capitalism. The Nation:558.

Criminal Justice Newsletter. (12/15/88). Defendants' Rights Not a Great Bar to Prosecution, Panel Finds.

————. (3/1/89). Bush Budget for Justice Department an Increase over Reagan's.

————. (3/15/89). Survey Shows Declining Rate of Drug Use by High School Seniors.

————. (7/3/89). Courts: Preventive Detention Sometimes Lasts Years, Senate Panel Told.

Crittenden, Ann. (12/29/89). Prison Can Be a Dumb Solution. New York Times:29A.

Currie, Elliott. (1985). Confronting Crime. New York: Pantheon Books.

Cushman, John H., Jr. (2/7/90). Truck Deaths Linked to Alcohol or Drugs. New York Times:A11.

Data Clearinghouse for Drugs and Crime. (May 1989). Telephone interview with analyst.

Davis, Debra. (6/7/91). War Machines Now Help Fight Illegal Drug Activity. Montgomery Advertiser:2C.

Decker, Scott H., and Barbara Salert. (1987). Selective Incapacitation: A Note on Its Impact on Minorities. Journal of Criminal Justice, 15:287–299.

del Olmo, Rosa. (1987). Aerobiology and the War on Drugs: A Transnational Crime. Social Justice, No. 30:28–44.

DeParle, Jason. (10/29/90). Talk Grows of Government Being Out to Get Blacks. New York Times:C10.

Deutsch, Linda. (8/11/90). Government Illegally Kidnapped Mexican Doctor, Federal Judge Rules. Montgomery Advertiser:1.

Diskin, Marton, and Kenneth E. Sharpe. (1986). El Salvador. In Morris J. Blackman, William M. LeoGrande, and Kenneth E. Sharpe, eds., Confronting Revolution: Security through Diplomacy in Central America. New York: Pantheon Books.

Dixler, Elsa. (5/15/89). Just Who Is This We? The Nation:650, 678–679.

Dorris, Michael. (6/25/90). A Desperate Crack Legacy. Newsweek:8.

Downey, Thomas J., and George Miller. (7/10/90). Ten Years Later: Foster Care, Again. Christian Science Monitor:18.

Drug Policy Foundation. (1989). Mr. Bush and the 1988 Anti-Drug Abuse Act. *Drug Policy Letter*, 1, 1.

Duston, Diane. (6/1/90). Smoking Will Kill Five Million Youths, Surgeon General Says. *Montgomery Advertiser*:4A.

Earle, Joe, and Betsy White. (9/27/89). Area Teens Not Surprised Drug Use Higher. *Atlanta Journal Constitution*:1A.

Eddy, Paul, Hugo Sabogal, and Sara Walden. (1988). *The Cocaine Wars*. New York: W. W. Norton and Company.

Efron, Sonni. (2/1/89). Bahamas: Indictments Are Political. *Anchorage Daily News*:1.

Eitzen, D. Stanley, and Doug A. Timmer. (1985). *Criminology: Crime and Criminal Justice*. New York: John Wiley.

Elias, Marilyn. (5/3/90). Crack Causes Brain Seizures in Some Teens. *USA Today*:D1.

Engelberg, Stephen. (3/6/89). Antidrug Effort Floundering, Former Cocaine Dealer Says. *New York Times*:1.

———. (1/9/90). In Search of Missions to Justify Outlays. *New York Times*:6.

Epstein, Edward Jay. (1977). *Agency of Fear: Opiates and Political Power in America*. New York: Putnam's.

Epstein, Gail. (9/8/89). Drug Suspect Implicated in Kidnap Threat. *Atlanta Journal and Constitution*:1A.

Fagan, Richard R. (1987). *Forging Peace: The Challenge of Central America*. New York: Basil Blackwell.

Fairbanks Daily News. (12/18/88). Palmer Mother Indicted for Endangering Unborn:A1.

Farnsworth, Clyde H. (1/9/90). U.S. Falls Short on Its Debt Plan for Third World. *New York Times*:1.

———. (6/15/90). Congress Voices Concern over Trade Pact with Mexico. *New York Times*:C2.

Feinberg, Richard E., and Bruce M. Bagley. (1986). *Development Postponed: The Political Economy of Central America in the 1980s*. Boulder, Colo: Westview.

Fialka, John J. (3/1/90). How a Big Drug Cartel Laundered $1.2 Billion with Aid of U.S. Firms. *Wall Street Journal*:1.

Foss, Shelton. (2/20/90). New Trial for Sims Ruled Out. *Montgomery Advertiser*:3A.

Foster, Catherine. (6/13/90). Sullivan Calls for Action on Smoking, Crack Babies. *Christian Science Monitor*:9.

———. (6/19/90). Major Change in U.S. System Urged. *Christian Science Monitor*:8.

Fowler, Elizabeth M. (9/12/89). Careers: More Stress Found in the Workplace. *New York Times*:46.

Freemantle, Brian. (1986). *The Fix*. New York: Tom Doherty Associates.

Freudenheim, Milt. (1/3/90). Booming Business: Drug Use Tests. *New York Times*:23.

Friedman, Thomas L. (12/18/89). U.S. Assails Shooting of Officer in Panama and Hints at Military Response. *New York Times*:6.

———. (12/31/89). Bush Says Troops Erred in Searches of Home of Envoy. *New York Times*:1.

Garcia, Rodolfo. (1/3/90). Nicaraguan Troops Surround Embassy. *Montgomery Advertiser*:A4.

Gemini News Service. (1990). London. Excerpted in *World Press Review* (June 1990):6.

Gerber, Jurg, Eric L. Jensen, Myron Schreck, and Ginna M. Babcock. (1990). Drug Testing and Social Control: Implications for State Theory. *Contemporary Crisis, 14*: 243–258.

Gerharz, George. (1/29/90). Wisconsin's Learnfare: A Bust. *New York Times*:A19.

Gerth, Jeff. (5/6/90). Israeli Arms, Ticketed to Antigua, End Up in Colombia Drug Arsenal. *New York Times*:1.

———. (6/13/90). Management Woes Hobble U.S. Air Fleet in Drug War. *New York Times*:1.

Gest, Ted. (12/23/85). Using Drugs? You May Not Get Hired. *U.S. News and World Report*:45.

Gibbs, Nancy. (4/24/89). How America Has Run Out of Time. *Time*:58–67.

Gimbel, Michael M. (12/29/89). Boot Camps Are Creative Way to Reach Nation's Drug Addicts. *Montgomery Advertiser*:13A.

Gladwell, Malcolm. (6/1/88). Plan to Curb Drug Trade in Peru Set Back. *Washington Post*:A15.

Goldberg, Fred T., Jr. (3/13/90). IRS Needs to Know Who's Paying in Cash. *USA Today*:10A.

Goldstein, Paul J., Henry H. Brownstein, Patrick J. Ryan, and Patricia A. Bellucci. (1989). Crack and Homicide in New York City, 1988: A Conceptually Based Event Analysis. Unpublished manuscript.

Goleman, Daniel. (9/21/89). Pushing Toddlers in Preschool May Be Pointless. *New York Times*:15.

Gorman, Peter. (12/30/90). Marijuana McCarthyism. *New York Times*:15.

Gottfredson, S. D. (1985). Predication. In D. Gottfredson and M. Tonry, eds., *Crime and Justice: An Annual Review of Research*. Chicago: University of Chicago Press.

Gottfredson, S. D., and D. M. Gottfredson. (1984). Accuracy of Prediction Models. Paper presented to the National Academy of Sciences Center, July.

Greenhouse, Linda. (4/18/89). Court to Decide on Foreign Searches. *New York Times*:10A.

———. (5/17/89). Abortion for Florida Teen-Ager Blocked by Supreme Court. *New York Times*:7A.

———. (9/22/89). Judicial Panel Urges Limit on Death Row Appeals. *New York Times*:13.

———. (1/1/90). Chief Justice Makes Plea for More Federal Judgeships. *New York Times*:8.

———. (3/1/90). Justices Back Property Searches of Foreigners in Foreign Nations. *New York Times*:1.

———. (3/11/90). The Court Cuts Off Another Exit from Death Row. *New York Times*:5E.

———. (5/16/90). Rehnquist Urges Curb on Appeals of Death Penalty. *New York Times*:1.

————. (4/25/91). Thornburgh Goes to Court on Death Penalty Precedents. *New York Times*:A12.

Gross, Jane. (2/10/90). Drug-Shooting Casualty Inspires a City to Resist. *New York Times*:8.

Hackel, Joy, and Daniel Siegel. (1987). *In Contempt of Congress: The Reagan Record on Central America*. Washington, D.C.: Institute for Policy Studies.

Hamm, Mark S. (1988). Drug Policy and Applied Research: A Study of Users, Abusers and Politicians. *Journal of Crime and Justice*, 11(2):103–121.

Harper, Sam. (1/17/90). Mayor, Police Chief to Target Youthful Offenders. *Montgomery Advertiser*:1C.

————. (2/18/90). Agents Take Dangerous Forays in Effort to Eradicate Marijuana. *Montgomery Advertiser*:B1.

Hayeslip, David W. (1990). Methodological Issues in Defining the Public Housing Drug Trafficking Problem and What to Do about It. Paper presented at the annual meeting of the American Society of Criminology, November.

Helmer, John. (1975). *Drugs and Minority Oppression*. New York: Seabury Press.

Henry, Tamara. (1/22/90). College Freshmen Say No to Drugs. *Montgomery Advertiser*:9A.

————. (9/2/90). First Big Wave of Youngsters. *Mongtomery Advertiser*:1B.

Herman, Edward S. (1987). U.S. Sponsorship of International Terrorism: An Overview. *Crime and Social Justice*, Nos. 27–28:1–31.

————. (11/89). The War on Drugs? *Z Magazine*:19–20.

Herring, Amy. (1/25/90). Panels OK 14 of Hunt's Drug Bills. *Montgomery Advertiser*:3A.

Hey, Robert P. (6/29/90). Rate of Abuse Hits Emergency Level. *Christian Science Monitor*:6.

————. (7/9/90). Tentacles of S&L Mess Reach to Other Issues. *Christian Science Monitor*:1.

————. (7/13/90). U.S. Scrambles to Continue Funds for Key U.S. Food Subsidy Program. *Christian Science Monitor*:7.

Hills, Stuart (Ed.). (1987). *Corporate Violence: Injury and Death for Profit*. Totowa, N.J.: Rowman and Littlefield.

Hilts, Phillip. (9/19/90). Treatment Helps Addicts Avoid AIDS. *New York Times*:16A.

Hilts, Philip J. (5/18/90). Health Department Backs Away on Criticism of Tobacco Exports. *New York Times*:1.

Hinds, Michael deCourcy. (7/18/90). Number of Killings Soars in Big Cities across the U.S. *New York Times*:A10.

Hobsbawm, Eric. (11/20/86). Murderous Colombia. *New York Review of Books*, 33:27–30,35.

Hockstader, Lee, and Joanne Omang. (12/31/89). U.S. Officials' Accounts Are Contradictory. *Washington Post*:1A.

Hoffman, Jan. (8/19/90). Pregnant, Addicted—and Guilty? *New York Times Magazine*:33.

Holmes, Steven A. (1/21/90). Fewer Turf Battles, More Drug Arrests. *New York Times*:22E.

————. (1/24/90). A Dealer Finds Many Eager to Launder His Drug Money. *New York Times*:1.

Holts, Philip J. (9/19/90). Few Get Treatments That Help Addicts Avoid AIDS. *New York Times*:A12.

Huggins, Martha K. (1987). U.S. Supported State Terror: A History of Police Training in Latin America. *Crime and Social Justice*, Nos. 27–28:149–171.

Hunnicutt, Benjamin K. (1/4/90). Are We All Work: No Time for God or Family. *Wall Street Journal*:A12.

Ingram, Ragan. (5/23/90). Grand Jury Indicts State Employee. *Montgomery Advertiser*:F1.

In These Times. (9/19–/25/90a). If You Can't Beat 'Em, Shoot 'Em:6.

———. (9/19–/25/90b). Kristolschlock:15.

Isikoff, Michael. (6/8/88). Federal Aid May Be Lever in Drug War. *Washington Post*:1.

———. (6/5–/11/89). The Losing Battle to Stem the Tide of Cocaine. *Washington Post National Weekly Edition*:31.

———. (11/6–/12/89). Drafting Banks into the War on Drugs. *Washington Post National Weekly Edition*:33.

———. (1/14–/20/90). Florida's Crackdown on Crime Is Setting Criminals Free. *Washington Post National Weekly Edition*:31.

———. (2/19–/25/90). Youths Deal a Snub to Drugs. *Washington Post National Weekly Edition*:19.

Isikoff, Michael, and Tracy Thompson. (11/4/90). Getting Too Tough on Drugs: Draconian Sentences Hurt Small Offenders More Than Kingpins. *Washington Post*:C1.

Jacobs, James B., and Lynn Zimmer. (1991). Drug Treatment and Workplace Drug Testing: Politics, Symbolism and Organizational Dilemmas. Draft of manuscript to appear in *Behavioral Sciences and the Law*, 9, 3.

Jacoby, Tamar. (11/14/88). Drug Testing in the Dock. *Newsweek*:66.

Johns, Richard, and Robert Graham. (1990). Drawing Closer to Mexico. From *Financial Times of London*, excerpted in *World Press Review*, (August 1990):58–59.

Johnson, Dirk. (6/17/90). Road Checks: Where the Police Put Drunken Drivers to the Test. *New York Times*:1.

———. (11/1/90). More Prisons Using Iron Hand to Control Inmates. *New York Times*:A8.

Johnson, Julie. (12/13/89). Dinkins, in Senate, Tells of Drug Toll. *New York Times*:16.

Jordan, Mary. (2/26/88). New Anti-Drug Efforts Needed, Officials Say. *Washington Post*:29.

Kadish, S. H. (1971). Overcriminalization. In L. Radzinowicz and M. E. Wolfang, eds., *Crime and Justice*, vol. 1, The Criminal and Society:56–71. New York: Basic Books.

Kamen, Al. (7/10–/16/89). The Reagan Revolution Takes a Seat at the Supreme Court. *Washington Post National Weekly Edition*:31.

Karel, Richard. (1990). News Briefs. *National Drug Strategy Network*:1.

Katz, Jack. (6/5–/11/89). No Way to Fight Street Crime. *Washington Post National Weekly Edition*:29.

Kawell, Jo Ann. (10/25–/31/89). Sending in Army Could Drag U.S. into Morass. *In These Times*:11.

Keen, Judy. (4/16/90). Study: Bill Falls Due for Poor Kids. *USA Today*:3A.

Kelley, Jack. (5/15/90). Hospital Cocaine Cases Drop Sharply. *USA Today*:1.

———. (5/17/90). Drug Tactics Raise Rights Fears. *USA Today*:3A.

———. (7/17/90). Trend Shift Has Agents Wondering. *USA Today*:3A.

Kelley, Jack, and Sam Meddis. (5/3/90). $150M Sought for Drug War Gadgetry. *USA Today*:3A.

Kerr, Peter. (4/17/88). Bolivia with U.S. Aid. *New York Times*:14.

Kidder, Rushworth M. (9/21/89). America Needs a "Fix" For Its Values. *Atlanta Journal Constitution*:A4.

Kifner, John. (9/8/89). Bush's Drug Plan: Scorn on Besieged Streets. *New York Times*:1A.

Kiley, Robert R. (2/17/90). The Homeless Are Dying in the Subway. *New York Times*:17.

King, Patricia. (2/19/90). The City as Patient. *Newsweek*:58–59.

Klare, Michael T. (1/1/90). Fighting Drugs with the Military. *The Nation*:8.

Knickerbocker, Brad. (8/27/90). Military Drafted in Effort to Find, Eradicate American 'Pot' Growers. *Christian Science Monitor*:7.

Kolata, Gina. (7/20/90). Racial Bias Seen in Prosecuting Pregnant Addicts. *New York Times*:A10.

Krauss, Clifford. (9/25/90). Salvadoran Chief, in U.S., Vows to Solve Jesuit Case. *New York Times*:3A.

Kristol, Irving. (3/28/88). *Washington Post*:24.

Kwitny, Jonathan. (9/10/90). The Mafia in the S&L's? *New York Times*:A15.

Labaton, Stephen. (9/25/89). Unassuming Storefronts Believed to Launder Drug Dealers' Profits. *New York Times*:1.

———. (12/6/89).The Cost of Drug Abuse: $60 Billion a Year. *New York Times*:27.

———. (12/29/89). New Tactics in the War on Drugs Tilt Scales of Justice Off Balance. *New York Times*:1.

———. (6/19/90). Glutted Probation System Puts Communities in Peril. *New York Times*:1.

LaCroix, Susan. (5/1/89). Jailing Mothers for Drug Abuse. *The Nation*:585–588.

Lait, Matt. (4/17/88). California's New Role: Leading PCP Supplier. *Washington Post*:26.

Langer, Gary. (10/2/89). Poll: Few Back Bush Drug Policy. *Montgomery Advertiser*:1A.

Lawlor, Julia. (7/25/90). Unions Attack High Cost of Health Care. *USA Today*:1.

Leary, Warren E. (1/24/90). Generic Drug Recalled after Questions on Data. *New York Times*:2D.

———. (6/9/90). Bloomy Report on Teen-Ager's Health. *New York Times*:8A.

Lernoux, Penny. (2/13/89). Playing Golf While Drugs Flow. *The Nation*:188–192.

Lewin, Tamar. (1/9/89). When Courts Take Charge of the Unborn. *New York Times*:1.

———. (2/10/90). Johns Hopkins to Institute Drug Tests on Its Physicians. *New York Times*:8.

———. (9/13/90). Drug-Testing Kit for Parents Spurs Stormy Debate. *New York Times*:12A.

Lewis, Anthony. (4/13/90). Time for Change. *New York Times*:A15.

Lewis, Neil A. (12/29/89). U.S. to Use the Military to Cut Latin Drug Routes. *New York Times*:14.

———. (1/10/90). Scholars Say the Arrest of Noriega Had Little Legal Justification. *New York Times*:8.

———. (1/30/90). Experts Fault Strategy of Noriega as "P.O.W." *New York Times*:A9.

———. (2/9/90). Drug Lawyers' Quandary: Lure of Money vs. Ethics. *New York Times*:1.

———. (6/25/90). Court Bars H.U.D. Plan to Evict Drug Dealers. *New York Times*:A10.

———. (2/24/91). How Drugs Launched, and Then Destroyed, Career of a Thornburgh Aide. *New York Times*:15.

Lewis, Pat. (5/29/90). Officials: Just Saying No Won't Work. *Montgomery Advertiser*:1.

Lewis, Paul. (2/21/90). Drugs Pit Baker vs. Third World at U.N. *New York Times*:A3.

———. (10/11/90). Security Council Shuns a Fight against Drugs. *New York Times*:4.

Lipman, Joanne. (2/23/90). Lumping Alcohol into Drug War Isn't Idea Industry's Warming To. *Wall Street Journal*:B5.

McAllister, Bill. (4/25/88). Meese Asks Drug Testing for 'Most' Workers. *Washington Post*:1.

McCartney, Tracey, and John Gerome. (2/15/90). Sting Ends in Officers' Resignations. *Montgomery Advertiser*:1.

MacDonald, Scott B. (1988). *Dancing on a Volcano: The Latin American Drug Trade*. New York: Praeger.

McFarren, Peter. (5/19/91). South America's Health Problems Larger Than Cholera Epidemic. *Montgomery Advertiser*:11A.

McGinley, Laurie. (5/16/90). Attacks against Air Terrorists Urged by Panel. *Wall Street Journal*:A3.

MacNeil/Lehrer Newshour. (4/17/89). National Public Broadcasting.

McWilliams, John C. (1989). The Futility of the War on Drugs: "Deja Vu." Paper presented at the American Society of Criminology Conference, Reno, Nevada.

Magnuson, Ed. (1/22/90). More and More, a Real War. *Time*:22.

Mahan, Sue, and Julie Howkins. (1990). Cocaine Mothers and the Law. Paper presented at the annual meeting of the American Society of Criminology, Baltimore, Maryland.

Malcolm, Andrew H. (10/1/89). Crack, Bane of Inner City, Is Now Gripping Suburbs. *New York Times*:A1.

———. (11/19/89). In Making Drug Strategy, No Accord on Treatment. *New York Times*:1A.

———. (12/30/89). Explosive Drug Use in Prisons Is Creating a New Underworld. *New York Times*:1.

———. (12/31/89). More Americans Are Killing Each Other. *New York Times*:14.

———. (9/4/90). Many Police Forces Rearm to Counter Criminals' Guns. *New York Times*:A10.

Mann, Judy. (12/8/89). A Culture Made Sick by Drugs. *Washington Post*:B3.

Margasak, Larry. (4/20/91). GAO: Mismanagement of Seized Property Costly. *Montgomery Advertiser*:6A.

Marriott, Michel. (2/20/89). After 3 Years, Crack Plague in New York Grows Worse. *New York Times*.

———. (6/1/89). The 12 Worst Drug Bazaars: New York's Continuing Blight. *New York Times*:1A.

———. (1/10/90a). Drug Detection Methods Raise Pupil Rights Issues. *New York Times*:23.

———. (1/10/90b). For Addicts, A Long Scary Wait for Treatment. *New York Times*:1.

Martz, Larry. (2/19/90). A Dirty Drug Secret. *Newsweek*:74.

Meddis, Sam. (3/12/90). Cities Face "Hard-Core" Drug Cases. *USA Today*:1A.

Meier, Barry. (9/25/89). Police Using New Tests to Stop the Drugged Driver. *New York Times*:1.

Melman, Seymour. (5/20/91). Military State Capitalism. *The Nation*:1.

Mesce, Deborah. (1/14/91). Forced Use of New Contraceptive Raises Legal and Ethical Concerns. *Montgomery Advertiser*:3A.

Milloy, Courtland. (1/28/90). Wrong Way to Fight Drugs. *Washington Post*:D3.

Moffett, Matt. (5/14/90). Mexican Plan for Privatizing Banks Approved. *Wall Street Journal*:A10.

Mohr, Charles. (10/13/88). Senate Is Closer to Drug Bill Vote. *New York Times*:24.

———. (10/14/88). Penalty of Death Kept in Drug Bill. *New York Times*:23.

———. (10/30/88). Experts Say Impact of Drug Bill Remains Unclear. *New York Times*:25.

Montgomery Advertiser. (9/7/89). Troops' Role in Drug War Criticized:10A.

———. (11/15/89). Bill Requires Treatment for New Drug Offenders:3C.

———. (12/6/89), Teacher Cleared Files Lawsuit over Lost Job:5A.

———. (12/29/89). Former Policeman Returns Home after Stint in Prison:26.

———. (1/10/90). U.S. Plan Defended:4A.

———. (1/27/90). Sheriff Encourages Illegal Drug Deals:2A.

———. (2/2/90). Drug Pushers Must Pay Prison Costs:3A.

———. (3/18/90). Investigation Nets Cache of Cocaine:2A.

———. (5/24/90). Drug Deaths Decline:4A.

———. (6/5/90). Poverty's Effects May Linger for Generations, Study of Babies Shows:2A.

———. (6/22/90). Drug Bombings Up, Goverment Reports:1D.

———. (6/24/90). Prison Guards Charged:5A.

———. (7/25/90a). S&L Penalties Questioned:2A.

———. (7/25/90b). Tearful Mother Tells of Potty-Training Death in Trial of Her Husband:4A.

———. (8/9/90). Man Sets Self Afire, Accidently Kills Mother:1.

———. (8/15/90). Comatose Man Shows Apparent Signs of Life:3A.

———. (8/30/90a). Jail Term Possible in Mobile for Unexcused Absences:3C.

———. (8/30/90b). New Test Detects Drugs Instantly:4A.

———. (2/1/91). Cartel Blamed in Death:7A.

Moody, John. (7/23/90). The War That Will Not End. *Time*:33.

Morgan, John P. (May/June 1989). Impaired Statistics and the Unimpaired Worker. *Drug Policy Letter*:4.

Morganthau, Robert M. (9/27/89). A Drug War, with Little Ammunition. *New York Times*:27.

Morin, Richard. (9/8/89). Many in Poll Say Bush Plan Is Not Stringent Enough. *Washington Post*:A18.

———. (1/1/90). Americans Ill-Informed in Information Age. *Montgomery Advertiser*:1A.

Morley, Jefferson. (10/2/89). Contradictions of Cocaine Capitalism. *The Nation*:341–347.

Morse, Dan. (6/1/90). Housing Project Raided. *Montgomery Advertiser*:1.

———. (8/25/90). Police Storm Tulane Court. *Montgomery Advertiser*:1.

Moynihan, Daniel Patrick. (10/20/89). Assassinations: Can't We Learn? *New York Times*:27.

———. (7/16/90). Another War—The One on Poverty—Is Over, Too. *New York Times*:A11.

Mydans, Seth. (10/16/89). Powerful Arms of Drug War Arousing Concern for Rights. *New York Times*:1A.

———. (6/2/90). Tightening of Belts in Food Program Means Those of People on Welfare. *New York Times*:10.

Nader, Ralph, and Mark Green. (4/2/90). Passing On the Legacy of Shame. *Nation*, 444–446.

Nash, Nathaniel C. (10/8/90). Bill Eases Death Row Appeals Tied to Race Bias. *New York Times*:C10.

Nation, The. (7/3/89). Clearing the Air, Sort Of:1.

National Public Radio. (1/27/90). *Weekend Edition*.

———. (3/5/91). *Morning Edition*.

Nelson-Pallmeyer, Jack. (1989). *War against the Poor: Low-Intensity Conflict and Christian Faith*. New York: Orbis Books.

New York Times. (4/16/88). Seized Honduran: Drug Baron or a Robin Hood?:4A.

———. (10/10/88). Reagan Backs House Drug Bill:15.

———. (11/25/88). 3 Former Drug Agents Charged in Fraud Scheme:21A.

———. (11/30/88). U.S. Looking into Undercover Drug Manipulation:20A.

———. (1/22/89). Rightists Blamed in Colombia in Killings of 12 on Court Team:1.

———. (2/23/89). 33 Charged with Laundering $500 Million in Drug Profits:24.

———. (3/1/89). Washington Imposes Curfew to Fight Drug-Related Crime:1.

———. (3/23/89). Colombian Cocaine Network Is Target of U.S. Indictments:1.

———. (5/10/89). Mother Charged in Baby's Death from Cocaine:A10.

———. (5/28/89). Crack: A Disaster:E14.

———. (9/10/89). Appeals Court Backs Random Drug Testing:12A.

———. (9/27/89). Off-Duty Soldiers Trade Gunfire at a House Linked to Drug Sales:9.

———. (10/8/89). Colleges Balk at Enforcing Pledge on Student Aid and Drugs:14A.

———. (10/13/89). Court Upholds Drug Testing of Correctional Officers:10A.

———. (12/2/89). Thornburgh Asks Stiff Civil Fines in Cases of Small Drug Amounts:10.

———. (12/10/89a). Allotments for Guard in Drug War Approved:25.

———. (12/10/89b). Pregnant Addicts Are Focus of Suit:28.

———. (12/18/89). Study Finds Crisis in Rural Housing:11.

————. (12/21/89). Hungry Children Increase in Survey:20.

————. (12/24/89). The No-Parent Child:10.

————. (12/30/89). Human Rights: Now the Hard Part:14.

————. (12/31/89a). Spaniards Protest G.I. Intrusion in Panama:8.

————. (12/31/89b). U.S. Resists Easing Curb on Marijuana:14.

————. (1/1/90). Mindless Macho in Panama:18.

————. (1/9/90a). Nebraska Drug Curbs Proposed by Governor:6.

————. (1/9/90b). The Drug War: Toll Increases in U.S. Cities:6.

————. (1/10/90). Soldiers Violated Law in Raid, O.A.S. Says:8.

————. (1/25/90). 5 Officers Are Charged in 2 Miami Cocaine Cases:A11.

————. (1/26/90). First Victory in the Drug War:A14.

————. (2/1/90). Thornburgh Assails Death Penalty Delays:A12.

————. (3/11/90). Look Who's Hooked on Drug Dollars:20E.

————. (3/18/90). Yes: Drive Down the Deficit, No: Don't Punish the Poor:18.

————. (3/19/90). Report Shows Nation Is Lagging in Care for Well-Being of Children:A14.

————. (4/3/90). Military Bases as Drug Prisons:A14.

————. (4/25/90). Drug Abusers with AIDS Virus Are Selling Plasma, Study Finds:A10.

————. (4/26/90). House Passes Bank Bill on Money Laundering:C2.

————. (5/15/90). Health Chief Tells of a Decrease in the Number of Cocaine Addicts:A10.

————. (7/17/90). A Murder Case That Put Strains on Ties to Mexico Goes to a Jury:11A.

————. (8/17/90). Kentucky Law Officials Are Arrested in Drug Sting:A8.

————. (8/19/90). Thornburgh's Son Cleared in Inquiry:14.

————. (9/30/90). Criticizing Sentencing Rules, U.S. Judge Resigns:16A.

————. (10/2/90). A Challenge to Drug Testing Declined by the High Court:10A.

————. (11/11/90). Truant Student's Parents Are Threatened with Jail:33.

————. (1/16/91). Colombia Drug Baron Surrenders under Offer of Lenient Treatment:A2.

————. (1/25/91a). City Plans to Tell Employers of Drug Arrests:A10.

————. (1/25/91b) Release of Trafficker Shakes Hope in Colombian Drug Plan:A2.

————. (2/1/91). Colombia Ring Kills 2d Hostage:3A.

Oakes, John B. (1/26/90). Bush in Panama: A Tragicomedy. *New York Times*:A15.

Oreskes, Michael. (5/6/90). Study Finds Astonishing Indifference to Elections. *New York Times*:16A.

Passell, Peter. (9/5/89). How the Traffickers Profited from the War on Marijuana. *New York Times*:E14.

————. (3/4/90). America's Position in the Economic Race. *New York Times*:E5.

Pastor, Robert A., and George G. Castañeda. (1989). *Limits to Friendship*. New York: Vintage Books.

Pear, Robert. (5/27/90). Justice Department Scrambles to Explain Mexico Abduction. *New York Times*:14A.

————. (5/29/90). Many States Cut Food Allotments for Poor Families. *New York Times*:1.

————. (7/6/90). Administration Rejects Proposal for New Anti-Poverty Programs. *New York Times*:1.

———. (8/12/90). The Hard Thing about Cutting Infant Mortality Is Educating Mothers. *New York Times*:E5.

———. (8/15/90). Congress Acts to Admit More Skilled Immigrants. *New York Times*:A12.

Pedersen, Daniel. (3/5/90). The Swedish Model: Lessons for the Left. *Newsweek*:30.

Pereira, Joseph, and Ann Hagedorn. (1/29/90). Vermont Court Delays Civil Jury Trials. *Wall Street Journal*:B6.

Petras, James. (1987). Political Economy of State Terror: Chile, El Salvador, and Brazil. *Crime and Social Justice*, Nos. 27–28:149–171.

Pfost, Donald R. (1987). Reagan's Nicaraguan Policy: A Case Study of Political Deviance and Crime. *Crime and Social Justice*, Nos. 27–28:66–87.

Pitt, David. (9/30/88). New Drug Unit Checks Police on Corruption:B1.

Pitt, David E. (1/16/90). American Troops in Panama Sparring with 3 Embassies. *New York Times*:7.

Pittman, Robert W. (1/24/90). We're Talking the Wrong Language to "TV Babies." *New York Times*:A15.

President's Commission on Law Enforcement and Administration of Justice. (1967). *The Challenge of Crime in a Free Society*. Washington, D.C.: U.S. Government Printing Office.

Price, Debbie M., and Thomas W. Lippman. (12/31/89). President Apologizes for Troops' Blunder. *Washington Post*:1A.

Prowse, Michael. (1990). The Not-So-Great Society. From *Financial Times of London*, reprinted in *World Press Review*, (June 1990):79.

Public Broadcasting System. (1/6/90). Drug Seminar.

———. (2/14/90).

Purdum, Todd S. (2/18/90). New York City Is Out of the Needle Trade. *New York Times*:6E.

Purvis, Andrew. (12/11/89). Can Drugs Cure Addiction? *Time*:104.

Raber, Thomas. (3/12/90). Cocaine Crisis Hits Hospitals. *USA Today*:3A.

Rabinovitz, David. (12/29/89). Metal Detectors Make Schools Like Prisons. *New York Times*:28.

Radzinowicz, L., and R. Hood. (1980). Incapacitating the Habitual Criminal: The English Experience. *Michigan Law Review*, 78:1305–1389.

Rasky, Susan F. (6/10/88). Officials Urge a Wide Military Role in Drug Fight. *New York Times*:A32.

Raspberry, William. (1/11/88). Free Needles for Addicts. *Washington Post*:A27.

———. (9/26/89). Embryo Ruling Raises Questions. *Montgomery Advertiser*:10A.

Rawls, Phillip. (5/2/91). Panel Votes to Repeal School Drug Sales Law. *Montgomery Advertiser*:5A.

Reeves, Richard. (12/29/89). Assassins Can Work Both Ways. *Montgomery Advertiser*:12A.

———. (2/14/90). Just Don't Hurt Anyone's Feelings. *Montgomery Advertiser*:8A.

———. (8/27/90). Split along Racial Lines Frightens. *Montgomery Advertiser*:8A.

Reiman, Jeffrey. (1984). *The Rich Get Richer and the Poor Get Prison: Ideology, Class and Criminal Justice*. New York: Wiley.

Reveron, Derek. (2/18/90). The Living Dead. *Miami Herald Magazine*:9.

Richissin, Todd. (2/3/91). Alabama Case to Test Drug Death Penalty. *Montgomery Advertiser*:13A.

Riding, Alan. (2/27/89). Paraguay's Leader Denies Ties to Drugs. *New York Times*:A10.

Ring, Wilson. (2/26/88). Honduran Sought in Drug Crimes. *Washington Post*:10A.

Roberts, Peggy. (2/19/90). More Companies Say Yes to Drug Tests for Workers. *Montgomery Advertiser*:1.

Robinson, Mike. (9/1/90). Murder Toll May Break Record. *Montgomery Advertiser*:1.

Rohter, Larry. (12/12/88). Mexican Leader Vows Action against Drugs. *New York Times*:A5.

———. (3/1/89). Annual Lobbying for Mexico Begins. *New York Times*:14.

———. (4/16/89a). As Mexico Moves on Drug Dealers, More Move in. *New York Times*:3A.

———. (4/16/89b). Drugs' Roots Run Deep through a Mexican City. *New York Times*:1.

———. (12/31/89). Accounts by U.S. Differ on Search of Residence. *New York Times*:8.

———. (5/13/90). Drug Fight Targets U.S. Chemicals. *New York Times*:4A.

Rosenbaum, David E. (3/18/90). S&L's: Big Money, Little Outcry. *New York Times*:E1.

———. (6/6/90). A Financial Disaster with Many Culprits. *New York Times*:1A.

Rosenberg, Tina. (1/30/90). Military Can't Win Drug War. *Montgomery Advertiser*:13A.

Rosenthal, A. M. (3/3/89). The Giant Loophole. *New York Times*:E10.

Rosenthal, Andrew. (1/24/90). President Unveils New Drug Efforts. *New York Times*:A11.

———. (2/16/90). 3 Andean Leaders and Bush Pledge Drug Cooperation. *New York Times*:1.

———. (9/19/90). Did U.S. Overtures Give Wrong Idea to Hussein? *New York Times*:12A.

Rotstein, Arthur H. (5/19/90). Drug Tunnel Found beneath Border. *Montgomery Advertiser*:3A.

Rowan, Carl. (9/8/89). Waging a War on Drugs with a Popgun. *Atlanta Journal Constitution*:A15.

Ryan, Patrick J., Paul J. Goldstein, Henry H. Brownstein, and Patricia A. Bellucci. (1989). Drug-Related Homicides, New York City, 1988. Paper presented at the annual meeting of the American Society of Criminology, Reno, Nevada.

Safire, William. (1/26/90). The Lady in Red. *New York Times*:A15.

———. (8/14/90). Unequal Justice. *New York Times*:A15.

Salpukas, Agis. (1/27/90). Roadblock for Random Drug Tests. *New York Times*:21.

Sanchez, Carlos. (3/11/90). Fasters Protest Plan to Cut D.C. Aid to Homeless. *Washington Post*:C3.

Saul, John Ralston. (4/18/90). Drugs, Torture—and Western Cash. *New York Times*:A15.

Schmidt, William E. (12/14/89). Secret Fund of Detriot Police Is Investigated by Grand Jury. *New York Times*:16.

Schneider, Howard. (1/28/90). Schaefer's Anti-Drug Strategy Aimed at Middle Class. *Washington Post*:D1.

Schwartz, Jim. (7/3/89). Struggle for the Soul of the Union. *Nation*:8–10.

Sciolino, Elaine. (10/28/88). As Election Nears, Talk About Noriega Fades. *New York Times*:14.

———. (3/1/89). U.S. Study Praises Mexico on Drugs, State Department Says. *New York Times*:26.

———. (3/2/89). Drug Production Rising Worldwide. *New York Times*:10A.

Scott, David Clark. (4/17/91). Reforms Spur Exports, But Little Investment in Bid for Stable Growth. *Christian Science Monitor*:10.

Sesser, Stan. (1/17/90). Are Invasions Sometimes O.K.? *New York Times*:23.

Shank, Gregory. (1987). Counterterrorism and Foreign Policy. *Crime and Social Justice*, Nos. 27–28:33–65.

Shenon, Philip. (4/5/90). Bush Officials Say War on Drugs in the Nation's Capital Is a Failure. *New York Times*:1.

———. (4/22/90). The Score on Drugs: It Depends on How You See the Figures. *New York Times*:6E.

———. (5/13/90). Bush Administration Presents Bill Seeking Tougher Drug Penalties. *New York Times*:C19.

———. (5/23/90). Coast Guard Says It Suspects 10 of Drug Dealing. *New York Times*:A12.

Shepard, Scott. (4/20/90). Pregnant Addicts Find Few Places for Treatment. *Atlanta Journal and Constitution*:A12.

Silk, Leonard. (9/8/89). Robbing Peter to Fight Drugs. *New York Times*:26.

Skorneck, Carolyn. (9/27/89). Student Cocaine Use Drops. *Montgomery Advertiser*:4A.

———. (12/19/89). Survey: White High School Seniors More Likely to Use Drugs. *Montgomery Advertiser*:4A.

———. (2/21/90). U.S. May Enlist Bugs in Drug War. *Montgomery Advertiser*:1.

———. (9/6/90). Bush, Lawmakers Differ on Drug War. *Montgomery Advertiser*:4C.

Sonnett, Neal R. (3/13/90). Stop This IRS Assault on Lawyers. *USA Today*:10A.

Sourcebook of Criminal Justice Statistics, 1986. (1987). U.S. Department of Justice. Washington D.C.: GAO.

Specter, Michael, and Howard Kurtz, (2/11/90). Overlapping Epidemics Plague New York Hospitals. *Washington Post*:1A.

———. (2/19–/25/90). A Hospital System Near Collapse. *Washington Post National Weekly Edition*:9.

Sperling, Dan. (6/27/90). U.S. Men Face Highest Murder Risk. *USA Today*:1.

Squitieri, Tom. (5/15/90). U.S. Base of Smuggled Gun Network. *USA Today*:6A.

———. (5/21/90). Tunnel Hot Line May Dig Up Drug Clues. *USA Today*:3A.

———. (6/25/90). Public Housing Drug Suspects Get the Boot. *USA Today*:3A.

Stark, Pete. (8/12/90). Not All Drug Lords Are Outlaws. *New York Times*:E21.

Sullivan, Ronald. (4/25/90). Judge Voids a Drug Search, Charging Bus-Terminal Bias. *New York Times*:A16.

———. (4/26/90). Law Authorities Say Drug-Program Profiles Do Not Discriminate. *New York Times*:B12.

Tarlow, Barry. (1989). RICO Report. *National Association of Criminal Defense Lawyers* (September/October).

Taylor, Paul. (8/13-/19/90). Be All That You Can Be. *Washington Post National Weekly Edition*:13.

Terry, Don. (5/6/90). In Harlem, Death Is an Old and Busy Neighbor. *New York Times*:1.

Time. (1/8/90). Florida: Kracking Down on Crack:53.

———. (1/22/90). Who Killed Camarena:25.

———. (9/10/90). Drugs: Just Spray No:46.

Tolchin, Martin. (3/8/89). Kemp Vows to Oust Tenants over Drugs. *New York Times*:1.

Trainor, Bernard E. (12/16/89). Drug Smugglers and the Marines Exchange Shots. *New York Times*:1.

———. (12/31/89). Flaws in Panama Attack. *New York Times*:1A.

Treaster, Joseph B. (9/24/89). Coffee Impasse Imperils Colombia's Drug Fight. *New York Times*:8.

———. (12/16/89). A Top Medellín Drug Trafficker Dies in a Shootout in Colombia. *New York Times*:1.

———. (1/1/90). Battle against Drug Trafficking is Languishing in South America. *New York Times*:1.

———. (2/16/90). A Peruvian Peasant Fails to See Bush. *New York Times*:A9.

———. (4/29/90). Bypassing Borders, More Drugs Flood Ports. *New York Times*:1.

———. (5/6/90). Is Fight on Drugs Eroding Civil Rights? *New York Times*:5.

———. (6/14/90). Cocaine Prices Rise, and Police Efforts May Be Responsible. *New York Times*:1.

———. (7/1/90). Cocaine Epidemic Has Peaked, Some Suggest. *New York Times*:11.

———. (1/21/91). Little Effect Is Seen in Drug Smuggler's Surrender. *New York Times*:A12.

———. (2/23/91). Miami Beach's New Drug Weapon Will Fire Off Letters to the Employer. *New York Times*:9.

Turner, Robert F. (11/11/90). Is Assassination Acceptable? *Montgomery Advertiser*:13A.

Uchitelle, Louis. (8/14/90). Unequal Pay Widespread in U.S. *New York Times*:C1.

Uhlig, Mark A. (12/28/89). Managua Economy Hinges on Panama. *New York Times*:9.

———. (1/1/90). Ortega Says Search Made U.S. Relations the Worst in Years. *New York Times*:4.

———. (6/5/91). Mexico to Combat Police Corruption. *New York Times*:A6.

USA Today. (4/11/90). Spoils of Drug War:3A.

———. (5/16/90). Louisiana:6A.

———. (5/21/90). Mississippi:11A.

———. (5/23/90a). Don't Risk Rights in the War on Drugs:10A.

———. (5/23/90b). Drug Probe:3A.

———. (7/30/90). From Every State:8A.

———. (8/2/90). DEA Men Wanted:4A.

U.S. Senate. Committee on Foreign Relations. Subcommittee on Terrorism, Narcotics, and International Operations. 1989. *Drugs, Law Enforcement, and Foreign Policy*. Washington, DC: U.S. Government Printing Office.

von Hirsch, A., and D. Gottfredson. (1984). Selective Incapacitation: Some Queries about Research Design and Equity. *New York University Review of Law and Social Change*, 12:11–51.

Wachsman, Harvey F. (6/21/90). Trial Lawyers as S&L Bounty Hunters. *New York Times*:A15.

Wall Street Journal. (12/29/89). The Devil You Know:A6.

———. (1/10/90). Thousands of Panamanians Celebrated:1A.

———. (1/18/90). U.S. Exercised Its Veto:1A.

———. (1/19/90). Drugs Drop in Intensity:1A.

———. (1/22/90). Drug Case Overdose:7B.

———. (2/1/90). Bankers Fight Drugs:1.

———. (2/5/90). GM Hires an Investigator to Fight Drugs at Plant:B3.

———. (6/8/90). Review & Outlook: Poindexter's Punishment:A10.

Walsh, Elsa, and Nancy Lewis. (6/27/87). Probers Told Police Lied under Oath. *Washington Post*:A12.

Washington Post. (10/24/86). Police Said to Net $700,000 Each on Drugs:1.

———. (7/15/87). 12 Ex-Policemen Indicted in Miami:14.

———. (2/24/88). Arms and the Cartels:A14.

———. (4/27/88). Civil Rights Alarm:14.

———. (1/28/90). Fighting the Drug Wars:C6.

———. (3/11/90). Subway Motorman Suspended for Alleged Use of Cocaine: A25.

Washington Post National Weekly Edition. (2/26–3/4/90). Bugging Out:26.

Weatherford, Jack. (9/27/89). The Real Drug War Is in U.S. *Atlanta Journal and Constitution*:A27.

Weiner, Eric. (2/9/90). Loss of Balloons Hinders Drug Vigil. *New York Times*:A5.

Weinraub, Bernard. (9/8/89). States Would Pay Much of the Bill for the Drug War. *New York Times*:1A.

Wenner, Jann S. (6/22/90). Drug War: A New Vietnam. *New York Times*:15.

Wermiel, Stephen. (2/6/90). Drug Cases Crowd Out Civil Federal-Court Trials as Judge Calls Business Litigation a 'Stepchild.' *Wall Street Journal*:A20.

White, Jack E. (1/22/90). Genocide Mumbo Jumbo. *Time*:20.

Whitt, Richard. (9/5/89). System at Work: More Dealers Being Imprisoned, More Being Freed. *Atlanta Constitution*:A9.

Wicker, Tom. (10/10/89). Covert Means Fiasco. *New York Times*:27.

———. (11/28/89). Rights vs. Testing. *New York Times*:27.

———. (12/1/89). Warning about Tests. *New York Times*:31.

Wilkerson, Isabel. (12/11/89). Costly Absences: Wisconsin Ties Welfare to Attendance in School. *New York Times*:1.

Wilkins, L. T. (1980). Problems with Existing Prediction Studies and Figure Research Needs. *Journal of Criminal Law*, 71:98.

Williams, Cecil. (2/15/90). Crack Is Genocide, 1990s Style. *New York Times*:A19.

Wines, Michael. (3/30/89). Drug Money Ring Smashed, U.S. Says. *New York Times*:10.

———. (4/3/89). Law Enabled U.S. to Seize Proceeds of Drug Money Scheme. *New York Times*:12.

————. (11/17/89). U.S. Plans New Effort to Oust Noriega. *New York Times*:3A.

Winslow, Ron. (3/1/90). Malpractice Study Finds 7,000 Died in New York in 1984 Due to Negligence. *Wall Street Journal*:B4.

Woodiwiss, Michael. (1988). *Crime, Crusades and Corruption: Prohibitions in the United States, 1900–1987*. Totowa, N.J.: Barnes and Noble.

Worker's World. (1/1/87). Paraquat Kills People:14.

Wright, John. (5/27/90). News Reports Say Mexico Wants U.S. Agent Arrested. *Montgomery Advertiser* (AP):1A.

Zimmer, Lynn. (1989). Employment Drug Testing and Its Effectiveness in the War against Drugs. Paper Presented at the annual meeting of the American Society of Criminology, Reno, Nevada.

INDEX

acetone, 39, 41

AIDS: blood supply and, 27; children and, 70; education, 65; needle exchange programs and, 27, 69; needle sharing and, 10, 26; testing, 67

alcohol: addictive quality of, 59; industry, 57, 59; and performance, 96; presence in infants, 5; prohibition, 1; public perception of seriousness of use, 58; use, 80; use among homeless, 3; use among teenagers

alienation, 80–86

American Civil Liberties Union (ACLU), 90, 95, 103, 107

Andean countries: anti-drug efforts in, 34, 52; drug production in, 34. *See also names of specific countries*

Anti–Drug Abuse Act (1988), 26, 39, 95, 109

Antigua, 149

assassination, U.S.-sponsored, 157–59

asset seizures, 12, 117–19

Bahamas: drug corruption in, 48, 149, 151; drugs smuggled from, 20

Barry, Marion, 25, 61, 78

Bennett, William, 2, 15, 23, 26, 61, 79; alcohol advertising and, 59;

civil liberties and, 90; claims of success in drug war, 3, 10–13; harsher punishments, 111

Biden, Joseph, 2, 15, 85, 110

bifurcation of the population, 77, 101

Bolivia: advisors sent to, 42; aerial spraying in, 51–52; coca production in, 35, 41, 51; corruption in, 48; economy and drugs, 51, 145, 148; eradication programs in, 55; investment of drug profits in, 46; poverty, 134; seizures of cocaine in, 4; U.S. aid to, 55, 160

Brazil, 35, 39

Brennan, William, 25, 51

budget deficit, as obstacle to new programs, 64

Bush, George, 13; claims of success in drug war, 3; and Operation Greenback, 17

Bush administration: claims of success, 10–13; expenditures on the War on Drugs, 14–15, 16; ideological work in War on Drugs, 57; money laundering and, 23; political manipulation of figures on War on Drugs, 4; social programs, 64, 67–68

Cali cartel, 35

California v. Greenwood, 91

ABOUT THE AUTHOR

CHRISTINA JACQUELINE JOHNS is Assistant Professor in the Graduate Program in Criminology at Alabama State University. She has published widely on the topic of drug policy, both in the United States and in Latin America.

ISBN 0-275-94167-1

EAN

9 780275 941673

HARDCOVER BAR CODE